Managing Migration

Managing Migration

The Promise of Cooperation

Philip Martin, Susan Martin, and Patrick Weil

LEXINGTON BOOKS

A division of
ROWMAN & LITTLEFIELD PUBLISHERS, INC.
Lanham • Boulder • New York • Toronto • Oxford

LEXINGTON BOOKS

A division of Rowman & Littlefield Publishers, Inc.
A wholly owned subsidiary of The Rowman & Littlefield Publishing Group, Inc.
4501 Forbes Boulevard, Suite 200
Lanham, MD 20706

PO Box 317
Oxford
OX2 9RU, UK

British Library Cataloguing in Publication Information Available

Library of Congress Cataloging-in-Publication Data

Martin, Philip L., 1949–
  Managing migration : the promise of cooperation / Philip Martin, Susan Martin, and
Patrick Weil.
      p. cm.
  Includes bibliographical references and index.
  ISBN-13: 978-0-7391-1340-0 (cloth : alk. paper)
  ISBN-10: 0-7391-1340-2 (cloth : alk. paper)
  ISBN-13: 978-0-7391-1341-7 (pbk. : alk. paper)
  ISBN-10: 0-7391-1341-0 (pbk. : alk. paper)
  1. Emigration and immigration—Government policy. 2. Emigration and immigration—
Economic aspects. I. Martin, Susan Forbes. II. Weil, Patrick, 1956– III. Title.
JV6038.M38 2006
325'.1—dc22   2005032349

Printed in the United States of America

Contents

Acknowledgments

This book is a result of a unique experiment that brought together twenty-five researchers, policy makers, and administrators to conduct background research and visit sites in areas that offered potential best practices to manage migration. From Albania to Andalusia, and from Mali to Manila, the Cooperative Efforts to Manage Emigration (CEME) project was able to discuss innovative policies to manage migration with migrants, governments, employers, unions, and non-governmental organizations (NGOs). A full list of the participants and site visits is included in appendix 1.

We are grateful to the German Marshall Fund of the United States and the William and Flora Hewlett Foundation for their support of this project. In addition, we received support from the International Labor Office, International Organization for Migration, the Centro Studi Politica Internazionale, Fundación José Ortega y Gasset, the American Embassy in Santo Domingo, and the Canadian Embassy in Beijing.

Earlier versions of several of the chapters appeared in *International Migration* (vol. 40/3, 2002 and vol. 43/5, 2005) and *International Migration Review* (vol. 35/134, vol. 39/1, and vol. 38/4). Several of the members of the CEME expert panel contributed to the writing of the case studies. Thomas Straubhaur contributed to the Romania case study; Ferruccio Pastore to Italy/Albania; Elizabeth Midgely and Michael Teitelbaum to Turkey and the Dominican Republic/Haiti; Joaquin Arango to Spain/Morocco; Manolo Abella and Elizabeth Midgely to the Phillippines; and Irena Omelaniuk to China.

Many migrants, employers, NGO leaders, and government officials freely gave their time to explain their experiences and provide their perspectives on international migration. We thank them very much, and hope that this book can contribute to improving the world of migration.

CHAPTER ONE

Introduction

A growing share of the world's people live in the 175 developing countries, while global income and wealth are increasingly concentrated in the 25 developed countries. This disparity has led to increasing migration from the developing or "source countries" to developed or "destination" countries. The migration process has proven problematic for both source and destination countries. It has led to fears of brain drain and retarded development in the former and strained public resources and public attitudes toward migrants in the latter. While the need for cooperation among source, destination, and transit countries has been recognized, migration is proving difficult to manage at national, regional, and global levels. One solution to stemming the economic, political and social dislocations prompted by migration and making it work toward mutual gain lies in the economic arena where "industrial and developing nations have an equal stake in strengthening the credibility of the global economy" and where destination countries can aid the development of source countries through trade, aid, and political reforms that lead to economic convergence between the nations.[1]

The Cooperative Efforts to Manage Emigration (CEME) project is a bottom-up effort to identify models and best practices for spurring economic development and respect for human rights in migrant countries of origin, helping migrants abroad to work with their communities of origin to reduce emigration pressures, and promoting cooperation and regular dialogue among countries of origin, transit, and destination. In a series of site visits over four years, twenty leading migration researchers from North

America and Europe examined migration pressures in a variety of sending countries, integration efforts in receiving countries, and forums that promote cooperation between migrant sending and receiving countries.

We concluded that there is no one-size-fits-all framework for managing migration, but there are common elements of best-practice migration management policies. The major goal of virtually all sending and receiving countries is to achieve the economic development, human security, and confidence in the future that make unwanted, irregular, and forced migration unnecessary. One way to speed up the economic and political changes needed to achieve stay-at-home development is to tap the migrant diaspora abroad, so that migrants can participate in the development of their countries of origin via remittances and by returning with ideas and energies that accelerate economic and job growth as well as respect for human rights and democratic principles. Successful migration management requires an ongoing dialogue between sending and receiving countries to anticipate and deal with the challenges and opportunities that arise from the movement of people over national borders.

Development

Economic development can speed countries that currently send migrants abroad on the road to more jobs and higher wages. Migration can also expose those leaving repressive societies to principles and practices that respect human rights and participation in democratic political systems. When it works properly, migration can be a "win-win-win" for countries of origin, countries of destination, and the migrants themselves. Chapters 2 and 3 discuss the processes at work when migration is used in this way, as a resource for the economic and political development, respectively, of home countries. They also discuss barriers that limit the positive impacts of migration and suggest policies and practices to overcome the problems identified.

The European Union (EU) model for the economic integration of new members emphasizes political reforms, aid, and free trade prior to permitting free movement for work purposes. By the time nationals of Spain, Portugal, and Greece obtained freedom of movement rights, there was little labor emigration because of high growth rates and job opportunities in their own countries. A similar process is underway with the new and prospective members of the European Union.

The North American Free Trade Agreement (NAFTA) also aims to reduce emigration pressures in Mexico, although NAFTA does not envision eventual free labor movement. However, freer trade led to widespread labor displacement, especially in Mexican agriculture, while the promised economic and job growth was slower to offer workers incentives to stay at home. As a result, there has been a Mexico-U.S. migration hump in the past decade, but the tensions associated with it have been dealt with in part by new bilateral and regional cooperative mechanisms.

Other models of development that have reduced emigration include the Asian example of attracting foreign direct investment to build factories that employ potential migrants to produce goods that are exported, as in South Korea. In western Romania, for example, foreign direct investment is having the seemingly contradictory effect of both promoting stay-at-home behavior by offering good jobs and encouraging emigration to Italy, as the economic ties fostered by Italian investments have increased migration for training as well as for employment in Italy.

More generally, official development assistance granted by one country to assist the development of another can speed development and reduce emigration pressures. However, aid needs to be targeted more effectively to reduce emigration pressures, providing micro-credit for would-be migrants so they can invest in their home communities, income-generation opportunities for women left behind by migrating spouses, infrastructure development to create new markets and economic opportunities, and education and health care services for families in emigration areas.

At present, the financial contributions of migrants to developing countries far exceeds official development assistance, and in some cases, foreign trade and foreign direct investment. Migrants can contribute to economic development in their countries of origin through their financial resources as well as their skills, entrepreneurial activities, and support for democratization and human rights. The most visible socioeconomic contributions of migrants are often the new or improved health clinics, schools, churches, and roads their donations fund, the houses they build or improve, and the small business enterprises they launch in their home communities.

Many governments of emigration countries have recognized the development potential of their diasporas abroad and taken steps to facilitate remittances by working to reduce transfer fees and to match the portion of remittances that are invested to spur economic development. Such programs exist in diverse locations, including Mexico and Mali. The cooperation of host country governments can increase migrant circulation and returns that lead to job creation by identifying migrants with needed skills and encouraging them to return at least temporarily by giving them a secure residence status so they can return and subsidizing their employment during their temporary returns.

Democratization

Diasporas can also help to stimulate political reforms that improve conditions in home countries, as exemplified by Mexican migrants in the United States pushing for democratization and better governance at home or Serbs abroad helping to establish new democratic institutions in the Federal Republic of Yugoslavia.[2] Migrants who learn to participate in decision-making processes in their work places, schools, and community groups often return and expect to continue to have their voices heard at home, fostering democracy.

As more women migrate, particularly as principal wage earners, they take on new roles and press for new rights for women in both source and destination countries.

In many cases, however, stimulating democratization through migration requires far more of migrants than they can accomplish on their own. Many people are forced to migrate because of conflict and repression in their home countries. For them, migration is not a choice, it is a necessity forced upon them by circumstances out of their control. Forced migration presents special challenges for the international community, particularly when generated by protracted conflicts, such as in the former Yugoslavia, which leave large numbers of displaced people without a permanent resolution to their status. When conflicts end and refugees are able to return home, they along with economic migrants can play an important role in helping their home countries to restore normalcy and stability.

Dialogue

We found that cooperation between countries of origin and destination can maximize the benefits of migration, as with bilateral negotiations between Mexico and the United States and between France and Mali. Joint working groups discuss Mexico-U.S. border issues, which promotes cooperation in combating smuggling and trafficking, while cooperation in West Africa involves discussions of the integration of immigrants in France and development of the migrants' areas of origin in Mali. In North America and Europe, bilateral cooperation has evolved into regional cooperation to improve migration management.

We found cases of cooperation even when it appeared initially that the interests of immigration and emigration countries might be in conflict. For example, Albania looks at emigration as a safety valve, but the corruption and dangers involved in crossing the Adriatic in high-speed boats prompted a joint Italy-Albania police program to combat the smuggling and trafficking of migrants passing through Albania en route to Italy. Similar cooperation was achieved by the United States and the Dominican Republic to stem the smuggling and trafficking of third country nationals via Puerto Rico to the U.S. mainland.

In some cases, cooperation helped countries to establish systems to manage migration, as when the European Union and international organizations helped the Albanian government to sign the 1951 UN Convention Relating to the Status of Refugees and to develop appropriate domestic legislation and institutions to deal with foreigners seeking asylum. The EU similarly helped the Federal Republic of Yugoslavia to develop legislation and mechanisms for adjudicating asylum applications and to demilitarize its border police.

Structure of the Book

Development, democratization, and dialogue are major milestones on the path to cooperative migration management, but implementing them is neither simple nor straightforward. Part 1 of this book outlines the framework that guided our efforts, the results of our investigations, and our recommendations. Chapter 2 explains the migration challenge, discussing the reasons that international movements of people are expanding both numerically and in terms of diverse forms of migration. The third chapter focuses on labor migration, examining the interlinkages between migration and development and asking how recruitment, remittances, and returns can be harnessed to benefit migrant countries of origin. Chapter 4 deals with forced migration, particularly the movements of people to escape violence, repression, and persecution. It assesses policies that destination countries can pursue to avert mass migration while protecting the rights of those seeking safety. Part 2 includes our site visit reports: Chapter 5 discusses the relationship between the European Union and the countries seeking to enter it. Chapter 6 focuses on the relationship between Europe and African countries of emigration. Chapter 7 addresses migration relationships in the Americas. Chapter 8 focuses on countries of global immigration: China and the Philippines. Part 3 (chapter 9) lays out a framework for sustainable migration management that supports the interests of source countries, destination countries and the migrants themselves.

Notes

1. See www.tradepovertyforum.org.

2. At the time of the CEME site visit, the name used to describe the republics of Serbia and Montenegro was the Federal Republic of Yugoslavia. Although now changed, this book uses the terminology in place when the study team made its visit.

PART ONE

CHAPTER TWO

⁂

The Migration Challenge

In an ideal world, there would be few barriers to migration, and very little unwanted migration. In particular, there would be no migration resulting from severe economic, social, and political pressures. For most of human history, there were few governmental barriers to migration, and the challenge of too many people for available resources and technologies meant that it was "natural" for people to move from one place to another in response to famine, war, and displacement. However, nascent communication and transportation networks as well as institutions such as serfdom that limited human mobility often restricted migration.

The first age of mass migration was during the nineteenth and early twentieth centuries when 55 to 60 million Europeans migrated to the Americas. Even though many of the migrants were birds of passage seeking higher wages to finance upward mobility at home, most settled in the New World, and a combination of rapid population growth and displacement from agriculture in Europe as well as a need for labor in the New World and the evolution of networks linking settled immigrants abroad to their communities of origin facilitated transatlantic migration. The major sources of migrants changed from northern and western Europe to southern and eastern Europe by the end of the nineteenth century, and war and later quotas prevented a resumption of migration across the Atlantic in the 1920s.[1]

The second age of mass migration began during and after World War II. In Europe, the Iron Curtain limited migration from the east, and the result was the recruitment of guest workers in southern Europe, some of whom settled and unified their families, which turned previous emigration nations into immigrant destinations. Canada and the United States in the mid-1960s switched from selecting immigrants on the basis of their countries of origin to giving preference to relatives seeking to unify their families, and opened doors for foreigners requested by employers and for refugees resettled away from governments that were persecuting them. The result was a change in the origins of immigrants from Europe to Latin America and Asia.

Over the past quarter century, migration has become a global phenomenon, with most countries of the world participating in international migration as countries of origin, transit, or destination. The United Nations Population Division defines migrants as persons outside their country of birth or citizenship for at least twelve months, for any reason and in any legal status, and estimated there were 175 million international migrants in 2000,[2] including 60 percent or 105 million in what the UN calls "more developed" nations, and 40 percent or 70 million in developing countries.[3] Between 1975 and 2000, the number of international migrants doubled, with the fastest growth between 1985 and 1995, when the stock of migrants rose by about six million a year in response to, among other things, the fall of Communism, wars and persecution in the ex-Yugoslavia, Africa, and Afghanistan and Iraq, and freer trade that displaced workers who then migrated, as occurred under the North American Free Trade Agreement linking Mexico and the United States.

The people who share the migrant label are very different. Most are moving over borders for greater economic opportunity, others are joining family members settled abroad, and some are fleeing persecution and violence. Most individual motivations for migration can be traced to differences between origin and destination areas such as differences in demography, economics, and security that make one place more attractive than another. Differences between countries are growing, prompting more international migration, and per capita incomes that are six times higher in the United States than in Mexico and ten times higher in Germany than in Turkey help to explain the migration between Mexico and the United States and between Turkey and Germany.[4]

Yet, despite large and growing per capita income differences between countries, international migration remains the exception, not the rule. First, most people do not want to leave family and friends for another country, and most governments with migrants have border police to prevent illegal entries over borders and control systems that regulate the entry and settlement of foreigners. Second, many industrial country governments have increased their spending on border controls and asylum systems so much that migration management expenditures, most of which aim to limit the entry and stay of migrants from developing countries, are close to official development aid flows of about $50 billion a year.[5]

The third reason migration remains the exception in a globalizing world is that economic growth can narrow differences and reduce the motivation for migration. The migration transition that takes a country from a net emigration area to a net immigration area occurred in southern European nations such as Italy and Spain in the 1960s and 1970s and in Asian nations such as Korea in the 1980s. The challenge is to ensure that the globalization reflected in rising flows of goods and people across national borders leads to economic and political convergence rather than divergence between countries.

Inertia, controls, and development have reduced the differences that motivate migration in some areas, but in others differences have been widening, prompting millions of people to cross borders in search of opportunity. There are relatively few front doors for legal immigrants in most destination countries, so most of the world's migrants are classified by receiving countries as either temporary migrants; foreigners legally in the country for a specific time and purpose such as students, asylum seekers, and guest workers; or as unauthorized, undocumented, or irregular foreigners.

We expect that more international migration will occur in the twenty-first century, and we believe that most will involve people moving from developing to more developed countries. The challenge is to make this migration a win-win situation that speeds up the migration transition, allowing border barriers to fall without spawning out-of-control migration.

Factors Influencing Migration

Migration is a response to differences. Increasing differences in demographics, economics, and security—plus revolutions in communications, transportation, and rights that facilitate movement over borders—have created networks that bridge borders and allow people to cross them. Migration networks transmit information and advice about opportunities abroad and often provide both the funds to travel legally or illegally and shelter and jobs for new arrivals. A world of growing differences between nations and stronger networks over borders means there are more reasons and additional means to cross borders, promising more international migration and making more urgent the quest for effective and sustainable migration management.

Demographic Differences
At the dawn of agriculture in 8000 BC, the population of the world was about 5 million. The world's population rose to about 300 million in 1 AD

and was about 500 million in 1650. The global population reached the 1 billion mark in 1800, the 2 billion mark in 1930, 3 billion in 1960, 4 billion in 1974, 5 billion in 1987, 6 billion in 1999, and is projected to grow to 9 billion by 2050, with almost all of the growth in what are currently developing countries.[6]

The twentieth century may prove, in retrospect, to have been the "demographic century," a century in which the world's population quadrupled. Much of this population growth has been in developing countries, as decreased infant mortality produced millions of young people who then had families. During the 1960s, there were fears that a population explosion would lead to famines and similar catastrophes that would kill millions, and these fears prompted many countries to launch family planning programs that were often successful in reducing fertility. In the early 1970s, for example, Mexico's population was growing by 3.5 percent a year, one of the world's fastest growth rates, and Mexican women averaged 6.2 children each. Family planning programs, economic growth, and changing social mores sharply reduced fertility to 2.8 babies per woman today, and Mexico's population growth rate has fallen to about 2 percent a year.

World conferences such as the United Nations–sponsored International Conference on Population and Development held in Cairo in 1994 emphasized that educating girls and providing women with contraceptive information can reduce fertility, often dramatically. The Final Document from Cairo asserted: "All couples and individuals have the basic right to decide freely and responsibly the number and spacing of their children and to have the information, education and means to do so,"[7] and stressed the need to involve women in their heath care and reproductive decisions. Evidence and experience suggest that, when parents are assured their children will survive and as incomes rise with economic development, empowered women have fewer children.

However, the momentum from past and present fertility means that the world's population will continue to grow even as fertility falls. About 85 percent of the world's population—6.3 billion in 2004—is in the 175 developing countries, where women average 3.1 babies each (3.5 if China is excluded). About 15 percent of the world's residents live in 25 developed countries, where women average 1.5 children each. The fastest growth is in Africa, whose population is projected to more than double, and the sharpest decline in Europe, where the population is projected to shrink by 10 percent. Without immigration, these very different fertility gradients mean that the population shares or weights of the world's continents will change radically.[8]

Table 2.1.   Europe and Africa Demography: 1800–2050

	Share of World Population—%		
	1800	2000	2050
Africa	8	13	20
Europe	20	12	7
World population (billions)	1	6	9

One of the most dramatic examples of shifting population shares is evident in the comparison of Europe and Africa. Europe had 20 percent of the world's residents in 1800, when Africa had 8 percent.[9] In 2000 Europe and Africa had about equal population shares, but by 2050, Africa is projected to have 20 percent of global residents and Europe 7 percent, a reversal of each continent's global demographic weight within 250 years. Demographic heavyweight Europe was the major source of migrants in the nineteenth century and, if history repeats itself, Africa could be a major source of migrants in the twenty-first century.

In 2000, the UN Population Division (UNPD) issued a controversial report, *Replacement Migration: Is It a Solution to Declining and Ageing Populations?*[10] In the report, "replacement migration refers to the international migration that would be needed to offset declines in the size of population, the declines in the population of working age, as well as to offset the overall ageing of a population." To answer the question posed in the title, UNPD calculated:

- the migration required to maintain the size of the total population at the highest level it would reach in the absence of migration after 1995;
- the migration required to maintain the size of the working-age population (15 to 64 years) at the highest level it would reach in the absence of migration after 1995; and
- the migration required to maintain the potential support ratio (PSR), i.e., the ratio of the working-age population (15 to 64 years) to the old-age population (65 years or older), at the highest level it would reach in the absence of migration after 1995.

Noting extremely low fertility and increased longevity in many developed countries, the report cites immigration as the principal contributor to any population increase. In the absence of immigration, most countries would experience population decline. Maintaining *total population size* would require about the same current flow of migrants for France, the UK, the United States, and the EU states; but for Italy, Japan, the Republic of Korea, and Europe as a whole, offsetting population decline would require a level of immigration much higher than recent experience. Most countries, except the United States, would need a significantly larger number of migrants to offset declines in the *working-age population*. And, according to the report, "the levels of migration needed to offset *population ageing* (i.e., maintain potential support ratios) are extremely large, and in all cases entail vastly more immigration than occurred in the past." For example, in the absence of other changes (e.g., increasing retirement age and labor force participation), the United States would require almost 12 million immigrants per year, and Europe would require more than 27 million immigrants per year.

Among the large European nations, Italy is expected to have the greatest population loss, declining 28 percent in size by 2050. Germany is in the middle of the pack, while the United Kingdom and Northern Ireland are forecast to have the smallest decline of the large European nations. Quite in contrast, higher fertility and immigration rates generate forecasts of population growth in Canada and the United States. The elderly population is forecast to increase significantly in all of these countries—growing in size between about 50 percent (U.S.) and 90 percent (Italy).

The report reinforced for many academics and some policymakers in Europe in particular that international migration must be an important part of any strategy to combat population decline and aging. However, as the report pointed out, "maintaining potential support ratios at current levels through replacement migration alone seems out of reach, because of the extraordinarily large numbers of migrants that would be required." The report advised governments to reassess policies and programs relating to international migration, in particular replacement migration, and the integration of large numbers of recent migrants and their descendants.

While it is a fact that population decline in developed regions like Western Europe has been slowed by positive net immigration,[11] the debate continues about what role immigration can and should play in addressing demographic changes in the future. Opposition to immigration remains strong in many countries, and public opinion may well restrict any policy options that require substantial increases in admission. During the past decade, however, even countries with little tradition of immigration have acknowledged that they have sizeable immigrant populations and are likely to continue to admit immigrants.

Economic Security

Economic differences between nation states are widening, increasing the motivation for economically motivated migration. The world's gross domestic product (GDP) was $30 trillion in 2000, making the average per capita income $5,000 a year, but the range was from $100 per person in Ethiopia to $38,000 in Switzerland. When countries are ranked by their per capita GDPs, it is apparent that the gap between high-income countries, with $9,300 or more per person per year, versus low (below $750 per person per year) and middle (between $750 and $9,300) income countries has been widening, and very few low and middle income countries have been able to climb into the high-income ranks over the past quarter century.[12]

For example, per capita GDPs in the high-income countries in 1975 were on average forty-one times higher than in low-income countries and eight times higher than in middle-income countries. By 2000, high-income countries had per capita GDPs that were sixty-six times those in low-income countries and fourteen times those in middle-income countries, which helps to explain why so many migrants from low- and middle-income countries take big risks to enter high-income countries.

Most migrants are young people looking for work. The world's labor force was 3 billion in 2000, and it is growing much faster in developing than in developed countries. For example, between 2001 and 2010, the labor force in developing countries is projected to grow four times faster than the labor force in developed or high-income countries. Since many low-income countries have more workers than formal sector jobs and more new entrants into the labor force than additional jobs created, there is widespread unemployment and underemployment. Meanwhile, many high-income countries have social welfare systems based on contributions from those currently employed, so that immigration could help to stabilize their labor forces and pension systems. However, immigration only postpones inevitable adjustments in high-income countries, since migrants also age, so that countries pursuing immigration as the only solution to lower fertility and longer life spans commit themselves to ever more immigration.

A second dimension of increasing economic differences between countries adds to international migration. Some 1.3 billion or 43 percent of the world's workers are employed in agriculture, usually as small farmers or hired workers. In the poorer countries in which they are a majority of workers, farmers are taxed, while subsidies are common in rich countries where farmers represent a small share of workers. This means that farmers in poor countries generally have lower-than-average incomes, as taxes are extracted from

Table 2.2.   Global Migrants and Incomes, 1975–2000

	Migrants (millions)	World Population (billions)	Migrants World Population	Year Change (millions)	Countries Grouped by Per Capita GDP ($)			Ratios	
					Low	Middle	High	High-low	High-middle
1975	85	4.1	2.1%	1	150	750	6,200	41	8
1985	105	4.8	2.2%	2	270	1,290	11,810	44	9
1990	154	5.3	2.9%	10	350	2,220	19,590	56	9
1995	164	5.7	2.9%	2	430	2,390	24,930	58	10
2000	175	6.1	2.9%	2	420	1,970	27,510	66	14

Sources: UN Population Division and World Bank Development Indicators; 1975 income data are 1976. The UN migrant estimate for 1990 was raised from 120 million to 154 million, largely to reflect the break-up of the USSR, which added about 30 million migrants to the global stock. Many of these additional migrants did not move; they were, e.g., Russians considered foreigners in Estonia. Migrants are defined as persons outside their country of birth or citizenship for 12 months or more.

Table 2.3. Global Labor Force, 1980, 2001, 2010

	Labor Force (millions)			Average Annual Growth Rate	
	1980	2001	2010	1980–2001	2001–2010
World	2,036	2,983	3,377	1.8	1.4
Developing Countries	1,662	2,517	2,894	2	1.6
High-income Countries	373	467	483	1.1	0.4

Source: World Bank. 2003. *World Development Indicators,* p. 44

them via input suppliers who provide seeds or fertilizers at high prices or via monopoly purchasers of farm commodities who set prices that are below world prices and pocket the difference when the coffee or cocoa is sold on world markets.[13] Low farm incomes encourage migration off the farm.

Many industrial countries had a "Great Migration" off the land in the 1950s and 1960s, and similar "Great Migrations" are underway in many major emigration countries, including China, Mexico, and Turkey. Such Great Migrations have three implications for international labor migration. First, ex-farmers everywhere are most likely to accept so-called 3-D (dirty, dangerous, difficult) jobs in urban areas, either inside their countries or abroad. Second, ex-farmers who must find new jobs often make physical as well as cultural transitions when they move to cities, and some may find adaptation in a foreign city as easy as integration in larger cities within their countries because past migration has resulted in settled friends and relatives abroad. Third, rural-urban migrants get closer to the networks that can provide visas and documents for legal migration or help them arrange for irregular migration.

Human Security
Rising demographic and economic differences combine with a third major difference among countries: human security. By conservative estimates, about 50 million migrants are living outside of their home communities, forced to flee to obtain some measure of safety and security. Forced migration has many causes and takes many forms. People leave because of persecution, human rights violations, repression, conflict, and natural and human-made disasters. Many depart on their own initiative to escape these life-threatening situations, although in a growing number of cases people are driven from their homes by governments and insurgent groups intent on depopulating or shifting the ethnic, religious, or other composition of an area.[14] The majority of forced migrants are internally displaced. Also of concern are persons who are at high risk of forced migration, particularly war-affected civilian populations and stateless persons.

After the global conflict between capitalism and communism ended in the early 1990s, local conflicts erupted in many areas, leading to separatist movements, new nations, and more migrants, as in the ex-Yugoslavia and the ex-Soviet Union. Massive population movements from Bosnia and Kosovo, in particular, affected much of Europe. To avoid reification of ethnic cleansing, most of those forced to flee or evicted from their home countries received temporary protection, with the understanding that they would return when conditions permitted. After the Dayton Peace Accords ended the fighting in Bosnia and NATO forces drove the Milosevic government forces out of Kosovo, many refugees returned, although others remained in exile and new displacements occurred (particularly ethnic Serbs and Roma who fled Kosovo).

At the same time, asylum seekers from Asia, Africa, and Latin America sought refuge in developed countries, adding to a growing population of persons seeking protection in developed countries. While many of the asylum seekers failed in their bid for refugee status because they could not demonstrate a well founded fear of persecution, they were permitted to remain in destination countries because of conflict and other destabilizing factors in their home countries. Still others eluded authorities and remained without authorization. Far fewer were removed to their home countries under either voluntary or mandatory repatriation programs.

As noted, the 1990s also saw a proliferation of new states formed from the break-up of countries with artificial borders and surging nationalism within sub-regions. Creating new nations is almost always accompanied by migration, as populations are reshuffled so that the "right" people are inside the "right" borders.[15] Finally, with more nations, there are more international borders to cross: there were 191 generally recognized nation-states in 2000,[16] up from 43 in 1900.

Gender Differences

Women represent a growing share of migrants, as economies of destination countries offer more service jobs and barriers to migration erode for women in sending countries. As of 2000, about 49 percent of the world's migrants were women, up from 47 percent in 1960,[17] and the proportion of migrants who are women has grown to 51 percent in more developed regions. The highest proportions of women are in Europe and the lowest proportions are in Northern Africa.

The gender distribution of international migrants varies substantially by country. The proportion of legal immigrants who are women is particularly high in the traditional immigration countries (United States, Canada, and

Australia). For example, about 55 percent of legal immigrants to the United States are women.[18] In places that permit only temporary migration, the proportion of men migrating tends to be higher, particularly if admission is limited to certain types of occupations typically dominated by men (e.g., farm workers, miners, or information technology workers).

Differences can be seen among different emigration countries. While Mexico has many more male emigrants (69 percent in a census conducted in 1995), the Philippines has a considerably higher proportion of female migrants abroad (about 60 percent in data collected during the 1990s).[19] A million Filipinos a year—some 2,700 a day—are "deployed" or sent under government auspices to work abroad to be domestic helpers, entertainers, and nurses. High unemployment and low wages, combined with a well-developed migration infrastructure, have encouraged emigration as the fastest and surest route to upward mobility at home. The most common first-time Filipino migrant is a 25-year-old female college graduate going abroad to work as a domestic helper on a two-year contract, and the 1,200 licensed recruitment agencies make labor brokerage a major industry.[20]

During the past decades there has been an increase in the absolute and proportional number of women migrating as primary wage earners within their families. Several distinct categories of women migrate for work purposes, differentiated by their skills, the permanence of their residence in the host country, and their legal status. At the lower end of the skills spectrum, women migrants pick fruits and vegetables, manufacture garments and other items, process meat and poultry, work as nursing home and hospital aides, clean restaurants and hotels, and provide myriad other services. Overseas domestic service is a common occupation for migrant women. As women in developed countries enter the labor force in higher and higher numbers, the demand for migrant women to perform domestic work and child and elder care services has been increasing as well. Women may migrate through official contract labor programs that match workers and employers, or they may obtain such employment after migrating, often through informal networks.

At the higher end of the skill spectrum, women migrants engage in equally diverse activities. They fill jobs requiring specialized skills, run multinational corporations, teach in universities, supply research and development expertise to industry and academia, and design, build, and program computers, to name only a few activities. Sizeable numbers of migrant women are in the health professions, particularly nursing and physical therapy.

Because of the high proportion of women who migrate into domestic service and other potentially exploitable jobs, protecting female migrants has emerged as a major challenge for governments, with major labor exporters such as the Philippines taking the lead in developing mechanisms to help ensure the safety of female migrants. One government mechanism that aims to protect female migrants abroad is joint liability between local recruiters and foreign employers for the provisions of the contracts given to each legal worker. Since it may be difficult for the migrant to recoup unpaid wages or benefits from the foreign employer, a migrant who is underpaid can seek compensation from her Filipino recruiter after her return. However, joint liability is more effective to deal with wages than with working condition provisions of the contract, since those of domestic helpers vary enormously. The labor laws of many destination countries do not cover domestic helpers, and few countries have effective mechanisms that allow maids to report abuses and punish employers convicted of abusing foreign maids.

International migration profoundly affects gender relations, particularly the role of women in households and communities. In many respects, migration enhances the autonomy and power of women, as women from traditional societies migrate to advanced industrial societies and become familiar with new norms regarding women's rights and opportunities. If they take outside employment, women may have access to financial resources that had never before compensated their labor. Even if their pay is pooled with that of other family members, this new wage-earning capacity often gives women greater ability to direct household priorities.

Women who are left at home as their husbands migrate also experience changes in their roles. The stay-at-home spouses may now have greater household and economic responsibilities. Although they may be financially dependent on remittances from their overseas relatives, the women may have substantial autonomy over decisions about how the funds will be used. Should their husbands not return home, or should they stop sending remittances, the women may have to assume even greater responsibility for themselves and their children.

In other respects, migration can serve to reinforce traditional gender roles. This is particularly the case when women are expected to preserve cultural and religious norms that appear to be under attack. This process could be seen, for example, in Afghan refugee camps in Pakistan, where *purdah*, the separation of men and women, was practiced more rigidly than in Afghanistan itself. Upon return to Afghanistan, the Taliban leaders intensified the practice, imposing it throughout the whole country.

For women who migrate from developing to developed countries, adjustment to the new culture can be a difficult process. Barriers to successful adjustment include those within the host society as well as individual or personal ones. Among the former are racial intolerance and sexual and cultural discrimination against foreign women. Many migrants are of a different race from the majority of the population of their new country and, as women, they may face the dual problem of racism and sexism in seeking employment or training or otherwise participating in the activities of the new country.

A particularly troubling trend in recent years has been the emergence of professional trafficking operations that exploit primarily women and children. Trafficking is defined as: "the recruitment, transportation, transfer, harboring or receipt of persons, by means of the threat or use of force or other forms of coercion, of abduction, of fraud, of deception, of the abuse of power or of a position of vulnerability or of the giving or receiving of payments or benefits to achieve the consent of a person having control over another person, for the purpose of exploitation."[21] The trafficking of people for prostitution and forced labor is one of the fastest growing areas of international criminal activity and one that is of increasing concern to the international community.

Generally, trafficking moves people from less developed countries to industrialized nations or toward neighboring countries with marginally higher standards of living. Since trafficking is an underground criminal enterprise, there are no precise statistics on the extent of the problem, but even conservative estimates suggest the problem is enormous. The largest numbers of victims trafficked internationally come from Asia, with over 225,000 victims each year coming from Southeast Asia and over 150,000 from South Asia. The former Soviet Union is the largest new source of trafficking for prostitution and the sex industry, with over 100,000 persons trafficked each year. An additional 75,000 or more are trafficked from Eastern Europe. Over 100,000 victims are from Latin America and the Caribbean, and over 50,000 victims are from Africa.[22] Trafficking is now considered the third largest source of profits for organized crime, behind only drugs and guns, generating billions of dollars annually. Most of the victims are sent to Asia and the Middle East, Western Europe and North America, where they usually end up in large cities, vacation and tourist areas, or near military bases, where the demand is highest.

Traffickers acquire their victims in a number of ways. Sometimes women are kidnapped outright in one country and taken forcibly to another. In other cases, traffickers entice victims to migrate voluntarily with false promises of good paying jobs in foreign countries as au pairs, models, dancers, domestic workers, etc. Traffickers advertise these phony jobs as well as marriage opportunities abroad in local newspapers and use marriage agency databases and matchmaking parties to find their victims. In some instances, traffickers approach women or their families directly with offers of lucrative jobs elsewhere. After providing transportation and false travel documents to get victims to their destinations, they subsequently charge exorbitant fees for those services, creating lifetime debt bondage.

While there is no single victim stereotype, a majority of trafficked women are under the age of twenty-five, with many in their mid to late teens.[23] The fear among customers of HIV and AIDS infection has driven traffickers to recruit younger women and girls, some as young as seven. Victims of severe forms of trafficking are often subject to cruel mental and physical abuse in order to keep them in servitude, including beating and battering, rape, starvation, forced drug use, confinement, and seclusion. Once victims are brought to their destinations, their passports are often confiscated and they are forced to have sex, often unprotected, with large number of partners and to work unsustainably long hours. Many victims suffer mental breakdowns and they are exposed to sexually transmitted diseases, including HIV and AIDS. They are often denied medical care, and those who become ill are sometimes killed.

Recognizing the growth of trafficking operations, states agreed to a UN Protocol to Prevent, Suppress and Punish Trafficking in Persons, Especially Women and Children. This instrument, in combination with its companion protocol on human smuggling, requires international cooperation in combating smuggling and trafficking and encourages states to pass measures for the prevention of those who have been trafficked. The trafficking protocol entered into force on December 31, 2003, and the smuggling protocol entered into force on January 28, 2004, filling a void by laying out a mechanism to enable governments to cooperate to prohibit and prosecute smugglers and traffickers of humans.

Networks

Differences encourage migration, but it takes links between sending and receiving areas for people to move over borders. Demographic, economic, gender, and security differences are sometimes likened to negative and positive battery poles, and networks to the links that enable a current to flow. Migration networks are a broad concept and include factors that enable people to learn about opportunities abroad as well as the migration infrastructure that enables migrants to cross national borders and remain abroad.[24]

Migration networks have been shaped and strengthened by three major revolutions in the past half-century: in communications, transportation, and rights. The communications revolution helps potential migrants to learn about opportunities abroad and often provides both the motivation and the funds that encourage and enable people to move over national borders. The best information about opportunities abroad comes from migrants already in the destination, since they can inform family and friends at home in a context both understand. Those without family and friends abroad may see movies and TV shows produced in high-income countries that make recruiters' stories about the riches available seem plausible.[25]

The transportation revolution highlights the declining cost of long-distance travel. British migrants unable to pay passage to the colonies in the eighteenth century often indentured themselves, promising to work for three to six years to repay one-way transportation costs to the Americas. Migrants would sign contracts before departure, and settlers looking for workers would meet arriving ships, pay the fare, and obtain a worker who was obliged to stay with the master to pay off the transportation debt. Transportation costs today are far less, $2,500 to travel almost anywhere in the world legally, and $1,000 to $20,000 for unauthorized migration. Most studies suggest payback times for migrants are much quicker, so that even migrants who paid high smuggling fees can usually repay them within two or three years.[26]

The rights revolution refers to the spread of the rights of individuals vis-à-vis governments that allows some foreigners to stay abroad. Many countries have ratified the major UN human rights and refugee conventions[27] that commit them to providing all persons with basic rights such as due process. As a result, in many countries, migrants without legal status can nevertheless stay several years by applying for various forms of relief from deportation or removal, or be smuggled into a country, work in the underground economy, and apply for relief when apprehended. Most industrial countries extend eligibility for at least basic services to all residents, regardless of legal status, making it easier for migrants to survive while trying to establish a foothold.

Growing demographic, economic, and security differences increase potential migration, and the communications, transportation, and rights revolutions strengthen the networks that enable migrants to learn about opportunities, move over borders, and stay abroad. The high-income countries experiencing "unwanted immigration" can do little in the short-term about the differences that promote migration, and they have limited capacities and less desire to reverse the communications and transportation revolutions that, as a by product of connecting the global village, inform migrants about opportunities abroad and make it less costly for them to travel.

However, governments create and enforce rights, and the default policy instruments many have used to manage migration include new or modified laws that restrict the rights of migrants. For example, the United States in 1996 enacted laws that restricted the access of unauthorized as well as many legal immigrants to social assistance program benefits, under the theory that some migrants were arriving for a "hand out, not a hand up." Many European countries revised their laws in the 1990s to require foreigners to apply for asylum soon after arrival in order to receive housing and support, and shortened the appeal process in an effort to expedite the removal of those found to be not in need of protection.

Adjusting the rights of migrants to "control migration" often results in hardships for individuals without changing the fundamental forces encouraging migration. Unilateral efforts to manage migration by restricting the rights of migrants, as exemplified by Proposition 187 in California in 1994,[28] can also be divisive at home and provoke protests from migrant countries of origin. Instead of unilateral actions that are hard to implement, it makes more sense to understand how migration affects development and development affects migration, so that bilateral and regional dialogues can explore ways of managing migration for mutual benefits.

Notes

1. In their article "What Drove Mass Migrations from Europe in the Late Nineteenth Century?" Timothy Hatton and Jeffrey Williamson concluded that Europe was on the downside of its migration hump by the 1920s, so that even "without the imposition of quotas by the US government," migration would have decreased (Hatton and Williamson, "What Drove Mass Migrations from Europe in the Late Nineteenth Century?" in *Population and Development Review* 20, no. 3 [September 1994]: 556).

2. Of these 175 million migrants, about 145 million moved over borders, and 30 million became foreigners without moving, as with Russians in the Baltic countries after the breakup of the USSR. United Nations Population Division, *Trends in Total Migrant Stock: The 2003 Revision* (New York: United Nations, 2003).

3. The 105 million migrants in developed countries are 11 percent of the 955 million people in what the World Bank calls high-income countries.

4. In 2001, according to the World Bank's 2003 *World Development Report*, US gross national income (GNI) per person was $34,870 and in Mexico $5,540; in Germany, GNI was $23,700, versus $2,540 in Turkey. The high-income countries with 15 percent of the world's 6.1 billion people had 81 percent of the world's $31.5 trillion GDP. *World Development Report 2003: Sustainable Development in a Dynamic World*, (New York: Oxford University Press, 2003).

5. Philip Martin, *Trade and Migration: NAFTA and Agriculture*, Washington, D.C.: Institute for International Economics, 1993.

6. Global fertility is expected to decline to replacement levels—if it remained at current levels, the world's population would be 134 trillion in 2300. Alene Gelbard, Carl Haub, and Mary M. Kent, *World Population: Beyond Six Billion*, Population Reference Bureau 54, no. 1 (March 1999).

7. UN World Population Plan of Action, Section B, paragraph 14 (f).

8. Population Reference Bureau, *The 2004 World Population Data Sheet: 2004* www.prb.org/Template.cfm?Section=PRB&template=/Content/ContentGroups/ Datasheets/2004_World_Population_Data_Sheet.htm%20%20.

9. Europe's share of the global population (including Asian Russia) peaked at 25 percent between 1910 and 1920.

10. UN Population Division, *Replacement Migration: Is It a Solution to Declining and Ageing Populations?* (New York: UNPD, 2000).

11. See UN Population Division, *Replacement Migration*, which cites statistics on the major contribution that positive net migration has made to the population growth of countries such as Austria, Denmark, Germany, Greece, Italy, Luxembourg, Spain, and Switzerland, as well as in North America.

12. For example, Portugal and South Korea moved from the middle- to the high-income group between 1985 and 1995, while Zimbabwe and Mauritania moved from the middle- to the low-income group. See World Bank, *World Development Report* (Washington, DC: World Bank, various years).

13. In the high-income countries, farmers' incomes are generally higher than those of non-farmers, in part because high-income countries transfer funds from consumers to producers of food and fiber.

14. This definition of forced migrants includes persons who cross international borders in search of refuge as well as those who are internally displaced.

15. Governments have in the past sometimes sent migrants to areas that later broke away and formed a new nation, and these internal migrants and their descendants can become international migrants without moving again, as with Russians in the newly independent Baltics or Indonesians in East Timor.

16. The CIA factbook lists 191 "independent states," plus 1 "other" (Taiwan), and 6 miscellaneous entities, including Gaza Strip, West Bank, and Western Sahara (www.cia.gov/cia/publications/factbook/index.html).

17. See UN Division for the Advancement of Women, *2004 World Survey on the Role of Women in Development: Women and International Migration* (New York: United Nations, 2004) for a fuller discussion of the role of gender in international migration. One of this book's authors, Susan Martin, was the lead author of the Survey.

18. See U.S. Office of Immigration Statistics, *U.S. Legal Permanent Residents: 2004*, at uscis.gov/graphics/shared/statistics/publications/FlowReportLegalPerm Residents2004.pdf.

19. International Labor Organization, *International Labor Migration Database*, Geneva, 1999

20. Many women complete five or more two-year contracts abroad before returning home to stay. About nine hundred recruitment agencies specialize in placing Filipinos in land-based jobs abroad, and three hundred in sea-based jobs. Most are small—the Philippines Overseas Employment Administration (POEA) deployed about 10,000 Overseas Filipino Workers (OFWs) directly in 2003, and the largest agencies deployed 3,000 to 5,000.

21. Protocol To Prevent, Suppress And Punish Trafficking In Persons, Especially Women And Children, Supplementing The United Nations Convention Against Transnational Organized Crime, went into force in 2004.

22. US Congressional Research Service, Report 98-649C, *Trafficking in Women and Children: The US and International Response*, May 10, 2000 (Washington: CRS, 2000).

23. UN Division on the Advancement of Women, *2004 World Survey on Women and International Development: Women and Migration* (New York: United Nations, 2004).

24. Douglas S. Massey, Joaquin Arango, Graeme Hugo, Ali Kouaouci, Adela Pellegrino, and J. Edward Taylor, *Worlds in Motion: Understanding International Migration at the End of the Millennium* (New York: Oxford University Press, 1998).

25. Even if migrants know that movies and TV shows portray exaggerated lifestyles, some who move and find themselves in slave-like conditions abroad report that they did not believe that things in rich countries could be "that bad."

26. David Kyle and Rey Koslowski, eds., *Global Human Smuggling: Comparative Perspectives* (Baltimore: Johns Hopkins University Press, 2001).

27. The 1951 UN Convention Relating to the Status of Refugees (1951 Geneva Convention) obliges signatory countries not to *refoul* or return to danger persons who are outside their countries because of a well-founded fear of persecution related to race, religion, nationality, membership in a particular social group, or political opinion. In 2003, there were 10.4 million refugees, 1 million asylum seekers, 2.4 million refugees who recently returned to their countries of origin, and almost 7 million internally displaced and stateless persons, for a total of 20.6 million persons "of concern" to UNHCR (UNHCR, 2003).

28. Proposition 187 was an initiative approved 59 to 41 by California voters that would have established a state-financed screening system to ensure that unauthorized foreigners did not gain access to, among other things, K–12 schools; publicly-paid, non-emergency health care services; and welfare benefits, and would have required public employees to report suspected unauthorized foreigners to the California Attorney General. See "Prop. 187 Approved in California," *Migration News* 1, No. 12 (December 1994).

CHAPTER THREE

Migration and Economic Development: The 3 R's

International migration moves people from one country to another, and the 3 R's summarize the range of impacts that migrants can have on the development of their countries of origin. *Recruitment* deals with who migrates, asking whether migrants are persons who would have been unemployed or under-employed at home or key employees of business and government whose departure leads to layoffs and reduced services. *Remittances* are the monies sent home by migrants abroad, and questions include their volume and the impacts of their spending and investment on the lives of recipients as well as the communities and regions of origin of the migrants. *Returns* refer to migrants who come back to their countries of origin and ask whether returning migrants bring back new technologies and ideas and stay to foster development, circulate between home and abroad, or return to rest and retire.

The impact of the 3 R's on the differences that prompt international migration vary across countries, which is one reason why the link between migration and development is often described as uncertain or unsettled. Economically motivated migration can set in motion *virtuous circles*, as when young workers who would have been unemployed at home find jobs abroad, send home remittances that reduce poverty and are invested to accelerate economic and job growth, and return with new skills and technologies that lead to new industries and jobs. The result is a convergence in economic conditions and opportunities between sending and receiving areas. The alternative *vicious circle* can unfold if employed nurses, teachers, or engineers are recruited for overseas jobs so that quality and accessibility in health and schooling declines, and factories lay off workers for lack of key managers. In the vicious circle, migrants abroad do not send home significant remittances or send home remittances that fuel inflation rather than lead to job creation and economic growth. In the vicious circle, migrants abroad do not return or return only to rest and retire, so that there is only a limited transfer of new ideas, energies, and entrepreneurial abilities from developed to developing countries via international migration.

Recruitment

Migration is not random: Young people are most likely to move over borders because they have the least "invested" in jobs and careers at home and the most time to recoup their "investment in migration" abroad. Among young people who could move, those who actually migrate over borders depend significantly on the recruitment efforts of employers in destination areas, agents in sending areas, and networks that link the migrants to their final destinations. For example, if employers want information technology (IT) professionals and nurses, networks will evolve to help them move abroad, but if the demand abroad is for maids and farm workers, networks will evolve to move unskilled migrants over borders.

The recruitment of migrants has been concentrated at the extremes of the education ladder, as employers in destination countries seek both migrants with a college education and unskilled migrants. The overseas recruitment of well-educated professional workers is generally done openly, as employers advertise for workers and brokers or agents sign up nurses and computer specialists for overseas jobs. Recruiting college graduates can set in motion virtuous or vicious circles, and the experiences of India with IT specialists and Africa with doctors and nurses frames the virtuous and vicious extremes that link recruitment and development.

IT versus Health Care

India had about $10 billion in revenues from exports of computer-related products in 2003, including services provided to foreign firms in India (outsourcing). India had only 7,000 IT specialists in the mid-1980s, but multinationals recognized their skills and began moving some Indian IT specialists to their operations in other countries in the early 1990s. This led to the creation of brokers who specialized in the recruitment and deployment of Indian IT workers, and India soon became the world's major source of migrant IT workers.

Some of the Indian migrants returned with contracts to provide computer services to firms abroad, and the government bolstered India's budding IT industry that exported services instead of people by reducing barriers to imports of computers, upgrading the communications infrastructure, and allowing the state-supported Indian Institutes of Technologies to admit students on merit, setting quality benchmarks for IT education. Employing Indians in India to do computer work became a growing industry that had important spillover effects, including making improvements to the electricity and telecommunications infrastructure a higher government priority, wider acceptance of merit-based selection systems, and better IT services in India, since it made economic sense to offer Indians the same world-class level of services that were being offered to foreign firms. The virtuous circle was completed with a sharp jump in enrollment in science and engineering schools, pushing the number of IT specialists to 700,000 and making India the world's leading provider of low-cost and high-quality IT specialists and services.

By contrast, the recruitment of African doctors and nurses by hospitals and nursing homes in high-income countries seems to have set in motion a vicious circle of poorer health care that can lower productivity just when the need for health care is growing because of AIDS and initiatives to improve immunization. Many African countries retained colonial-era education systems, so doctors and nurses are trained to colonial-power standards, but financially strained health care systems in Africa find it hard to recruit and retain health care workers, especially in poorer rural areas. In an effort to provide health care services in rural areas, many countries require new graduates who received government support for their education to serve in rural areas, withholding licenses until a year or two of service is completed. Instead of staying in the country, the result is often a rush to emigrate, so that in South Africa, about 40 percent of the 1,300 doctors and 2,500 nurses who graduate each year plan to emigrate as soon as possible. The South African government estimates that it has spent $1 billion educating health workers who emigrated over the past decade, the equivalent of a third of all development aid it received from 1994 to 2000.[1]

How should governments in countries sending and receiving health care workers respond? In May 2004, African countries at the annual assembly of the World Health Organization (WHO) urged developed nations to compensate them for their lost investment in training health care workers, and won a pledge to study ways to reduce the damage from the emigration of nurses. One target of their concern is the British National Health Service (NHS), where starting pay is $31,000 a year, and a recent expansion to reduce waiting times for services has increased the demand for nurses. Since 2001, the NHS has promised not to engage in "aggressive recruitment" of African nurses unless their governments agree, but this promise does not apply to private British hospitals, where African nurses often get their first jobs and later switch to the NHS.

Health care is a peculiar sector, with governments influencing demand via the provision of clinics and charges for patients and drugs, and affecting supply by subsiding training and by setting salaries and working conditions. Local African observers emphasize that compensation may not solve understaffing in rural areas unless there are more fundamental reforms, including raising the wage premium for working in rural areas. Furthermore, there are trained health care workers in many African countries who are not working within their chosen field. For example, there were about 32,000 unfilled nursing jobs in South Africa in 2002, when there were 7,000 South African nurses abroad and 35,000 nurses in South Africa who were not working as nurses.[2]

Countries such as the Philippines and India seek to "market" their health care workers abroad by allowing and promoting training in private, tuition-charging schools, with students taking out loans to get their education and private recruitment firms finding jobs abroad for graduates. In the Philippines, about 15,000 nurses emigrated in 2003, and some doctors were reportedly retraining as nurses in order to increase their opportunities to go abroad.[3] Pay for Filipino nurses abroad was $3,000 to $4,000 a month in 2003, versus $170 a month in urban areas of the Philippines and $75 to $95 a month in rural areas.[4] Patricia Sto. Tomas, Philippines Labor Secretary, says that nurses are "the new growth area for overseas employment," and that Filipinas have a comparative advantage in care giving because they speak English, adding that "We won't lose nurses. The older ones, those in their mid-40s, are not likely to leave. Besides, the student population reacts to markets quickly. Enrollment is high. We won't lack nurses."

Some countries are promoting health tourism, which brings fee-paying private patients to private hospitals in developing countries that provide high-quality care at lower-than-home-country prices. For example, Malaysia has identified "health tourism" as a growth industry, reporting revenue of M$36 million in 2002 and M$54 million in 2003.[5] India is also promoting itself as a health tourism destination, creating a task force in January 2004 to "assess the opportunities for promoting India as a health destination and recommend specific types of health facilities which can be made available for this purpose."[6] As with IT services, the future could be a world in which migrants move from developing to developed countries to provide services and patients arrive in developing countries to obtain services, meaning that there could be more migration of health care workers as well as more trade in health services.

The migration of professionals refers to persons who have completed their education before they cross borders. There is an associated issue involving students from developing countries who study in developed countries. In many ways, foreign student programs are ideal "probationary immigrant" systems, since foreign students can generally stay in the country only if they successfully complete their studies, which require learning the host-country language and becoming familiar with host country ways of study and work. If foreign students find an employer to hire them after graduation, more countries are permitting them to remain.

In 2000, there were two million foreign students in the Organization for Economic Cooperation and Development (OECD) countries, half from outside the OECD, including 34 percent in the United States, 16 percent in the UK, 13 percent in Germany, 11 percent in France, and 8 percent in Australia (OECD, 2002, 52). Foreign students tend to study subjects that impart skills transferable internationally, e.g., science and engineering rather than law, and many institutions of higher education have become dependent on the revenues from foreign students. Michael Teitelbaum (2003) argues that the high percentage of foreign students in U.S. doctoral programs reflects labor market deficiencies and student desires for immigrant visas, not necessarily a "national need" for more PhDs in basic sciences. In many basic sciences, six or more years of graduate study are followed by five to ten years of low-paid postdoctoral research, so that graduates do not get "real jobs" until age 35 or 40.[7]

Unskilled Migrants

Few migrants set off blindly in search of better opportunities abroad. Instead, they move with the help of networks created by employers in destination countries who employ migrants as domestic helpers, farm workers, and service workers, usually with the blessing or at least toleration of their governments. After an initial period of recruitment sets migration flows in motion, networks often allow migration to expand, as experienced migrants recruit families and friends into workplaces that offer low-wage and high-turnover jobs.

The fact that the origins of most unskilled migrant flows lie inside destination countries has important implications for migration management. When destination country governments stop legal recruitment or announce that they will no longer tolerate unauthorized flows, they are attempting to break a link that has evolved to serve the interests of both migrants and their employers. A common mistake in many destination countries is to imagine that stopping legal recruitment will stop the flow of migrants, much as placing a dam across a river will stop the flow of water. But migration networks are like rivulets that form a delta, so that stopping recruitment is like placing one barrier on a multifaceted flow, and migrants can respond to one migration barrier by using other channels to cross borders.

The story of employers and migrants becoming dependent on each other and migration networks diversifying over time to make governmental controls more difficult is a familiar one on both sides of the Atlantic. The United States allowed the recruitment of Mexican bracero workers between 1942 and 1964, and most European governments allowed the recruitment of guest workers in the 1960s and early 1970s. Governments assumed that stopping recruitment would stop migration, and they were wrong—migration continued, but with workers arriving through different and often harder-to-manage channels. Experience shows that labor recruitment in one channel in one period can lead to migration in defiance of laws and via different channels in later periods, with the development of a private migration infrastructure contributing to the loss of governmental control. This means that unless remittances and return promote stay-at-home, the recruitment of guest workers can beget more migration.

Remittances

Remittances, the portion of migrant incomes abroad that are sent home, can reduce poverty and the incentive to emigrate. Remittances have risen with numbers of migrants and surpassed official development assistance as a source of capital in developing countries in the mid-1990s. In recent years, as foreign direct investment and capital market flows to developing countries have

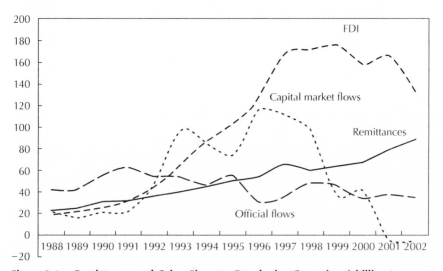

Figure 3.1.   Remittances and Other Flows to Developing Countries ($ billions)

Source: Ratha, Dilip. 2003. Workers' Remittances: An Important and Stable Source of External Development Finance. Chapter 7 in *Global Development Finance 2003.* World Bank. www.worldbank.org/prospects/gdf2003/.

decreased, remittances are the only financial flow to developing countries still on an upward path.

The growth of remittances has stirred hopes that they can become the foreign capital needed to reduce poverty and stimulate development. The International Monetary Fund (IMF) estimates remittances for each country in its Balance of Payments Statistics Yearbook, and distinguishes two major types of funds transferred: worker remittances, the wages and salaries sent home by migrants abroad for twelve or more months;[8] and compensation of employees (called labor income until 1995), the wages and benefits of migrants sent home by those abroad less than twelve months.[9] The volume of remittances depends on the number of migrants abroad, their earnings, and their willingness to remit. Global remittances to developing countries more than doubled between the late 1980s and the late 1990s, after experiencing drops in 1991 (Gulf War) and in 1998 (Asian financial crisis). There has been especially strong growth in remittances since 2000, with remittances approaching $150 billion a year.

A handful of developing countries receive most of the remittances. The three largest recipients are India, Mexico, and the Philippines, and they received a third of total remittances to developing countries in recent years. The top six recipients, these three plus Morocco, Egypt, and Turkey, receive half of all remittances to developing countries. Remittances are most

Table 3.1. Remittances to Developing Countries, 1988–2002

	Remits ($million)	Percent Change
1988	28,340	
1989	32,136	13%
1990	39,052	22%
1991	33,050	−15%
1992	37,196	13%
1993	38,872	5%
1994	44,134	14%
1995	50,632	15%
1996	54,851	8%
1997	65,021	19%
1998	60,895	−6%
1999	65,325	7%
2000	64,500	−1%
2001	72,300	12%
2002	80,000	11%
Total	766,304	
1988–2002		182%

Source: www.worldbank.org/prospects/gdf2003/gdf_statApp_web.pdf (p. 198).

Table 3.2.   Remittances to Selected Countries, 1995–2001

	1995	1996	1997	1998	1999	2000	2001
Developing Countries ($billion)	48	53	63	60	65	65	72
India	6.2	8.8	10.3	9.5	11.1	9.2	10
Mexico	4.4	5	5.5	6.5	6.6	7.6	9.9
Philippines	5.4	4.9	6.8	5.1	6.9	6.2	6.4
Morocco	2	2.2	1.9	2	1.9	2.2	3.3
Egypt	3.2	3.1	3.7	3.4	3.2	2.9	2.9
Turkey	3.3	3.5	4.2	5.4	4.5	4.6	2.8
Subtotal	24.5	27.5	32.4	31.9	34.2	32.7	35.3
Share of Total (percent)							
India	13	17	16	16	17	14	14
Mexico	9	10	9	11	10	12	14
Philippines	11	9	11	9	11	10	9
Morocco	4	4	3	3	3	3	5
Egypt	7	6	6	6	5	4	4
Turkey	7	7	7	9	7	7	4
Big 6 share	51	52	52	54	53	51	49

Source: www.worldbank.org/prospects/gdf2003/gdf_statApp_web.pdf (p. 198).

important in smaller nations, where they can be equivalent to 20 to 40 percent of GDP. In 2001, remittances were 37 percent of GDP in Tonga, 26 percent in Lesotho, 23 percent in Jordan, and 15 to 17 percent in Albania, Nicaragua, Yemen, and Moldova. The major sources of remittances were the United States, $28 billion in 2001; Saudi Arabia, $15 billion; and Germany, Belgium, and Switzerland, $8 billion each.

In order to increase the development payoff of remittances, the World Bank's *Global Development Finance Report*[10] investigated how to increase the access of workers to official banking channels, which would allow governments to borrow against expected remittances,[11] as well as how to lower transfer fees, which average 13 percent of the amount transferred. Many countries are taking steps to make it easier for migrants to open bank accounts, which has the side effect of increasing competition in the money transfer business, a sector with high fixed and low marginal costs.

Remittance Fees

Studies demonstrate convincingly that the best way to maximize the volume of remittances is to have an appropriate exchange rate and economic policies that promise growth.[12] Migrants whose families remain in their countries of origin generally remit over half of their earnings and are more likely to remit more, invest, and return if they see opportunities for profitable investment at home. Migrants whose families join them abroad are likely to remit less, although many provide support to parents and other relatives at home.

Since the September 11, 2001, terrorism attacks, there has been a new emphasis on how migrants remit funds. Most governments want remittances to arrive via formal channels such as banks so they enter the country's monetary system, add to the stock of foreign exchange, and can be more easily measured (and perhaps taxed). Migrants have demonstrated a willingness to transfer money via official channels, especially if bank transfers are easy and cheap, but this usually requires banking outlets in migrant communities at home and abroad and competition to lower transfer costs.

There has been considerable progress to reduce remittance fees and to encourage transfers via banks. However, in one of the largest transfer markets, that between the United States and Mexico, about 40 percent of the 25 million consumer money transfers in 2000 went through First Data Corp's Western Union subsidiary. Western Union offers several options, each with different fees and services, such as a 3-minute telephone call and the funds within an hour versus 24 hours.[13] Average charges are $5 to $20, or 2 to 7 percent of the $300 typically sent.[14]

The U.S.-Mexico remittance market is unregulated, in the sense that Mexicans in the United States decide how and how much to remit. Several Asian countries have specified both the amount of remittances migrants must send home and the form in which remittances are sent. For example, many Korean migrants in the Middle East in the late 1970s and early 1980s were considered employees of their Korean construction company while abroad and had their earnings sent to their families in Korea while receiving a stipend in local currency abroad. Many Chinese and Vietnamese migrants go abroad as employees of Chinese and Vietnamese firms, and their wages are paid in a similar way—most go to the migrant's family or bank account in the country of origin currency. The Philippines, in a policy unpopular with migrants, attempted to specify how much each migrant should remit in the 1980s, but later abandoned the policy.

Forced savings programs are unpopular with migrants. Migrants from Jamaica, Barbados, Saint Lucia, and Dominica have been recruited by U.S. farmers since 1943 under the auspices of the British West Indies Central Labor Organization (BWICLO), which required migrants to sign a contract agreeing to pay a fee of five percent of their earnings to BWICLO for its services and to have U.S. employers deposit 20 percent of each workers' earnings in a Jamaican savings bank. Migrants complained that they had difficulty getting back these forced savings, or received them with no interest. After protests, the Jamaican bank belatedly began to pay interest. Between 1942 and 1946, Mexican braceros had 10 percent of their earnings sent from U.S. employers to a U.S. bank and then on to the Bank of Mexico, but many war-time braceros complain they never received these forced savings after they returned to Mexico. The Mexican government says it has no records of what happened to the money, but after suits were filed in the United States, the Mexican government in 2005 established a $27 million fund to reimburse ex-braceros, illustrating how the aftereffects of this guest worker program persist sixty years later.

Impacts of Remittance

Remittances improve the lives of recipients, and can under some circumstances accelerate development that reduces poverty. A study of seventy-four low- and middle-income developing countries found that a 10 percent increase in the share of remittances in a country's gross domestic product (GDP) was associated with a 1.2 percent decline in the share of people living on less than $1 per person per day.[15] This poverty-reduction effect is associated with the spending of remittances, which can generate jobs and thus benefit non-migrants as well. Most studies suggest that each $1 in remittances generates a $2 to $3 increase in economic output, as recipients buy goods or invest in housing, education, or health care, and these additional jobs can reduce poverty.

Most remittances are used for consumption, helping to explain their stability[16] even as exchange rates and investment outlooks change in migrant countries of origin. Dilip Ratha noted that remittances to high-debt and less-transparent countries were more stable than those to middle-income open economies because the latter include more remittances destined for investment.[17] In an effort to attract remittances and spur development, many developing countries made their exchange rates more realistic in the 1990s, which improved the climate for foreign investment, including migrant investments.

Classical theories of migration suggested that the emigration of men in the prime of their working lives would reduce economic output in migrant areas of origin or leave output unchanged in Lewis-type economic development models in which a country's surplus labor was trapped in agriculture.[18] Empirical research suggests that while emigration may initially reduce output in local economies, remittances quickly lead to adjustments that maintain output, as when migrant families that lose males to migration shift from growing crops to less labor-intensive livestock or hire labor to continue to produce crops. In some cases, the exit of men and the return of remittances can increase output, as when agricultural productivity was constrained by the unavailability of credit to buy machinery or construct irrigation systems, and remittances provide the funds for the machinery or irrigation that increases output.

Remittances have many other effects in the communities in which they arrive. A very visible effect of remittances is new and improved housing. Many migrant families build more housing than they need, introducing rental housing in areas that previously had none. This can have follow-on socio-economic consequences, as when newlyweds began to live away from in-laws in rural Turkey as rental housing became available.[19]

Women often assume new roles in the absence of migrant husbands, and some become moneylenders in their villages, a remarkable change in often-traditional areas. Remittances may also allow children to remain in school for longer periods and to improve nutrition, which can have long-term benefits for development. There is a growing literature on risk and relativity reasons to migrate and remit, as when a farmer is more likely to try planting new seeds or crops if he is receiving remittances from abroad that cushion the risk of crop failure. Alternatively, if one family uses remittances to buy a TV and a satellite dish, there is pressure on other families to send out migrants and get remittances to keep up with their neighbors.[20]

The role of remittances in reducing poverty and speeding development has attracted the attention of the leaders of many major emigration countries. Mexican President Vicente Fox, for example, calls Mexican migrants in the U.S. "heroes" for the remittances Fox says are vital to Mexico's development. The Mexican government has expanded programs under which federal, state, and local governments match remittances that are invested to improve infrastructure in migrant communities of origin under so-called 3-for-1 programs—each $1 of remittances invested in government-approved infrastructure projects receives an additional $3 match from federal, state, and local governments, so that in 2004 the $20 million in remittance donations were matched to support $80 million of infrastructure projects. Some Mexican states such as Zacatecas have teamed up with the InterAmerican Development Bank to match remittance funds devoted to infrastructure improvement and to support returned migrants who invest in job-creating enterprises such as the value-added processing of farm commodities.[21]

In addition to remittances, migrants can steer investments to their countries of origin and sometimes persuade their foreign employers to buy products from their countries of origin. For example, professionals abroad can steer investments to their countries of origin as well as invest at home. Migration increases travel and tourism between countries as well as trade in ethnic foods and other home-country items. Migrants abroad may un-dertake many other activities, including organizing themselves to provide funds for political parties and candidates.

Returns

The third R in the migration and development equation is returns. Ideally, entrepreneurial migrants who have been abroad return and provide the en-ergy and ideas needed to start or expand businesses at home, and workers re-turn with the skills and discipline needed to raise productivity at home. Mi-grants are generally drawn from the ranks of the risk takers at home, and if their savings from work abroad are combined with risk-taking behavior, the result can be a new impetus for economic development. On the other hand, if migrants settle abroad and cut ties to their countries of origin, or if they re-turn only to rest and retire, their return may have limited development im-pacts. In the extreme, returning to rest and retire can slow development if workers acquire a work-abroad and rest-at-home mentality. There is also the possibility of back-and-forth circulation, which can under some conditions contribute to economic growth in both countries.

Government programs and policies can sometimes plant the seeds that lead to the return of migrants and investment and job creation. For example, Taiwan invested most of its educational resources in primary and secondary education in the 1970s, so that Taiwanese seeking higher education often went abroad for study, and over 90 percent remained overseas despite rapid economic growth in Taiwan.[22] During the 1980s, before the end of martial law, more Taiwanese graduates began to return as they perceived economic opportunities, and others maintained "homes" in North America and spent so much time commuting that they were called "astronauts" because of the time they spent on planes.

A major governmental effort that attracted migrants home was the Hin-schu Science-based Industrial Park, begun in 1980 to create a concentration of creative expertise in Taiwan to rival Silicon Valley. The government pro-vided financial incentives for high-tech businesses to locate in Hinschu, in-cluding subsidized Western-style housing (Luo and Wang, 2002). By 2000, Hinschu park was a major success, employing over 100,000 workers in 300 companies that had sales of $28 billion. About 40 percent of the companies were headed by returned overseas migrants, and 10 percent of the 4,100 re-turned migrants employed in the park had PhD degrees.

The Taiwanese experience suggests that investing heavily in the type of education appropriate to the stage of economic development and then tapping the "brain reserve overseas" when the country's economy demands more brainpower can be a very successful strategy. Mainland China has adopted this model, with leader Premier Zhao Ziyang calling overseas Chinese "stored brainpower overseas," and encouraging Chinese cities to offer financial subsidies to attract migrants home, which explains why many Chinese cities have "Returning Student Entrepreneur Buildings."[23] However, most Chinese who studied abroad remain abroad: 580,000 went abroad since 1979, but only 25 percent returned by 2002.

The poorest countries pose the largest return challenges. The International Organization for Migration (IOM) operates a return-of-talent program for professional Africans abroad, providing them with travel and wage subsidies if they sign two-year contracts to work in the public sector of their country of origin. The UN Development Program (UNDP) has a similar Transfer of Knowledge Through Expatriate Nationals (TOKTEN) program that subsidizes the return of teachers and researchers. Most returning professionals under these programs have an immigrant or long-term secure status abroad. By one estimate, there are 250,000 African-born professionals outside Africa, and 100,000 mostly non-African professionals working in Africa for UN agencies and under the auspices of other aid programs, prompting Sussex University's Richard Black to call subsidized return-of-talent programs "expensive failures," since they bring temporary return but not the "investment that [long-term return] should bring."[24]

Even if migrants do not return immediately, they can contribute to development by maintaining links with their countries of origin, increasing the probability of an eventual return. One way for sending countries to maintain links to their nationals abroad is to permit dual nationality or dual citizenship. Jagdish Bhagwati emphasizes that dual nationality can lead to "a Diaspora model [of development], which integrates past and present citizens into a web of rights and obligations in the extended community defined with the home country as the center."[25] Bhagwati notes that migrants abroad can generate "political remittances," including ideas that help to speed up change in often-traditional sending countries.

There are two caveats to the potential benefits of the Diaspora for development in their countries of origin. First, it is often asserted that instead of promoting returns with subsidies or asking international organizations to subsidize returns, sending countries could retain far more migrants by reducing discrimination, as occurs when only those from the right tribe or political party are allowed to work in the government. Second, the Diaspora can be a force for conflict rather than development at home, as when migrants provide the funds to prolong civil wars or conflicts.[26]

Development and Migration

Poverty is seen as a root cause of migration and development or a reduction in poverty as the solution for unwanted migration. For this reason, attacking the "root causes" of migration is widely heralded as the surest path to decrease irregular and unwanted migration. For example, the European Union in Seville in 2002 declared that "an integrated, comprehensive and balanced approach to tackle the root causes of irregular migration must remain the European Union's constant long-term objective."

The 3 R's can operate in a manner that helps to make migration self-stopping, as migration promotes convergence in wages between countries, as occurred between Europe and North America in the late nineteenth and early twentieth centuries and between southern and northern Europe in the 1960s and 1970s.[27] However, economic theory teaches that convergence can also be achieved as jobs move to workers via freer trade and investment, so that trade can be a substitute for migration. The U.S. Commission for the Study of International Migration and Cooperative Economic Development, in searching for "mutually beneficial" ways to reduce unwanted migration, concluded that freer trade was preferable to more migration as a way to promote the convergence that would reduce unwanted migration: "Expanded trade between the sending countries and the United States is the single most important remedy."[28]

Trade means that a product is produced in one country, taken over borders, and bought and consumed in another. Economic theory teaches that comparative advantage increases global income. The argument is as follows. If countries specialize in producing those goods in which they have a relative advantage because of their resources, location, or capital-labor costs then, even if one country can produce all goods cheaper than another, both are still better off specializing in the production of the goods they can produce most efficiently, exporting some, and importing goods they cannot produce as efficiently. Trade can also lead to economies of scale, which lowers the cost of production as output increases for a larger market.

Most political leaders assume that if the trade and migration are both substitutes in the long run, they are also substitutes in the short-run. This is why then-Mexican President Carlos Salinas, in arguing in favor of NAFTA in the early 1990s, asserted that freer trade means "more jobs . . . [and] higher wages in Mexico, and this in turn will mean fewer migrants to the United States and Canada. We want to export goods, not people."[29]

However, there can be job-displacement in emigration areas in response to freer trade, as when TV factories in the United States close and reopen in lower-wage Mexico, and Mexican farmers quit growing corn because of cheaper imports. The displaced U.S. workers are not likely to migrate to Mexico, but since rural Mexicans were migrating to the United States before there was freer trade, more may emigrate because of freer trade. The U.S. Commission anticipated this temporary increase in migration, warning that "the economic development process itself tends in the short to medium term to stimulate migration." Thus, there can be a migration hump—a temporary increase in migration that accompanies freer trade.[30]

The Migration Hump

A migration hump in response to economic integration between labor-sending and -receiving countries leads to a paradox: The same economic policies that can reduce migration in the long run can increase it in the short run, or, in the words of the U.S. Commission, there is "a very real short-term versus long-term dilemma" to persuade a skeptical public that freer trade is the best long-run way to reduce unwanted migration.[31] Political leaders can explain that the short-run increase in migration associated with freer trade is a worthwhile price to pay for policies that reduce unwanted immigration in the long run, but they must first understand why trade and migration can rise together.

The steadily rising line in figure 3.2 represents the status-quo migration flow, and the hump line depicts the additional migration associated with freer trade and economic integration; the number of migrants is measured on the Y-axis and time on the X-axis. Without economic integration, migration rises

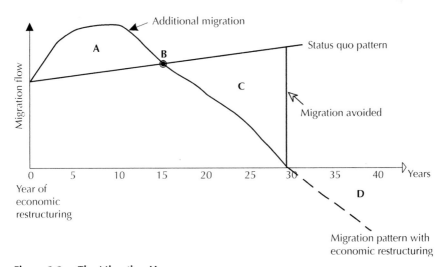

Figure 3.2. The Migration Hump

in the status-quo scenario because of faster demographic growth and slower economic growth in emigration countries. Economic integration, on the other hand, leads to a temporary increase in migration, represented by A. However, economic integration should also speed up economic and job growth, and the downside of the hump is shown in the movement toward B. As economic integration accelerates convergence, area C represents the migration avoided by economic integration, while area D represents the migration transition, which occurs when a net migrant sending country becomes a net receiving country.

The critical policy parameters are A, B, and C—how much does migration increase as a result of economic integration (A), how soon does this hump disappear (B), and how much migration is "avoided" by economic integration (C)? Generally, three factors must be present to create a migration hump: a continued demand-pull for migrants in the destination country, an increased supply-push in the origin country as a result of labor displacement and slow job growth, and migration networks that can move workers across borders. The usual comparative static economic analysis involves comparisons of equilibrium points before and after economic changes, not the process of adjustment to a new equilibrium; the migration hump is precisely this process of adjustment.

Trade Theory and the Migration Hump

Standard trade theory allows trade and migration to be complements, meaning they increase together, when some of its basic assumptions do not hold. These assumptions are in five major areas: including identical production technologies; factor homogeneity; constant returns to scale; instantaneous adjustment; and perfect competition, full employment, and complete markets. By relaxing these assumptions, we can see why there can be a migration hump.

Suppose a country in the North (N) is capital rich, and a country in the South (S) is capital poor. If the two countries share the same technologies or production functions, and if the same two factors of production, capital, and labor are used in each country to produce two items, free trade means that each country will export the product that is more intensive in the factor that is relatively more abundant. This means that Country N will import labor-intensive goods from Country S, and Country S will import capital-intensive goods from Country N.

Wolfgang Stolper and Paul Samuelson considered the effect on factor prices (wages and the return on capital) of an import tariff that increases the domestic price of the import-competing product relative to the price of the export product.[32]

Table 3.3. Theoretical Rationales for Migration Humps

Theoretical Rationale	Complementarity between Trade and Migration in the Short Run	Substitutability between Trade and Migration in the Long Run	Reason for Larger Migration Hump
Technology Differences	Labor-intensive production in south cannot compete with capital-intensive production in north	Production of goods in which south has a comparative advantage generates jobs	Poor infrastructure and public services may retard new job creation
Factor Productivity Differences	Wage differences are insufficient to create comparative advantage in labor-intensive production in south	Public investment in education and infrastructure closes the productivity gap	Failure of public policies to close productivity gap over time
Economies of Scale	Industries using migrant labor in the north expand, lowering costs of production and south cannot compete	Public investment in education and infrastructure in south closes the productivity gap	Failure of public policies to counteract scale economies in northern migrant-intensive industries
Adjustment Lags and Costs	Lags between economic integration and job creation Factor specificity: displaced corn farmers not hired as factory workers, so loss of subsidies prompts emigration	Economic integration creates jobs in south, especially for better educated younger workers most prone to migrate	Poor public services discourage investment, extend the investment-employment lag, and fail to overcome factor specificity problems
Market Failures	New jobs in south provide the funds to undertake risky migration	New jobs and factor market development offer alternatives for migration	Limited employment expansion to provide attractive alternatives to migration, due to above

Source: see text

If the underlying trade pattern is not altered by the tariff, the import tariff increases the real reward of the relatively-scarce factor and lowers the real reward of the other factor, meaning that a tariff levied against labor-intensive imports in Country N will increase Country N wages. Free trade would thus shift the production of labor-intensive goods from Country N to S, and shift capital-intensive goods from Country S to N. One result of freer trade is thus more jobs producing labor-intensive goods and upward pressure on Country S wages, which should discourage emigration.[33]

However, if there are technology differences, trade and migration can be complements despite freer trade. For example, corn production has been highly protected by Mexican government policies that in the early 1990s guaranteed farmers twice the world price. The 3 to 4 million Mexican corn farmers produced half as much corn as the 75,000 Iowa corn farmers, and the Iowa farmers used herbicides and other capital inputs rather than the oxen and intermittent rainfall on which many small Mexican farmers depended. With freer trade, the Iowa farmers can export corn to Mexico and undercut Mexican farmers who use labor-intensive production methods, illustrating the fact that if the basis for trade is differences in technology, trade and migration can increase together.

Factor productivity differences between countries are one reason to trade, but the *reasons* for these productivity differences can help to explain migration behavior. If Mexican workers are more productive in the United States than they are in Mexico because of the better U.S. public and private infrastructure, migration and trade can rise together. This is what occurred in the 1980s, when much of the Mexican shoe industry moved from Leon, Mexico, to Los Angeles, resulting in shoes produced with Mexican workers in Los Angeles being exported to Mexico. Migration and trade, by converting less productive Mexican workers into more productive U.S. workers, in this case discouraged the production a labor-intensive product in Mexico and encouraged migration to the United States.[34]

A third assumption of the standard trade model is that (identical) production functions in the two countries exhibit constant returns to scale, which means that increasing all inputs by 10 percent increases output by 10 percent. However, if costs of production fall as output expands, especially in industries that employ migrant workers, freer trade may expand production in the immigration country, increasing the demand-pull for migrants. This is what occurred in the 1960s in France and Germany, when importing guest workers and free trade helped car companies achieve economies of scale and discouraged the production of cars in countries sending guest workers abroad. When the basis of trade is economies of scale, migration and trade can be complements.

The fourth assumption of the standard trade model is that adjustments to changing prices and wages are instantaneous, and that the process of adjustment does not affect the eventual equilibrium. However, free trade and economic integration often lead to restructuring that displaces workers, and the unemployed may require some time to find new jobs. For example, freeing up trade in corn can immediately displace Mexican farmers but not immediately create new jobs in the areas in which farmers were displaced. Factor specificity, meaning that displaced farmers can work in agriculture but are not hired by factories, means that freer trade encourages more ex-farmers to migrate to work in agriculture abroad.

The fifth assumption of trade theory is that markets are perfect, individuals are rational and have full information, and there are no transaction costs. The realities of missing or incomplete markets, imperfect information, and high transaction costs are the hallmarks of the so-called new economics of labor migration, and they can explain why migration may not fall as quickly as trade economists predict. For example, people confronting market imperfections may respond by migrating, as when there is no (or no affordable) insurance available in rural areas, so that if the crop fails or a family member gets sick and runs up health care bills, the only or fastest way to repay emergency loans may be to emigrate. Similarly, if poor people who want to build a house cannot borrow the needed money, one response is emigration.

Risk also affects migration patterns. If migration is irregular, not all of those attempting to migrate over borders will succeed; some will be apprehended and returned. For example, suppose freer trade leads to export processing zones (EPZ) that employ mostly young women holding their first job. In such cases, a farm family may send daughters to the EPZ and, with the security of this income from legal internal migration, be willing to borrow to send sons on the much riskier international migration circuit.

The Migration Transition

Trade and migration can increase together when income differences between labor-sending and -receiving countries are more than four or five to one. Once wage differences narrow to four to one or less and job growth offers opportunities at home, the "hope factor" can deter especially irregular migration—most people prefer to stay near family and friends rather than cross national borders, especially if their migration is irregular.[35] Continued economic and job growth should eventually reduce migration pressures, offering a powerful argument for freer trade and investment.[36]

Economic factors determine the speed of income convergence, but migration networks can play a role that shortens or lengthens the migration hump. If there are dense and efficient networks, the sensitivity or elasticity of migration to wage and employment changes at home and abroad is likely to be greater. This helps to explain why trade-induced changes in rural Mexico are more likely to be translated into international migration to the United States than similar free trade effects in Chile.

Industrial countries that want to reduce the size of the migration hump can also encourage foreign direct investment (FDI) and provide aid. FDI rose rapidly in the 1990s, peaking in 1997 at $196 billion, reflecting widespread privatization programs that allowed foreign investors to buy previously state-owned operations as well as industrial country firms seeking higher return opportunities abroad. However, FDI is concentrated: The top ten developing country recipients of FDI between 1992 and 2001 received 70 to 80 percent of the total, China, Brazil, Mexico, Argentina, Poland, Chile, Malaysia, Thailand, the Czech Republic, and Venezuela, with China alone accounting for almost 40 percent. The incentive to invest in developing countries is driven by expected profits, not the need for jobs to reduce emigration, and much FDI goes to low- and middle-income countries that are net immigration areas, including Argentina, Malaysia, Thailand, and the Czech Republic. In the case of Malaysia and Thailand, for example, foreign investors often create jobs that are filled by migrants.

What role can Official Development Assistance (ODA), the grants, and low-interest loans given by one government to assist development in another, play in reducing the migration hump? In 2000, the OECD nations that are members of the Development Assistance Committee provided $54 billion in ODA,[37] about the same as the $53 billion in 1990, but this aid represented a smaller percentage of donor and recipient GDP. Some countries, notably France, call their aid programs "co-development" to stress that they envision cooperation in economic development and other areas of mutual interest with the countries receiving their aid. Since 2000, for example, the annual Mali-France Consultation on Migration has dealt with the integration of Malians who want to stay in France; co-management of migration flows; and cooperative development in emigration areas of Mali to reduce migration pressures.

During the current Doha "development round" of trade reform talks, many developing countries have highlighted the obstacles erected by industrial countries to their farm commodity exports. Their case was bolstered by the World Bank, which concluded that freer trade in farm commodities is more important than more ODA in stimulating economic development: "Trade reform in both industrial and developing countries would have a larger impact

Table 3.4.　ODA and Farm Subsidies: 1990s

	ODA($billions)	Farm Support (PSE $billions)	
	2000	1999	1986–88
DAC/OECD 24	56	252	221
U.S.	10	54	42
Japan	13	59	54
EU	28	114	95

DAC is Development Assistance Committee members of the OECD
PSE is producer support equivalent
PSE is the value of transfers from taxpayers (payments) and consumers (higher prices) to farmers

on improving welfare in developing countries than any of the increases in aid. . . . Industrial countries spend more than $300 billion a year in agricultural subsidies, more than six times the amount they spend on foreign aid." If developing countries had unrestricted access to industrial country markets, their GDPs would rise 5 percent, according to the World Bank, more than they gain from remittances.[38]

Most migrant-receiving countries protect their farm sectors, generally by guaranteeing their farmers higher-than-world-market prices for the commodities they produce, and often donating or subsidizing the sale of the surplus, depressing world prices for farm commodities. This limits the incentives for farmers in developing countries to stay on the farm and promotes emigration.[39] Furthermore, farm subsidies in rich countries are rising: between the late 1980s and late 1990s, the producer support equivalent (PSE) level of subsidy for the farm sector in the United States, Japan, and the European Union (EU) rose from about four times their level of aid to five times. Prospects for reducing developed country farm subsidies are mixed.

Linking Aid and Migration Cooperation

Migration can reduce poverty via remittances, but the emigration safety valve and remittances can slow the impetus for the fundamental structural changes needed for development. Structural changes often threaten established interests in emigration countries, so that emigration can act like the discovery of natural resource wealth, relieving the pressure for the painful economic and political changes needed for long-run economic growth.

Several countries illustrate the dilemma and raise the question of whether aid should be linked to cooperation on migration management. Moldova, one of the smallest and most densely populated countries that arose from the breakup of the USSR, has perhaps 25 percent of its population abroad, including a disproportionate number of young people. Older residents nostalgic for the security of Soviet times have re-elected to power ex-communist leaders, one of whom said "emigration is better than revolution," suggesting that the changes that young people would demand if they were not abroad can be postponed.

Should the aid received by emigration countries such as Moldova be made conditional on cooperation to manage migration? Conditionality is increasing in the provision of aid, as with the U.S. Millennium Challenge Account, which adds $2 billion to the $16 billion the United States annually provides in ODA but provides these additional funds only to countries with per capita annual incomes below $1,435 that meet performance standards in the areas of human rights, democracy, and lack of corruption.

At their June 2002 meeting in Seville, the leaders of Spain, Italy, and Britain proposed sanctions including less aid for "uncooperative countries in the fight against illegal immigration." France and Sweden resisted, arguing that denying aid to such countries would simply increase poverty and emigration pressures. Decisions on immigration and asylum require unanimity, and EU leaders eventually agreed to "a systematic evaluation of relations with third countries that do not collaborate with the fight against illegal immigration."[40]

The Challenge: Cooperative Migration Management to Promote Development

International labor migration is a response to differences that encourage individuals to cross national borders. Voluntary migration increases incomes for migrants and, by lowering wages and prices in receiving countries, provides an extra increment to host-country GDP. Most governments want to reduce the differences that prompt migration by accelerating growth in sending countries, not reducing wages in receiving countries, to level up and not down. Most governments embrace the idea that the "root causes" of migration must be dealt with, but the past fifty years have demonstrated that reducing the inequalities that promote international migration is neither simple nor quick. The World Bank says that "migration is the most underresearched of the global flows," and a better understanding of migration could help to turn migration from a source of conflict into an area of cooperation (World Bank, 2002, 82).[41]

When there are few differences between countries, there tend to be few barriers to migration and little unwanted migration. Most industrial countries permit nationals of other developed countries to travel without visas, and a major issue within regional blocks such as the EU is how to increase the mobility of those with freedom of movement rights.

Developing countries can be arrayed along an emigration pressure spectrum, ranging from countries that are mostly sources of migrants, such as the Philippines and Myanmar, to countries that both send and receive significant numbers of migrants, such as Poland and Morocco, to countries that are more mostly destinations for migrants, such as most industrial countries. Each type of country has different migration interests: The mostly sending countries have a primary interest in protecting their nationals abroad and maximizing remittances, the senders and receivers have interests in protection and remittances but also in control, and integration, and the mostly receivers have development, control, and integration interests.

Top-Down vs. Bottom-Up

Most prescriptions for reconciling the interests of sending, transit, and receiving countries call for a "new international regime for the orderly movements of people," such as a World Migration Organization (WMO) analogous to the World Trade Organization (WTO).[42] Proponents of this top-down approach to migration management hope that a WMO could take the lead to establish rules for moving various kinds of migrants over national borders and develop norms that could eventually lead to more legal channels for migrants, much as the WTO is credited for keeping the world moving toward freer trade. A WMO could be launched as a result of a global conference on migration, and the UN in March 1999 sent letters to its permanent members asking whether a global conference on migration should be convened. Support was lukewarm, and so the UN launched a Global Commission on Migration in 2004 to place migration on the global agenda, examine gaps in migration management and linkages between migration and development, and make recommendations to maximize the benefits and reduce the costs of international migration.

The quest for a WMO highlights a key difference between trade and migration. Economic theory suggests that nations that do not trade hurt themselves and the global economy, but there is no comparable theory that unambiguously shows that countries failing to send or receive migrants hurt themselves or reduce global economic output. Using standard trade theory, Bob Hamilton and John Whalley estimated that global GDP could more than double with migration that equalized the marginal productivity of labor (and wages) among 179 countries grouped into seven world regions, adding $5 trillion to $16 trillion to global GDP, which was $8 trillion in 1977.[43]

However, the fact that most countries are not open to migrants suggests that they are ignoring huge potential economic gains, or that the assumptions underlying the estimates are overly optimistic.[44]

Challenges and Opportunities

Migration is generally a force for individual and global betterment. Individuals moving to take advantage of higher wages and more opportunities generally benefit themselves, their host countries, and sometimes the countries they left. However, there is no scientific basis for calculating an optimal rate of migration, which means that there is no agreement on whether the current 3 percent of the world's residents who are migrants is optimal, or whether the 10 percent of persons born in Mexico who are U.S. residents is optimal. The migrant share of the global population and work force, as well as migrant shares in particular countries, varies with economic, social, and political conditions, which is why a continuing dialogue that honestly evaluates the tradeoffs inherent in migration is the foundation for effective migration management.

Differences prompt migration, but most international and many national standards call for equal treatment of migrants. This complicates the discussion of tradeoffs in migration management, because there is an inverse relationship between the number of migrants and the rights of migrants—the number of migrants tends to fall as rights and equal treatment rise. Globally, the fastest growth in migrant employment is outside established channels designed to admit and protect foreign workers, that is, in unauthorized migration. This poses a fundamental challenge for governments and international organizations: Should they try to put unauthorized migrants and their jobs into established and legal channels by stepping up enforcement and having legalization programs, or should they accept a layered labor market and society in which rights and conditions for migrants vary with legal status and other factors?

Worker and migrant advocates believe strongly that there can be only one labor market and one set of rights and privileges, that labor rights are nonnegotiable human rights. Many reject a numbers and rights tradeoff, as when the AFL-CIO in the United States calls for legalization for unauthorized workers as well as an end to the enforcement of employer sanctions laws, arguing that sporadic enforcement only serves to intimidate unauthorized workers. On the other hand, most economists and employers acknowledge that there is a relationship between numbers and rights, emphasizing that if equality of wages and treatment were mandated and enforced strictly, there would likely be fewer migrant workers because trade, mechanization, or other changes would reduce the demand for them.

In searching for the proper balance between migrant numbers and rights, we must be mindful of the fact that in managing migration, the perfect can be the enemy of the good. The quest for comprehensive international labor migration conventions, for example, can lead to a panoply of rights for migrants but to very few ratifications that permit the monitoring of the efforts of governments to enforce these rights. Finding the proper balance between numbers and rights is a difficult and complex challenge for migrants, employers, and governments in the twenty-first century. We will return to this issue in the final chapter of this book.

Notes

1. Celia W. Dugger, "In Africa, an Exodus of Nurses," *New York Times*, July 12, 2004.

2. Physicians for Human Rights, winner of the Nobel Peace Prize in 1997 for its work to ban land mines, in July 2004 endorsed the Africans' call for compensation for the loss of health professionals educated at African government expense, but also emphasized that there is a tradeoff between the rights of African health professionals to seek a better life and the rights of people in their home countries to decent health care. It recommended against efforts to ban the emigration of African health care workers.

3. The Philippine Nurses Association Inc. (PNA) estimated in 2002 that 150,885 Filipino nurses were abroad, and noted that experienced nurses with specialty training were most in demand overseas.

4. Since it is easiest to go abroad as a nurse, some Filipino doctors, who earn $300 to $800 a month, are reportedly retraining as nurses so they can emigrate.

5. About 60 percent of foreigners who seek treatment in Malaysia are from Indonesia, and in October 2003, the Health Ministry set fees under three packages priced between RM450 and RM1,150, and has recommended floor and ceiling prices for 18 procedures performed for cardiology, orthopedics, and plastic surgery. "Robust Growth in Revenue for Health Tourism Sector," *Business Times* (Malaysia), February 4, 2004

6. "Government Sets Up Task Force on Health Tourism," *Financial Express*, January 11, 2004.

7. According to one study cited by Michael Teitelbaum, bioscientists can expect to earn $1 million less than MBAs graduating from the same university in their lifetimes, and $2 million less if stock options are taken into account, suggesting one explanation for the very different composition of students in MBA programs and graduate science programs. Teitelbaum, "Do We Need More Scientists?" *The Public Interest*, no. 153, Fall 2003, pp. 40–53.

8. Remittances are listed under current transfers and compensation of employees in a country's current account. Many countries do not know how long the migrants remitting funds have been abroad, so most analyses combine workers' remittances

and compensation of employees. For example, Mexico reports most money inflows under worker remittances, while the Philippines reports most under compensation of employees.

9. A third item not generally included in discussions of remittances is migrants' transfers, which is the net worth of migrants who move from one country to another. For example, if a person with stock migrates from one country to another, the value of the stock owned moves from one country to another in international accounts.

10. World Bank, *Global Development Finance Report* (Washington, DC: World Bank, 2003).

11. When the risk premium for borrowing funds abroad is very high, some countries have been able to float bonds secured by the anticipated future flow of remittances, as Brazil did in 2001.

12. Dilip Ratha, "Workers' Remittances: An Important and Stable Source of External Development Finance," in World Bank, *Global Development Finance*, 2003.

13. A recent survey of migrants found that money-transfer firms such as Western Union made 78 percent of the transfers to Latin America in 2004, people traveling carried 11 percent of the remittances, and U.S. banks had only a 7 percent share.

14. Since December 1998, Mexico's federal consumer protection agency, Profeco, has compared the cost of transferring $300 from the United States to Mexico weekly in six U.S. cities: Chicago, Los Angeles, New York, Dallas, Miami, and Houston (www.profeco.gob.mx/enviodinero/enviomnu.htm). The costs vary by city or origin and destination as well as the services provided with the transfer. For example, on April 23, 2001, when the interbank exchange rate was $1 = 9.3 pesos, the fee charged by most money transfer firms in Los Angeles was $8 to $15, and the exchange rate ranged from 8.9 to 9.2 pesos per dollar, making the total costs of a transfer $5 to $20, or 2 to 7 percent of the $300 typically sent.

15. R. H. Adams Jr. and J. Page, "International Migration, Remittances and Poverty in Developing Countries," World Bank Policy Research Working Paper, no. 3179 (Washington, DC: World Bank, 2003).

16. Automatic stabilizers in developed countries, such as unemployment insurance, help to stabilize the flow of remittances to developing countries that have the same economic cycles as the countries in which their migrants work.

17. Ratha, "Workers' Remittances."

18. Lewis assumed that the traditional agricultural sector of developing countries had an unlimited supply of labor that could be absorbed in an expanding modern industrial sector with no loss of farm output (W. Arthur Lewis, "Economic Development with Unlimited Supplies of Labour," *Manchester School of Economic and Social Studies* 22, 1954:139–91). Ranis and Fei extended the Lewis model so that, once the marginal product of labor and wages are equal in the traditional and modern sector, rural-urban migration stops (G. Ranis and J. C. H. Fei, "A Theory of Economic Development," *The American Economic Review* 51, 1961:533–65). Johnson noted that rural-urban migrants could take capital with them (H. G. Johnson, " Some Economic Aspects of the Brain Drain," *Pakistani Development Review* 7, 1967:379–411.

Todaro took a micro perspective, showing that rural and urban wages did not converge as expected in Lewis-style models because, with high and rigid urban wages, rural migrants continued to pour into cities despite high unemployment because their expected earnings (higher wages times the probability of employment) were higher in the cities. Todaro argued that the solution to unwanted rural-urban migration was urban wage subsidies and migration restrictions (Michael P. Todaro, "A Model of Migration and Urban Unemployment in Less-developed Countries," *American Economic Review* 59, 1967:138–48). Bhagwati and Srinivasan showed that tax and subsidy schemes could yield optimal migration levels without migration restrictions. (Jagdish Bhagwati and T. N. Srinivasan, "On Reanalyzing the Harris-Todaro Model: Policy Rankings in the Case of Sector-Specific Sticky Wages," *American Economic Review* 64 (3), 1974:502–8.

19. Philip L. Martin, *The Unfinished Story: Turkish Labor Migration to Western Europe, With Special Reference to the Federal Republic of Germany* (Geneva: International Labor Office, 1991).

20. Conspicuous consumption is a well-observed fact in migrant areas of origin; in eastern Turkey in the 1960s and 1970s, some migrant households displayed electric appliances from Germany even before their homes had electricity.

21. Some $20 million was spent on 308 three-for-one projects in Zacatecas, including bridges, paved roads, and providing drinking water, but one assessment concluded that three-for-one projects have improved the quality of life but not stimulated the Zacatecan economy. Ken Bensinger, "Mexico's Other Migrant Wave," *Christian Science Monitor*, October 8, 2004.

22. These students were highly motivated, since they had to complete two years of military service and obtain private or overseas financing to study abroad.

23. Shanghai reportedly has 30,000 returned professionals, 90 percent with MS or PhD degrees earned abroad, who are employed or starting businesses (Jonathan Kaufman, "China Reforms Bring Back Executives Schooled in U.S.," *Wall Street Journal*, March 6, 2003; Rone Tempest, "China Tries to Woo Its Tech Talent Back Home," *Los Angeles Times*, November 25, 2002.

24. Quoted in Alan Beattie, "Seeking Consensus on the Benefits of Immigration," *Financial Times*, July 22, 2002, p. 9.

25. Jagdish Bhagwati, "Borders Beyond Control," *Foreign Affairs*, Jan./Feb. 2003.

26. Some governments are reluctant to welcome home refugees, viewing with suspicion those who fled a conflict for refuge abroad.

27. Timothy Hatton and Jeffrey Williamson, *The Age of Mass Migration: Causes and Economic Impact* (Oxford: Oxford University Press, 1998, and Thomas Straubhaar, *On the Economics of International Labor Migration* (Bern/Stuttgart: Paul Haupt, 1988).

28. U.S. Commission for the Study of International Migration and Cooperative Economic Development, *Unauthorized Migration: An Economic Development Response*, Washington, D.C.: U.S. Government Printing Office, 1990, p. xv.

29. Quoted in Bush letter to Congress, May 1, 1991, p. 17.

30. U.S. Commission on International Migration and Economic Development, *Unauthorized Migration*, p. xvi.

31. U.S. Commission on International Migration and Economic Development, *Unauthorized Migration*, p. xvi.

32. Wolfgang F. Stolper and Paul A. Samuelson, "Protection and Real Wages," *Review of Economic Studies* 9, November 1941, pp. 58–73.

33. Both Stolper-Samuelson and the Heckscher-Ohlin theorem on which it is based rule out international factor movements, including migration.

34. This point is closely related to a long-standing debate in the trade literature concerning the definition of labor abundance, rooted in the Leontief Paradox. If labor supply is measured in efficiency units, and if workers are significantly more efficient in the North than in the South, then the North may be labor *abundant*. Migration, by converting southern workers into northern ones, can increase the amount of labor available in the North, measured in these efficiency units. The greater efficiency of labor in the North relative to the South may discourage the production of some labor-intensive goods in the South, and thus encourage South-North migration.

35. South Korea made one of the world's fastest migration transitions, sending 200,000 workers abroad in the early 1980s and having over 300,000 migrants today. However, some Koreans still want to emigrate, and about 11,000 a year do so. Private firms such as the Emigration Development Corporation advertise emigration opportunities to Koreans, and collect fees for helping Koreans who want to emigrate to navigate, for example, the Canadian point system.

36. Indeed, in countries that underwent a migration transition from labor-sender to receiver, the feedback effect of the 3 R's accelerated economic and job growth even if foreign investment and job creation were not directed to the major areas of migrant origin. For example, southern Italy was the source of many migrants, and as Italy grew in the 1960s, migrants moved south to north within Italy rather than over borders.

37. Another $6.9 billion in official aid was provided to so-called Part II countries, most in Eastern Europe and the ex-USSR. About a quarter of ODA is provided via technical cooperation grants, as when donors pay consultants to advise developing country governments.

38. Merlinda Ingco and John D. Nash, eds., *Agriculture and the WTO: Creating a Trading System for Development* (Washington, DC: World Bank, March 2004).

39. In the late 1990s, when global exports of manufactured goods were about $3.5 trillion a year, global exports of farm goods were less than $500 billion a year, including a third from developing countries. Another comparison is with global arms sales, some $26 billion in 2001, down from $40 billion in 2000, and two-thirds of global arms sales are to developing countries.

40. Quoted in EU, "Seville, Enlargement," *Migration News* 9, no. 7 (July 2002).

41. World Bank, *Globalization, Growth, and Poverty* (Washington, DC: World Bank, 2002), p. 82.

42. Bimal Ghosh, ed., *Managing Migration: Time for a New International Regime?* (New York: Oxford University Press, 2000), p. 6. Ghosh calls for "regulated openness" with participating countries sharing "common objectives," a "harmonized normative framework," and a "monitoring mechanism." P. 227).

43. Bob Hamilton and John Whalley, "Efficiency and Distributional Implications of Global Restrictions on Labour Mobility" in *Journal of Developmental Economics*, vol. 14, 1984: 61–75. Hamilton and Whalley assumed the world's labor supply was fully employed producing a single output, and used CES production functions to estimate differences in the marginal productivity of labor across seven multi-country regions—these differences were assumed to be due to migration restrictions. They estimate the efficiency gains that would result from labor moving until MPs and wages were equalized, that is, they assume factor-price convergence via migration, with workers losing and capital owners gaining in receiving areas and workers gaining and capital owners losing in sending areas.

44. There are many problems with the Hamilton and Whalley estimates. For example, the full employment assumption is necessary to assume that wages are determined by marginal productivity; it is assumed that the ratio of wages to profits is one in both rich and poor countries before migration barriers are lifted, and that capital does not move even as labor migrates.

CHAPTER FOUR

Averting Forced Migration

Many countries of emigration are in transition from conflict to peace and from authoritarian to democratic governments. Addressing population movements from these countries requires more than economic opportunities; equally important is the establishment of the rule of law, respect for human rights, and, in countries recovering from conflict, reconstruction of destroyed infrastructure and housing. Otherwise, fragile peace and democratization processes can easily break down, creating new waves of forced migrants and hampering efforts towards repatriation and reintegration of already displaced populations.

International migrants belong to two broad groups: voluntary migrants and forced migrants. Fuelled by a combination of push factors in source countries and pull factors in receiving countries, voluntary migration is sustained by well-developed networks that link the supply of labor with the demand of businesses for both highly skilled and unskilled workers. Forced migration is fuelled by conflicts, human rights abuses, and political repression that displace people from their home communities.

Distinguishing between voluntary and forced migrants can be difficult in practice. Voluntary migrants may feel compelled to seek new homes because of pressing problems at home; forced migrants may choose a particular place of refuge because of family and community ties or economic opportunities. Moreover, one form of migration often leads to another. Forced migrants who settle in a new country may then bring family members to join them. Voluntary migrants may find that situations change in their home countries, preventing their repatriation and making them into forced migrants.

Despite the difficulty of categorizing different types of migrants, the process is more than an exercise in semantics. Countries have different responsibilities toward different types of migrants. For example, more than 130 countries have signed the UN Convention Relating to the Status of Refugees obliging them not to return refugees to where they have a well-founded fear of persecution and to provide assistance and protection to refugees whom they admit. No similar legal obligation extends toward other international migrants, although international human rights law, national laws, and International Labor Organization conventions relating to conditions of recruitment and employment protect their rights in destination countries.

The complicated relationship between voluntary and forced migration challenges receiving States when they try to distinguish between refugees and other migrants. Many governments have established sometimes elaborate and costly asylum adjudication procedures to make these determinations. In some cases, where other immigration avenues are restrictive, these procedures are the only or the principal means through which migrants are able to gain admission, regardless of their reasons for emigration or the circumstances they would face on return. Fearing uncontrolled migration, states have imposed such mechanisms as visa requirements and carrier sanctions to limit access to their territory. Too often, however, these mechanisms fail to make distinctions between refugees and other migrants and limit the protection afforded to persons who, failing to find asylum elsewhere, find themselves endangered. In some cases, these mechanisms are also self-defeating, as would-be migrants, including bona fide refugees, turn to increasingly more sophisticated smuggling and trafficking operations that are able to circumvent the immigration controls. A vicious cycle then develops, with governments imposing new restrictions while smugglers find new ways to get around them.

In recent years, governments and the UN High Commissioner for Refugees (UNHCR) have begun to explore ways to address forced migration pressures at their sources and in regions of origin. The European Union has established a high level working group that has developed plans to address the causes of migration in the principal source countries of migration to Europe. The high level working group examined the causes of influx, including the human rights situation in the subject-country; assessed the effectiveness of aid and development strategies; identified the needs for humanitarian and rehabilitation assistance as well as ways to assist reception of displaced persons in the region; and identified areas of and means for cooperation with UNHCR and nongovernmental organizations (NGOs) in preparation for joint measures in the field of asylum and migration.

It must be emphasized that options for addressing forced migration in countries or regions of origin are by no means substitutes for well-functioning asylum systems. However, they do provide additional mechanisms for protecting and assisting those who, in their absence, may seek admission to countries in North America and Europe. This chapter outlines some of these approaches. The first section describes more fully the nature of forced migration today. The next section discusses some of the new contexts for addressing forced migration globally. The sections that follow outline a range of approaches to address the potential for forced migration, including preventive actions, in-country and regional protection mechanisms, and return and reintegration options. All of these approaches require significant levels of cooperation among destination, transit, and, in the case of return when conditions permit, source countries of migration.

Nature of Forced Migration

A large number of international migrants have been forced to leave their home countries and seek refuge in other nations. Many leave because of persecution, human rights violations, repression, or conflict. They depart on their own initiative to escape these life-threatening situations, although in a growing number of cases they are driven from their homes by governments and insurgent groups intent on depopulating or shifting the ethnic, religious, or other composition of an area. In other cases, migrants are forced to move by environmental degradation and natural and human-made disasters that make their homes uninhabitable for at least some period.[1] Because the legal frameworks for responding to these forms of forced migration differ, the two groups will be discussed separately.

Refugees have a special status in international law. A refugee is defined by the 1951 UN Convention Relating to the Status of Refugees as "a person who, owing to well-founded fear of being persecuted for reasons of race, religion, nationality, membership of a particular social group or political opinion, is outside the country of his nationality and is unable or, owing to such fear, is unwilling to avail himself of the protection of that country." Refugee status has been applied more broadly, however, to include others persons who are outside their country of origin because of armed conflict, generalized violence, foreign aggression, or other circumstances that have seriously disturbed public order, and who, therefore, require international protection. These statuses are often referred to as complementary or subsidiary to the convention definition described above.

Environmental degradation and natural disasters uproot another type of forced migrant. Unlike the refugees described above, environmental migrants do not need protection from persecution or violence, but like refugees, they are unable to return to now uninhabitable communities. Most environmental migrants move internally, some relocating temporarily until they are able to rebuild their homes and others seeking permanent new homes. Some environmental migrants, however, cross national boundaries.

The specific environmental factors that precipitate movements vary. Mass migration may result from such natural phenomena as earthquakes, volcanic eruptions, flooding, hurricanes, and other events that destroy housing, disrupt agriculture, and otherwise make it difficult for inhabitants to stay within their communities, particularly until reconstruction is completed. For example, periodic floods in Bangladesh have uprooted hundreds of thousands of persons and hurricanes George and Mitch provoked massive displacement in the Caribbean and Central America, respectively. While most of these flood victims are internally displaced, the recurrent environmental problems provide an impetus for external movements as well.

Manmade disasters also precipitate mass movements. Large-scale industrial and nuclear accidents, such as those that occurred in Bhopal and Chernobyl, can displace thousands of people within a very short period. Other manmade environmental problems lead to more gradual movements. Global warming, acid rain, pollution of rivers, depletion of resources, soil erosion, and desertification all hold the potential to uproot millions of people who can no longer reside or earn a living in their home communities. While some of this environmental degradation may be reversible, the most severe problems will require sustained attention and significant resources for reclamation. In the meantime, both internal and international migration can be expected.

New Contexts for Addressing Forced Migration

The post–Cold War era presents new opportunities as well as new challenges for migration regimes. The effects are most profound with regard to treatment of forced migration. Most of current refugee and asylum policy was formulated following World War II with the lessons of the Nazi era in mind and tensions between East and West growing. To a large degree, refugee policy was seen as an instrument of foreign policy at both international and domestic levels. Admission of refugees for permanent resettlement, asylum for victims of persecution and repression, and international aid to victims of surrogate Cold War fights (Central America, Ethiopia, Vietnam, etc.) were all part of the fight against communism.

The Cold War also made all but impossible some of the solutions to refugee crises, whether defined as attacking root causes or promoting return of refugees. With the end of the Cold War, new opportunities emerged. Many decades-old civil wars came to an end. Democratization and increased respect for human rights took hold in numerous countries throughout the globe. As a result, repatriation became a possibility for millions of refugees who had been displaced for years.

One of the most significant changes in recent years has been in the willingness of countries to intervene on behalf of internally displaced persons and others in need of assistance and protection within their home countries. Classic notions of sovereignty, which formerly precluded such intervention, are under considerable pressure. International human rights and humanitarian law have growing salience in defining sovereignty to include responsibility for the welfare of the residents of ones territory.

Intervention may be expected when the actions of a sovereign state threaten the security of another state. What is new is the recognition that actions that prompt mass exodus into a neighboring territory threaten international security. In a number of cases, beginning with Resolution 688 that in effect authorized humanitarian intervention in northern Iraq, the UN Security Council has determined that the way to reduce the threat to a neighboring state is to provide assistance and protection within the territory of the offending state.[2]

The changing geopolitical scene is a two-edged sword, however. The need for humanitarian intervention also is linked to the end of the Cold War. Rabid nationalism has replaced communism in some countries, while others have so destabilized that no government exists to protect the civilian population. Addressing these new situations is made all the more challenging now that the ideological supports for generous refugee responses have unraveled. That the principles of asylum and non-refoulement (non-return to places of persecution) appear to be under growing attack in Europe and North America is one manifestation of this issue. Further, as the failure of the international community to protect the so-called safe havens in Bosnia showed, humanitarian interests alone are often insufficient substitutes for political will to address the causes of the displacement.

Options to Address Forced Migration
from Countries in Transition

It is essential that governments have multiple tools to deal with complex flows of people. What are the elements of a comprehensive approach to migration that will most effectively address forced migration while protecting refugees and others at risk? Four aspects must be considered: ameliorating the causes of forced movements; strengthening mechanisms that enhance protection while minimizing abuses; resolving the longer-term status of forced migrants; and reintegration and reconstruction when return is possible.

Ameliorating the Causes of Unauthorized Migration

Ultimately, reducing the push and pull factors that lead to migration is the most sensible way to address increasing migration pressures. Peace, respect for human rights, and reduction in income differentials between rich and poor countries are the best long-term solutions to uncontrolled migration. Given the large number of people fleeing internal conflict and insecurity, as Sadako Ogata, then UN High Commissioner for Refugees, said before the Carnegie Commission on Preventing Deadly Conflict, UNHCR "has an obvious interest in the prevention or mitigation of deadly conflict. Not only are we in direct contact with the suffering of those who manage to escape persecution and mass violence, but we also witness the shrinking willingness to offer them sanctuary."[3]

The role that those concerned with forced migration can play regarding prevention is a limited but important one. Clearly, there are neither the resources nor the capacity to prevent conflict, ensure human rights, or promote economic security in all countries that may produce forced migrants. Those concerned with forced migration can, however, 1) advocate alleviation of the causes of forced migration; 2) stimulate early warning of and response to refugee emergencies to prevent displacements and mitigate longer-term impacts; 3) advocate utilization of humanitarian assistance in a manner that reduces tensions, stabilizes communities, limits the potential for its diversion to military purposes, and reaches those in need without unnecessarily requiring their movement toward the aid; and 4) encourage safe and orderly repatriation in a manner that supports peace and reconciliation. At the same time, it is important to emphasize that prevention does *not* mean preventing people from seeking safety and protection abroad.

One area worth exploring is the role that expatriate communities can play in supporting democratization and human rights in home countries, particularly promoting respect for minority rights. This proposal is in sharp contrast to a better-known role that expatriates play in supporting continued conflict, particularly by furnishing financial resources to purchase arms. Just as expatriates send remittances to their home communities, they can send information and support for the democratic practices and rule of law that are common in their adopted countries.

Helping establish the rule of law, including protection of minority rights, is a key element to any prevention strategy. Many of the countries in transition do not yet have fully operating judicial systems. Nor do they have mechanisms to prevent or prosecute discrimination against minorities or to help ensure that discrimination does not lead to acts that may precipitate flight. Legal procedures for reclaiming land and other property, particularly upon return, are also sorely lacking in many of these societies. To the extent that destination countries—including expatriates who have developed new skills in mediation, minority rights, and law—can help countries in transition to establish the rule of law, pressures for outward migration may be significantly diminished.

Strengthening Mechanisms that Promote Protection
Refugee protection is generally defined in relationship to the 1951 UN Convention Relating to the Status of Refugees and its 1967 Protocol. The core, fundamental precepts of protection are: non-refoulement, including non-rejection of asylum seekers at the frontier; admission to safety; access to fair and efficient procedures for determination of refugee status; basic standards of treatment that accord with human dignity and integrity; and appropriate lasting solutions. Key to ensuring such protection is unhindered access to asylum-seekers and refugees to monitor their situation and treatment.

One of the principal responsibilities of the UN High Commissioner for Refugees is reinforcing these protection principles. Given that numerous countries have not yet signed the refugee Convention nor implemented policies and procedures to protect refugees, UNHCR should continue to encourage signatories. Even with full accordance to the 1951 Convention, however, gaps in international protection will be seen. The Convention definition is narrow in scope, referencing a well-founded fear of persecution on specific grounds. Persons who flee generalized conflict, violence, and abuses do not necessarily fit the 1951 Convention definition. Although the Organization of African Unity (OAU) Convention and the Cartagena Declaration widen the scope to include those fleeing such situations, and UNHCR considers them to be of concern, states do not consistently apply the broader criteria.

Moreover, the Convention refers only to those who are already out of their countries of origin. It does not pertain to those who are still at home, even if they are subject to the types of conditions that would make them refugees if they left. In effect, the refugee system presents a fundamental dilemma for those concerned with protection: Only those who manage to flee are covered by the refugee Convention, but flight often requires refugees to break immigration laws and to subject themselves to danger and sometimes exploitation at the hands of smugglers and traffickers.

A challenge is to broaden the scope of refugee protection to fill these gaps and to do so in a manner that ensures the continued integrity of asylum while protecting the broadened system from potential abuse. A number of different approaches could be considered.

Encourage Forms of Protection that Complement Asylum

Complementary protection regimes are needed, in particular, for persons who flee generalized conflict and violence rather than persecution. States should set out minimum standards of treatment for those granted the complementary status, affording similar protections to those spelled out in the Convention. The principal obligation of states should be non-return of migrants to conditions in which they would be endangered. If such conditions continue for some time, however, states should be encouraged to permit those granted the complementary status to remain permanently.

Complementary statuses serve not only to protect the large number of asylum seekers who flee conflict rather than persecution; they also facilitate both the appearance and reality of migration control. At present, it appears as if states have less control over their asylum systems than is the case. Although a sometimes-small minority of applicants are accorded asylum, a much larger number are permitted to remain on other humanitarian grounds. Because the policies are framed solely as asylum policies, however, these other forms of relief tend to be disregarded. They do have value, apart from their humanitarian one, in allowing states to keep track of persons within their territory, determine what rights accrue to specific statuses, and require return if conditions permit.

Encourage Development of Mechanisms for In-Country Protection

Mechanisms to offer protection to would-be asylum seekers still within their own countries will help minimize the negative effects of migration controls such as visa requirements and carrier sanctions. In particular, states should explore the feasibility of establishing procedures through which would-be asylum seekers can request protection prior to departure. The options include creating special "refugee" visas that embassies and consulates would grant to persons who do not qualify for regular visas but who can demonstrate that they are or will be endangered if they do not leave their home countries; establishing UNHCR offices in countries of origin where would-be asylum seekers could request protection, with the understanding that they would be evacuated to countries willing and able to receive them; and broadening the responsibilities of pre-inspection personnel and other immigration officials assigned to overseas locations so that they can assess the asylum claims of persons seeking to board aircraft and other carriers without proper documentation.

These various mechanisms are largely untried, and they certainly are not substitutes for a functioning asylum system. The experience with in-country processing for refugee resettlement has been mixed, to say the least, for both refugee protection and migration management. For example, the Orderly Departure Program (ODP) from Vietnam and Cuba at least partially stemmed large-scale departures in unseaworthy boats, saving lives, and providing a safer avenue for departure. The departures were stemmed, however, because both governments agreed to halt the movements, which meant that bona fide refugees afraid to apply for orderly departure, thereby making them known to the government, had even more limited options for flight. In Haiti, the presence of in-country processing was used by the United States as a reason to return interdicted boats directly to Haiti without affording passengers the opportunity to apply for asylum.

From the immigration management vantage, ODP arrangements can hinder the capacity of the receiving country to set its own priorities for admission. In the Vietnamese ODP, for example, the United States established lists of persons who sought entry and met minimal criteria for admission, and Vietnam developed lists of those granted exit permission. Generally, only those who were on both lists were able to leave, but these individuals may not have been as high priorities as were other applicants. Despite these problems, and the necessity for UNHCR continually to reinforce that in-country procedures cannot be a substitute for asylum, in-country procedures provide opportunities for victims of persecution and other abuses to find safety without resort to subterfuge and further violation of their rights.

Establishing Regional Protection Mechanisms

Regional protection holds promise for helping states balance twin interests: providing protection to refugees without providing admission to persons who do not otherwise qualify for entry. As discussed above, international migration generally requires both push and pull factors. In the case of refugees seeking entry into the highly developed countries of North America and Europe, the push may be persecution or conflict, but the pull is generally better economic opportunities. Regional protection—that is, protection in neighboring or nearby countries with similar economies to those of the country of origin—offers safety without the potential magnet for unauthorized migration presented by admission to wealthier nations. It also presumably facilitates repatriation when conditions permit because the economic advantages of remaining outside of one's country are reduced.

Regional protection is hardly a new concept. The vast majority of refugees have always found asylum within their regions of origin, generally in neighboring countries. What is new is the interest of European and North American States in redirecting movements towards regional centers.

This approach was pioneered in Southeast Asia, when a processing center was established in Bataan, the Philippines, to receive refugees admitted to Thailand, Malaysia, Singapore, and Hong Kong for temporary asylum before they were resettled elsewhere. Because the numbers seeking entry outpaced the resettlement capacity, the processing center relieved the pressure on first asylum countries, keeping the door opened for protection, and allowed the resettlement countries to examine applications carefully to determine who was admissible. The processing center effectively served both protection and migration management ends.

A different form of regional protection was used in 1994 to address an increasing number of boat departures from Haiti.[4] In this case, regional protection was offered as an alternative to admission into the United States. Fearing that access to U.S. territory would serve as a magnet to further flight, the United States instead offered safe haven at Guantanamo Naval Base and, through a regional agreement, in Panama and the Turks and Caicos Islands, but emphasized that there would be no admission to the United States. The implementation of this policy led to an abrupt decline in boat departures, but not before about 40,000 Haitians afforded themselves of this regional protection. The need for safe haven lessened considerably when international pressure and the threat of military intervention led to a restoration of the elected government and the presence of peacekeeping forces. The vast majority of those offered protection chose to return home when conditions permitted. A small number were permitted entry into the United States to pursue asylum claims or to seek medical attention.

A third example of regional protection, supplemented by humanitarian evacuation to preserve first asylum, occurred during the Kosovo crisis. By far the largest number of refugees from Kosovo remained in the neighboring countries of Albania and the former Yugoslav Republic of Macedonia. However, to ensure that first asylum was maintained, and in recognition of Macedonia's concern about its own security, other states agreed to accept some refugees for temporary protection or resettlement. A regional approach was hence sustained by international responsibility sharing.

Costa Rica provides a fourth example. Costa Rica has provided temporary protection to persons fleeing civil conflict as well as natural disasters. Recognizing that many of the migrants would not be able to return home, the Costa Rican government is supporting integration programs in twenty-one Costa Rican communities, providing supplemental education, employment, health, and housing assistance to both migrants and other local residents.

With the help of the International Organization for Migration (IOM), these initiatives include education programs that involve migrants and local residents in building or refurbishing schooling facilities in areas with many migrants and in designing curricula that preserve cultural identity.

This brief review of the experience with regional protection shows it has utility, but it reinforces that regional protection must be accompanied by mechanisms for broader responsibility sharing—in both the costs of maintaining regional protection and in the resettlement or relocation of at least a portion of those requiring protection.

Resolving the Status of Forced Migrants

States increasingly are turning toward temporary mechanisms to address migration flows. The growing interest in temporary protection policies, along with the increased use even in traditional immigration countries of temporary work provisions, lead to many situations in which the longer-term status of migrants, including forced ones, remains in doubt for sometimes lengthy periods. There are two likely resolutions to these situations: return of migrants to their home countries or more permanent integration into their new communities. Third country resettlement is a less frequent though often important alternative for migrants in some type of temporary status.

At present, mechanisms for determining which solution is appropriate are sorely lacking. States have no agreed upon criteria for determining whether conditions justify return, particularly in the aftermath of conflict. Even in the case of voluntary migration, states differ as to the extent that they should take such considerations as brain drain into account in requiring return. Similarly, there is little agreement as to the circumstances under which local integration should be permitted or encouraged. Should temporary migrants who remain outside of their country for a specific period (let us say five years) be permitted to adjust to a permanent status because they have established roots and developed equities in the destination country? Should there be different criteria for those granted temporary protection versus those with temporary work permits? Should there be assistance toward return and/or integration? These are all questions that now beg adequate answers.

Resolving status is particularly important if temporary protection mechanisms are to work toward giving refuge to the largest number of persons needing such protection. If countries fear that temporary protection is merely and always a way station toward permanent admission, they may be less likely to be generous in its grant. On the other hand, if governments persist in arguing that all of those granted temporary protection should return regardless of how long it takes home country conditions to change, they are fighting against the realities of the equities that long-term mi-grants develop over time. More transparent policies that provide criteria for determining when and how return or adjustment to permanent status will occur will help to resolve some of the most difficult dilemmas now seen in temporary protection policies.

Reintegration and Reconstruction

An area of particular difficulty for receiving countries is return of rejected asylum seekers and persons no longer requiring temporary protection. Large-scale return movements to countries where personal security is at risk, that are devoid of economic opportunities, and where commitments to peace are fragile, pose more problems than they solve. Political leaders in host coun-tries and those in post-conflict countries of origin have legitimate and con-tradictory interests: the former face popular resistance to growing numbers of refugees; the latter contend they are unable to incorporate certain groups— or very large numbers—of returnees. This has been illustrated in areas as dif-ferent as the Balkans and Central America.

Contentious problems such as recovery of land, property, and professional licenses, political representation of minorities, and monitoring human rights are, at best, referenced in peace agreements but left for later solutions. These issues arise frequently, warrant far more attention than they have thus far re-ceived, and should be systematically analyzed by policy makers and experts.

Best practices in enabling return and reintegration to proceed smoothly can be found in many post-conflict societies, although many of these ap-proaches are practiced on a small scale. Among the best practices to be ex-amined are programs to promote reconciliation among formerly warring par-ties who return to the same communities; to protect the rights and safety of returnees who are minorities in their home communities (particularly in the context of attempts at ethnic cleansing); to help returnees reclaim property or obtain appropriate compensation; to bring community members, includ-ing returnees, together to rebuild destroyed homes, infrastructure, and com-munity resources (often called Quick Impact Projects—QIPs); to promote reintegration of women-headed and child-headed households; to demobilize and reintegrate soldiers, including child soldiers; and to help victims of vio-lence and sexual abuse to deal with conflict-induced trauma.

Settlement or Resettlement

When return and reintegration are impossible because home conditions do not change, settlement in countries of first asylum or temporary protection will be the next best solution for the migrants. Prolonging limbo statuses that prevent those needing protection from finding permanent shelter and employment only raises the costs of protection to both the receiving country and the forced migrants themselves. Such prolonged displacement is particularly troubling when the forced migrants must remain in camps or camp-like situations for years on end. Integration into local communities will help reduce their dependency and marginalization from the rest of society.

Local integration can pose short-term costs to countries that host large numbers of forced migrants. The international community may need to step in to help local integration occur with minimal disruption to the host communities. Financial aid can reduce the burden on host countries and help forced migrants to resume normal lives.

In some cases, however, local integration may not be possible even with international assistance. The situation in a host country may be too insecure to enable forced migrants to remain. Third country resettlement may be the more appropriate solution. While moving forced migrants to countries at some distance from their homes can involve major disruptions, particularly if the migrants do not speak the destination country's language or have transferable skills, their safety and security may require such a step to be taken. Moreover, third country resettlement may be the only or best option for them and their children to regain lives of dignity.

Conclusion

Averting future movements and returning and reintegrating migrants from countries in transition requires special attention when these countries are recovering from conflict, repressive governments, and a history of human rights repression. Without dealing with these fundamental issues, flight will continue, and it will be hard to return rejected asylum seekers and those no longer needing temporary protection. Countries of asylum and post-conflict countries of return do not generally have the resources or expertise needed to effect the necessary changes without help, which is why a comprehensive approach to managing migration requires cooperation among destination, transit, and source countries to prevent and respond to forced migration.

Notes

1. See Susan Martin et al., *The Uprooted: Improving Humanitarian Responses to Forced Migration* (Lanham, MD: Lexington Books, 2005) for more detailed discussion of the nature of forced migration today.

2. The changing context for humanitarian action also affects the roles and responsibilities of international organizations with regard to forced migrants. Formerly, most responsibility for handling forced migration crises went to UNHCR, which mobilized resources from other agencies. Today, new sets of actors drawn from security, military, human rights, and development communities have growing involvement, particularly in situations involving internal displacement.

3. Remarks by Mrs. Sadako Ogata, United Nations High Commissioner for Refugees, Conference of the Carnegie Commission on the Prevention of Deadly Conflict and UNHCR, on a Humanitarian Response and the Prevention of Deadly Conflict, Geneva, 17 February 1997.

4. Susan Martin, Andrew Schoenholtz, and Deborah Waller Meyers, "Temporary Protection: Towards a New Regional and Domestic Framework," in *Georgetown Immigration Law Journal* 12, no. 4 (Summer 1998).

PART TWO

CHAPTER FIVE

⁂

The Lure of the European Union

The European Union (EU) increasingly resembles the United States in considering itself an "unfinished nation" shaped and reshaped by immigration. However, there is far less agreement as to the desirability of the kind of immigration that transforms cultures and societies. Most EU political leaders consider more immigration inevitable, but surveys suggest that most European citizens want immigration reduced. This division of opinion promises increased tension about migration as the EU assumes more authority to coordinate national migration policies.

Most of the economically motivated migration within and to Europe after World War II reflected rural-urban migration within countries, and movements between colonies and home countries, such as between Algeria and France or India and Pakistan and the UK.[1] Faster postwar recovery in northern Europe prompted the recruitment of guest workers from southern Europe, where economic and job growth was slower. Government leaders in non-immigrant Germany and Austria asserted that Yugoslav and Turkish workers would rotate in and out of the country, returning home after a year or two and be replaced by countrymen if guest workers were still needed. In reality, however, guest workers were probationary immigrants, entitled to unify their families if their employers requested that their initial work and residence permits be renewed. Many did in fact stay and unify their families in their new countries of residence, producing populations and labor forces that today include 5 to 10 percent foreigners.

As the EU acquired more powers vis-à-vis member states, and as countries such as France and Germany realized they could not solve all migration issues within their borders, authority over migration policy began to shift to the EU.[2] Four cities lent their names to agreements that symbolize the growing authority of the EU in migration matters. In 1985, several EU countries meeting in Schengen, Luxembourg, agreed to develop a common list of countries whose nationals would require visas and inspect arrivals for each other so that there would be no more border controls between France and Germany or Portugal and Spain—border control agents would share the same database, the Schengen Information System, to determine who was to be refused entry to all Schengen member countries. Today, "Schengen" has become an anchor of EU cooperation on migration management, with all new EU entrants required to adhere to Schengen standards, which required significantly more border agents and upgrading of their equipment and infrastructure.[3]

The Maastricht Treaty, signed in a Dutch city in 1991, created an EU citizenship and paved the way for EU nationals to live, work, and vote in local elections in any EU nation. The Amsterdam Treaty, which went into effect in 1999, commits the EU to develop a common immigration and asylum policy by 2004. Developing a common asylum police has taken more time than expected. The Dublin Convention of 1990 required foreigners seeking asylum to apply in the first EU country they reached. The goal was to prevent migrants from traveling by boat to Greece or Italy, which provide few benefits to asylum seekers, and then traveling north to Germany or Scandinavia, where benefits for asylum seekers are better. However, it took until 2004 for eight EU nations—Ireland, Denmark, Belgium, Finland, Spain, Sweden, Britain, and Portugal—to enact common minimum rules for acquiring refugee status and procedures for processing asylum requests, and there are still problems with convincing EU countries to accept the return of asylum applicants who passed through them.

The EU's growing role in managing migration rests on the third of the three pillars of the Maastricht Treaty. The EU takes the lead in promoting economic integration under the rubric of completing the internal market. While member states remain in control of their foreign policies, there is to be ever-closer cooperation in justice and home affairs, which includes cooperation on immigration and asylum issues. The debate is over how much leaders of the EU should control debate and policy about immigration, especially since they are not elected and since many of them tend to favor increased immigration. The former Commissioner for Justice and Home Affairs, Antonio Vitorino, for example, asserted, "the zero immigration policies of the past 25 years are not working [and urged] new legal ways for immigrants to enter the EU."[4] Vitorino and many other EU leaders looked at low fertility rates and said that the EU must accept immigrants to prevent population decline. However, most Europeans oppose increased immigration, which sets the stage for anti-immigrant parties to make strong showings, especially in elections for the European Parliament, the EU's legislative body.[5]

At a summit meeting in Tampere, Finland, the EU gave its strongest recognition that unilateral decisions on migration were unlikely to be productive. Cooperation with transit and source countries would be essential to improved management of migration. Such cooperation would also be needed to address the root causes of irregular migration and to establish programs through which migrants could be returned to their home countries when appropriate.

For states seeking eventual entry into the European Union, the situation was even more strongly defined: cooperation over migration issues with the then fifteen members was a precondition for membership. Cooperative Efforts to Manage Migration (CEME) members visited a number of countries at various stages of discussions with the EU over membership. In some cases, irregular migration from these countries was a clear barrier to membership and the discussions generally focused on ways to increase control over these movements. In other cases, the membership path was very clear and the discussions were about the new member's own immigration policies, as they became the eastern or southern borders of an expanded EU. In all cases, but especially the former Yugoslavia, transition from countries with questionable human rights practices to ones in compliance with EU standards meant particular attention was given to asylum policies.

Turkey

Turkey is a country of 70 million that has been knocking on Europe's door for two decades. The major issues discussed during the March 2001 site visit included the economic development process, Turkish migration and EU entry, and immigration to and transit migration through Turkey. The Turkish government in the 1920s launched a top-down modernization effort, and in the 1960s the government began to promote the export of surplus labor in the hope that sending workers abroad from less-developed parts of the country would bring the remittances and returned workers with skills acquired abroad needed for modernization. Among the governments of labor-exporting countries, Turkey's has been unique in its high hopes for recruitment, remittances, and returns; they were expected to bring about a transformation of the country, and these high expectations help to explain widespread frustration with migration's actual effects in Turkey.

The Turkish government's current number-one goal is full membership in the EU as soon as possible. Ankara stresses that the EU should embrace full Turkish membership because of the country's strategic position between Europe and Asia and to send a signal to other Muslim societies, such as those of North Africa, that the EU will include Muslim societies that are secular and democratic. However, there are about 3.5 million Turks living abroad, including 3 million in Europe, and 70 percent in Germany. Many Europeans fear that Turkish EU membership would lead to another wave of migration; estimates are that 20 to 30 percent of Turkish youth would emigrate to seek higher wages in Europe if they could do so. Turkey hopes that admission to the EU will bring EU assistance and foreign direct investment that creates jobs and pushes up wages in Turkey, thus making migration insignificant.

Turkey is an emigration, transit, and immigration country. There are 3 to 4 million Turks abroad, 3 to 4 million foreigners living in Turkey (perhaps half Iranians), and tens of thousands of non-Turks who move through Turkey to Europe. Turkey is revising its asylum law in a manner that will allow persons fleeing persecution outside Europe to be considered refugees in Turkey and to establish a support system for refugees.

There is a sharp contrast between the role of migration in the efforts of Mexico (see chapter 7) and Turkey to integrate with larger economies nearby. In both cases, migration came before liberalization of trade, during eras in which governments pursued since-abandoned state-led industrialization policies. Mexico-U.S. migration probably expedited the acceptance of NAFTA in the United States, as NAFTA proponents promised that freer trade would prevent Mexican immigration from becoming even greater in the future. Turkey-EU migration has been reduced to 50,000–70,000 a year from 200,000 a year in the early 1970s, but fears of restarting Turkey-EU migration flows are one reason why many Europeans are reluctant to embrace Turkey's EU entry.

Most of the Turkish and Mexican migrants were and are unskilled workers from rural areas, and popular perceptions of Turks in the EU and Mexicans in the United States have been shaped by interactions with such workers and their families. In Europe, "unskilled Turks" are believed to have played an important role in creating attitudes that slow EU entry, and Turkish elites sometimes sympathize with Europeans trying to deal with Anatolian peasants.[6] It is in this sense that Turkish labor migration is sometimes described as a lose-lose proposition—Europe got unskilled Turks that have proved difficult to integrate, and the presence of Turkish migrants in the EU makes it harder for Turkey to win full EU membership.

Mexican economic integration with the United States has proceeded much faster than Turkish economic integration with the EU. Mexico proposed NAFTA in 1990, and the treaty went into effect less than four years later, on January 1, 1994. Turkey has been discussing integration with the EC/EU since the 1963 Ankara Agreement, but negotiations on Turkey's entry into the EU have not yet begun. Membership in the EU entails far more rights and responsibilities than does NAFTA membership, and the Turkish government does not believe that the Mexican experience holds many lessons for its efforts to join the EU. History plays a large role in Turkish attitudes toward Europe. The dissolution of the Ottoman Empire, including the never-implemented plans to divide Turkey after World War I and the forced return of many Turks from former Ottoman territories, has left a suspicion that outsiders are trying to take advantage of Turks.

Economy and Labor Market

Turkey, a country of 71 million people in 2003, generates goods and services worth $200 billion a year, $2,800 per capita. About 13 percent of Turkish gross domestic product (GDP) is from agriculture, 22 percent from manufacturing, and 65 percent from services, but employment shares are very different: agriculture has 45 percent of Turkish workers, manufacturing 15 percent, and services 40 percent, suggesting lower than average incomes in agriculture and higher than average incomes in manufacturing.

Turkey has had uneven economic growth, averaging 3.1 percent a year between 1990 and 2003. The Turkish economy shrank by 6 percent in 1994, expanded by 7 to 8 percent a year between 1995 and 1997, and shrank by 5 percent in 1999—the 1999 recession was due in part to an August 17, 1999, earthquake that killed 17,000 Turks and left 500,000 people homeless. In December 2000 the stock market plunged and interest rates rose on fears of bank failures due to unsecured loans made to those with close connections to political leaders. On February 22, 2001, when the president accused the prime minister of not doing enough to pursue corruption allegations, a panic led to an 18 percent one-day fall in the stock market and the Turkish lira dropped 30 percent, to 1 million lira to $1. Turkey agreed to additional economic reforms in order to obtain International Monetary Funds (IMF) support that stabilized its currency and economy, and growth exceeded 7 percent in 2004.

Turkey has a very high inflation rate, due in part to losses incurred by state enterprises and deficits in the social security system. These deficits are financed by internal and external borrowing, which pushes up real interest rates and drives down the Turkish lira. Turkey usually runs balance of trade deficits—there was a $10 billion deficit on goods trade in 1999—offset in part by a surplus in services exports (the tourism surplus was $5 billion in 1999 and the surplus from the activities of construction firms was $1.2 billion). Workers' remittances were $4.5 billion in 1999, making labor exports about as important as tourism as a source of foreign exchange.

Financial uncertainty is only one of many factors that put Turkey on a knife-edge. The image of Turkey teetering on a bridge between Europe and Asia helps to explain the uncertainty over Turkish EU entry in both Turkey and EU nations. For example, what priority should Turkey place on EU entry, especially if EU membership requires changes in areas that Turkey feels outsiders do not understand, including the rights of the Kurdish minority and the division of Cyprus into Turkish- and Greek-dominated areas?

There were 47 million Turks of working age in 2000, defined as persons twelve years or older. Half, 23 million, are in the labor force, including 9 million women—Turkey has a relatively low labor force participation rate. About half of Turkish workers are in formal jobs (covered by social security) and 45 percent are employed in agriculture—most Turkish women in the labor force are unpaid family workers in agriculture. The 11 million Turks employed in agriculture have lower than average wages; in 2003 the official unemployment rate was 11 percent, and more Turks in the work force were considered underemployed.[7] Unemployment insurance, enacted in 1998–1999, covers the half of the work force in the formal sector.

Two sectors—public employment and agriculture—need significant reforms. About 30 percent of Turkish workers are public employees, with many employed in State Economic Enterprises (SEE), public-sector companies that lose money producing textiles, food products, iron and steel, petrochemicals, tobacco, and electricity. SEE privatization has been slowed by union and popular opposition to layoffs, and by corruption—some past privatization efforts were marked by sweetheart deals with insiders or business people connected to politicians.[8]

Turkish agriculture, traditionally dominated by grains and sheep, contains many small units—70 percent of farms are less than 1.5 hectares or four acres. At the other end of the size spectrum, a handful of very large units take advantage of irrigation to produce high-value fruits and nuts,[9] especially in the Harran Plain below the Ataturk dam in the southeast—the dam is expected to irrigate 1.8 million hectares. To subsidize small farmers, the government offers higher than world prices for some crops, but these payments mostly benefit the largest producers. Agricultural subsidies were 7.5 percent of GDP in 1997.

Education and Human Rights

Education is compulsory for children aged eight to fourteen; until 1998, only five years of schooling was compulsory, and most of Turkey's 30,000 villages had schools that offered five years of instruction. After eight years of schooling, about two-thirds of children seek jobs, and one-third continue studying. Many of the children under fourteen seen working are considered by their parents to be "apprentices" learning an occupation. Most schools require uniforms that cost $75, and parents are expected to pay another $75 for textbooks. Turkey has 525,000 teachers, and class sizes average sixty-four students. Teachers earn $300 a month or $3,000 a year.

Government expenditure on education is equivalent to 10 percent of the GNP; expenditures on health are 2 percent of GDP, and 13 percent for social security. Many educated youth are unemployed; about one-fourth of the high school graduates fifteen to twenty-four were unemployed in late 1998.

The major minority rights issue involves Kurds, the 10 to 15 million people who have a separate language and culture, live in all parts of Turkey but are concentrated in the poorer southeastern part of Turkey, and are considered not to be a minority by the Turkish government. In 1984, the Kurdish Workers' Party or PKK began an armed struggle for an independent homeland for Kurds. The Turkish government says that Kurds have the same rights as other Turkish citizens, but allowing the establishment of Kurdish-language schools or television stations would weaken the unity of the state.

Some 30,000 people died in the struggle between 1984 and 1999, including 5,000 Turkish soldiers, and Turkey spent an estimated $100 billion trying to extirpate the rebels. In February 1999, Turkey arrested the most prominent Kurdish rebel, Abdullah Ocalan, head of the Kurdish Workers' Party (PKK), and Ocalan called for an end to an armed struggle for an independent Kurdistan. Martial law, which had been imposed in ten provinces, now applies in only four. Candidates associated with the Kurdish political party HADEP have run for office and been elected in local elections. March 2001, the Kurdish holiday Newruz could be celebrated in a more open manner than in the past.

Turkish Migration to the EU

The 3.5 million Turks abroad in 1998 were equivalent to 5 percent of Turkish residents, and the 1.3 million Turkish workers abroad in 1998 were equivalent to 6 percent of Turkish workers. Remittances peaked at $5.4 billion in 1998, fell to $4.5 billion in 1999, and were $2 billion in 2003.

Turkish labor migration began in the early 1960s. Much of the literature evaluating this migration has a negative flavor, because expectations in

Turkey as well as in Western European host countries were not fulfilled. Germany, France, and Belgium wound up with significant immigrant populations rather than workers who went home after a year or two. Nor did Turkey get what it wanted: an economic take-off toward developed country status from the recruitment, remittances, and return of migrant workers.

Organized Turkish labor migration began with an October 1961 agreement between Turkey and Germany. The annual exit of migrants rose to 66,000 in 1964, 130,000 in 1970, and peaked at 136,000 in 1973. Between 1961 and 1975, about 805,000 Turks were sent abroad through the Turkish Employment Service (TES); other Turks emigrated as tourists and then went to work. It is estimated that 1.5 to 2 million Turks went abroad for employment between 1961 and 1973, equivalent to 10 to 12 percent of Turkey's 1970 work force and 40 percent of men aged twenty to thirty-nine in the Turkish work force in 1970. When labor recruitment was stopped in 1973, there were 1 million Turks on waiting lists maintained by TES to go abroad for jobs.

The government promoted worker emigration and anticipated eventual free access to the European labor market. The September 1963 Ankara Association Agreement and the Additional Protocol of 1973 promised a steady reciprocal lowering of European Community (EC) tariff and eventually migration barriers, with Turks having "free access" to the European labor market by December 1986. However, the Ankara Agreement was not implemented. In December 1976, Turkey announced that it could not decrease its trade barriers as scheduled, and in January 1982 the European Parliament persuaded the EC Commission to suspend negotiations over closer EC-Turkish relations.

On April 14, 1987, Turkey applied for EC membership. On December 18, 1989, the EC Commission rebuffed Turkey's application, citing several factors that made Turkey not ready for EU membership, including its lack of adherence to basic human rights conventions and the gap between the Turkish and EU economies. In 1996, a Turkish-EU customs union went into effect that had a limited North American Free Trade Agreement (NAFTA)-like impact of increasing foreign investment in Turkey—foreign companies wanting to use low-cost Turkish labor to manufacture products such as autos for European markets invested in the country. However, imports also increased as a result of lower tariffs, reducing profits and employment in other Turkish industries.

Turkey is struggling with several chicken-egg problems related to EU entry. The EU wants Turkey to abolish the death penalty and increase respect for human rights, which Turkey believes it can do only after terrorism is eliminated. Similarly, the EU wants Turkey to restructure its economy before entry negotiations begin. Ankara argues that there will be more foreign investment (currently foreign direct investment or FDI is about $1 billion a year, versus $30 to $40 billion a year to Mexico)[10] and thus less restructuring pain if the EU makes a definite commitment to admit Turkey before workers are displaced from agriculture and SEEs. Turkey tends to have weak coalition governments, so higher unemployment could produce political protests that bring them down. In 2002, the Islamic Justice and Development Party (AKP) won the elections, marking the first time that a religious party has taken over government responsibilities in Turkey. The AKP has maintained the commitment of previous governments to join the EU.

In December 1999, EU leaders put Turkey on a list of countries eligible for future EU entry, but announced that political and economic reforms were required before accession negotiations could begin. In November 2000 the EU issued an Accession Partnership Document (APD) with a list of issues Turkey must deal with before negotiations can begin, including guaranteeing minority rights, reducing torture and the role of the military in politics, and supporting efforts to find a solution to the division of Cyprus. Turkey made many of the changes demanded by the EU, and accession negotiations were scheduled to begin in October 2005. Opinion polls suggest that a majority of Turks support EU membership, some 60–65 percent in March 2001 and 55 percent in spring 2005.

If admitted, Turkey would be the most populous EU country within a generation. Germany is projected to have 82 million residents in 2025 and Turkey 89 million. Turkey would have the largest land area in the EU, about 300,000 square miles, 50 percent larger than France.

Ankara hopes that EU aid and investment can create jobs for displaced workers and new labor force entrants. If this strategy failed, and Turkey entered the EU with immediate freedom of movement, there would almost certainly be large-scale emigration. Turkey has one of the fastest population growth rates in Europe, about 1.4 percent or a million per year, and a labor force of 31 million that is growing by almost 3 percent or 900,000 per year. Doubt that Turkey can meet this job-creation challenge lies at the root of some of the European fears surrounding Turkish entry into the EU. The Turkish government is explicit that "we do not want to overwhelm Europe with unskilled Turkish workers," but at the same time takes the position that full EU membership cannot be divorced from freedom of movement.

After Turkey applied for EU entry in 1987, there was an effort to project probable emigration if Turkey were to join the EU and Turks gained freedom of movement rights in 2005 or 2010. The opinions of key informants in Turkey and EU nations was that there would be an initial wave of Turks testing EU labor markets as soon as they could—25 to 35 percent of the twenty-to-twenty-nine-year old men were expected to seek jobs abroad—followed by a level of labor migration that depended on the evolution of European labor markets. If there were jobs available in Europe at high wages, Turks would stay and more might come. If not, Turkish migration would be expected to wane.

Turkish experts who projected low levels of migration (20 percent or less of twenty-to-twenty-nine-year olds would emigrate to see if they could find jobs outside Turkey) emphasized that Turkey was growing fast and that the jobs filled by Turks in Europe were difficult, dirty, and dangerous, living outside Turkey was expensive, and there was discrimination against Turks. Those who predicted high levels of emigration (50 percent or more of twenty-to-twenty-nine-year olds would emigrate) noted that there is significant east-west migration within Turkey that could become international migration, since internal migrants often have friends and relatives abroad; 1960s and 1970s migrants who are settled abroad are seen as economic successes by potential migrants in Turkey, as they return with cars and money for better housing; there is little prospect that enough formal sector jobs will be created for new labor force entrants, especially for young women in urban areas who now have very low labor force participation rates, and there is less room to absorb additional workers in agriculture.

Thus, most Turkish key informants projected an initial wave of emigration larger than that of the 1960s and 1970s. However, this migration hump was expected to be short-lived, because most European countries in the late 1980s projected fewer job openings for unskilled migrants. If the number of jobs for unskilled workers shrank as projected in most European countries, and if most Turkish migrants were unskilled, then migration to test the waters would be followed by far less migration, that is, it would appear as a migration hump.

During the 1990s, there was little opportunity for Turks to migrate for employment to Europe, but they could migrate for employment to Russia and the Middle East. In 1998, some 600,000 Turks were on waiting lists maintained by the Turkish Employment Service for overseas jobs; the TES sent 17,000 workers abroad in 1999, 26,000 in 1998, and 33,000 in 1997, down sharply from 60,000 a year in 1994–1995. The drop was due to the decline in the number of migrants sent to the ex-USSR, for example, 42,000 sent in 1994 and 7,000 in 1999.

Turkey has begun developing policies for migrants abroad. Two commissions were created on February 16, 1998, to deal with migrant issues: a Supreme Committee for Nationals Living Abroad chaired by the Prime Minister and a Coordinating Committee for Nationals Living Abroad, which includes representatives of Turks in twelve foreign countries. Turkey in 1995 made it easier for overseas Turks to naturalize abroad by creating a "special foreign nationality" symbolized by a pink card for Turks who gave up their Turkish citizenship, but want to preserve their right to buy and inherit land in Turkey. Also in 1995, Turks under age twenty were permitted to give up Turkish citizenship without fulfilling their Turkish military obligations.

Migration and Development

Turkey's May 27, 1960, constitution guaranteed Turks the right to a passport and travel abroad, and the Turkish government in the 1960s embraced exporting surplus labor as the best way to relieve un- and under-employment, especially in agricultural areas, where almost half of the population lived. The government played a significant role in 1960s labor migration, designating certain areas as priority areas for recruitment. Turkey sought to maximize and channel remittances with a variety of programs and policies that ranged from allowing tariff-free imports if returning migrants converted their foreign currency DM savings into lira and establishing Turkish workers companies to channel savings into job-creating factories in the migrants' areas of origin.

Turkey has been trying to modernize in a top-down fashion since Ataturk came to power in 1923, and migration was seen by the government as a way to export surplus labor and accelerate modernization. Migration did accelerate modernization, but not always in anticipated ways. It was very hard in the 1960s and 1970s to create small businesses or to establish businesses that relied on foreign capital or foreign partners. Turkey during these years had high tariff walls, an overvalued exchange rate, and a preference for state-run businesses, which encouraged migrants returning with savings of $2,000 to $5,000 to buy land or animals if they returned to farm, or to build better houses, buy vehicles to provide taxi or transport services, or to buy land and housing as investments.

The reasons for the failure of labor migration to transform Turkey lay as much in the economic policies of the government that made it hard to establish small businesses as in problems inherent in migration. Migration under a different set of economic policies might well have produced many of the new businesses and jobs desired by Turkey.

Turkey today has a relatively low-wage and low-productivity economy in which workers are moving from agriculture to seek non-farm jobs. The Turkish government wants to reform and restructure agriculture, the state-owned SEEs, the pension system, and the banking system. However, if Turkey is to be modernized, the government may have to foster bottom-up democracy rather than using the traditional top-down approach.

Immigration, Refugees, and Transit Migrants

Turkey is both a country of immigration and of transit. There are about 3.5 million foreigners in Turkey, half of them Iranians. In 1998, for the first time, the number of foreign workers officially entering Turkey was the same as the number of Turks going abroad for employment, about 25,000. Migrants from Iraq, Iran, and Afghanistan go through Turkey, which does not have re-admission agreements with EU-member states for constitutional reasons, and thus does not accept the return of migrants who travel through Turkey en route to Europe.

Many of the foreigners in Turkey are unauthorized. Apprehensions have increased rapidly in the 1990s, from 3,600 in 1995 to 65,600 in 2000. The police reportedly do not try very hard to apprehend unauthorized foreigners because police agencies bear the cost of detaining them. In some cases, organized criminals pay off police, who then do not search out or detain unauthorized foreigners who are being smuggled to other countries. There are three main types of smugglers—PKK sympathizers; international syndicates capable of moving large numbers of migrants by ship; and local, smaller and often opportunistic smugglers.

A 1937 law that permits only persons of ethnic Turkish origin to immigrate shapes Turkey's current immigration policies. Turkey accepted and provided support to some two million ethnic Turkish immigrants between 1923 and 1971, and again in 1989 when there was an influx of ethnic Turks from Bulgaria.

Turkey's asylum regulations were revised in 1994 to require foreigners to apply for asylum within five days of entry or be subject to deportation. Between 1994 and 2000, Turkish data suggest that some 20,000 foreigners—including 11,000 Iranians—applied for asylum in Turkey, and 7,300 (including 5,000 Iranians) were accepted as refugees. Some 3,700 applications were rejected, and 8,000 are pending. Most rejected asylum seekers were not removed from Turkey. The UN High Commissioner for Refugees (UNHCR) data for the same years report 31,000 asylum applications, 11,000 acceptances, and 18,000 rejections. Under Turkish law, anyone can appeal a government decision to the Council of State.

Under pressure from the EU, Turkey was developing a system of reception centers for asylum applicants, and plans to more closely adhere to UNHCR policies of interviewing applicants to determine if they qualify for refugee status. Some fear that this effort to bring Turkish practice into conformity with UNHCR policies may be bad for people in need of refuge, as Turkey may not provide informal refuge to foreigners in need of protection who do not qualify for asylum, something it often does now. Illegal immigration may also increase, as Iranians and Moldavians going to western Europe through

Turkish airports may be forced to travel illegally to and through Turkey rather than legally.

Turkish Migration to Germany

Germany is the major foreign destination of Turks. About 50,000 Turks a year emigrate, usually to join their families in Germany, and another 10,000 a year apply for asylum in Germany. The Istanbul consulate is the third largest in the German Foreign Service, issuing 102,000 visas in 2000 (the German consulate in Ankara issued 70,000). Most of these visas were issued for business visits—about 60,000, and most were issued within 48 hours of the application. Another 40,000 visa requests are for tourism or family visas, which cost DM40 for 30-day visits or DM60 for 90 days. The overall approval rate for visa applications is about 92 percent, but about 25,000 potential applicants a year are advised to return with better documentation of their jobs in and ties to Turkey and thus do not show up in rejection data.

Most decisions on applications for business or tourist visas are based on a review of documents submitted in support of the application—most applicants are not interviewed in person. Germany accepts photos of women wearing headscarves on visa applications; France does not.

Only 9,350 of the German visas issued in Istanbul in 2000 were for immigration, and they generally involved Turkish spouses and children moving to Germany to join a spouse/parent established abroad. The procedure is for a Turk to apply for a family unification visa in Turkey, which prompts the German consulate in Istanbul to request documents from the appropriate aliens authority in Germany in a process that takes six to eight weeks. If the visa application is rejected, the applicant can hire a lawyer in Germany and appeal the denial—about 20 percent of the 1,000 rejected applications for immigration visas each year are appealed.

German law gives consular offices a great deal of discretion about who should receive an immigration visa. For example, when considering a family unification visa application, German consular officers may decide that it is best for a sixteen-year-old who has been raised by grandparents in Turkey to stay in Turkey. The desire of many Turks to emigrate has given rise to migration via marriage, which prompts German and other EU nations to scrutinize carefully requests for visas for Turks in Turkey who marry Turks or others settled abroad in an effort to ferret out marriages of convenience. Neither Germany nor Turkey recognizes so-called imam marriages, civil marriages that can be regarded as legal after four years. Finally, German consulate staff are responsible for checking that asylum seekers returned from Germany to Turkey are not tortured in Turkey.

Many Europeans, and especially many Germans, are somewhat wary of more Turkish immigration because of difficulty integrating current Turkish residents. For example, the high unemployment rate among Turks in Germany— over 20 percent—and the relatively low rate at which second and third generation Turks earn certificates in an occupation suggest that admitting more Turks could add to unemployment as well as to employment.

Internal Migration

Internal migration remains a significant factor in Turkey. Istanbul has grown rapidly, from 1.5 million residents in 1955 to 10 to 12 million today, due to rural-urban migration as well as migration to Istanbul from other Turkish cities. Istanbul is unusual in that many non-Muslims left the city at the same time as more Muslims arrived from elsewhere in Turkey: in 1990, only 40 percent of Istanbul residents and 20 percent of heads of households, were born in the city. Some of the migration from southeastern Turkey to Istanbul resulted from efforts to escape fighting between PKK sympathizers seeking an independent Kurdistan and government troops.

CEME visited Kadikoy, a part of Istanbul across the Bosporus Strait, that is a recipient of migrants from Eastern Turkey. Kadikoy is a banana-shaped municipality; most residents work in other parts of Istanbul. At the time of the site visit, Kadikoy was one of only three of the twenty-eight municipalities in Istanbul with elected mayors who were not affiliated with the Islamist-oriented Virtue party, the successor to the banned Welfare Party (the governor of Istanbul is appointed by the federal government in Ankara). These Islamist parties became the Justice and Development Party (AKP) that won national elections in November 2002.

In 1994, Kadikoy launched family assistance centers to help women who had migrated with their families from rural areas to the shantytowns that ring the city and could serve as a base for fundamentalism. The family assistance centers are aimed at helping illiterate women to achieve basic literacy and the skills needed to improve their self-esteem, earnings, and prospects for self-employment. About six hundred women a year participate because they want to learn and because they receive a completion card that entitles them to various forms of municipal and voluntary services, including health care for themselves and their children, second-hand clothes and school uniforms, and basic foods such as milk and eggs. The women learn or refine cooking skills as well as computer, handicraft, and other skills during the twelve months they are enrolled.

CEME also visited APS Textile, a 550-employee sewing factory in Kadikoy established in 1982, that had sales in 2000 of $33 million. The company's major products are skirts and pants produced primarily with Turkish cotton for firms such as Banana Republic and Liz Claiborne. APS employees—whose average age is twenty-eight—are guaranteed Turkey's minimum wage of about $140 a month, but most work under piece rate wages and earn $200 to $400 a month. The factory can produce 100,000 pairs of pants a month, and has the capacity to produce another 350,000 pairs a month by using a network of 15 to 20 subcontractors that have 80 to 150 employees each.

APS says that Turkish entry into the EU would not have a significant effect on the company. Instead, APS stressed the problems associated with U.S. textile quotas—these quotas have encouraged APS to establish partnerships with producers in Bulgaria and Ukraine as much for access to the U.S. market as for the lower wages there.

Romania

Romania, a country of 22.5 million people, has land borders with Hungary in the northwest, Serbia in the southwest, Bulgaria in the south, Moldova in the northeast, and Ukraine in the north. The Black Sea connects the country to Russia, Georgia, and Turkey. Romania aims to join the EU in the second round of enlargement by 2007.

Economic development has been slower in Romania than in other Eastern European countries: GDP in 2000 was about $34 billion, and per capita GDP $1,600, one-tenth of the EU average. Living standards fell during the 1990s: in 2000 they were only a bit over half of what they were at the end of Communist rule. In 1996 they were at 73 percent of 1990 levels, in 2000 at 56 percent. Multi-party democracy has been established, but the government has not cleaned up the legacy of Communism by privatizing loss-making state industries or clarifying property rights or reforming the bureaucracy or reducing corruption to a tolerable level.

There is a significant emigration of highly educated workers, especially information technology (IT) professionals, of Roma, many of whom are unemployed, and of ethnic Germans, about half of whom have moved to Germany. Many more Romanians wish to emigrate. A May 2001 poll found that 17 percent would try to find a job in the EU if they had freedom of movement rights; 39 percent said they would definitely stay in Romania.[11]

The Romanian nation is struggling to modernize its society and economy amidst disruptive forces unleashed by the collapse in 1990 of a command economy and a ruthless dictatorship. Among them are widespread societal discrimination and police harassment against the Roma; demands by the legally established "national" minorities—chiefly ethnic Hungarians and

Germans—for more autonomy; and the rapid growth of the far-right Greater Romania Party, second-strongest in Parliament, which has attacked the demands of the minority groups and is pressing for the return of formerly Romanian territory in present-day Ukraine and Moldova.

In its annual report to the European Council on Romania's progress toward meeting the standards for accession, the EU described Romania as having a functioning democracy and reasonably stable institutions but listed grave deficiencies. Orphanages are underfunded and "still heavily dependent on humanitarian assistance provided by foreign donors." Abandonment of children and a significant population of street children are continuing problems. An approach to the problem of discrimination by public employees, private companies, and economic operators on grounds of race, ethnicity, and gender was made in a September 2000 ordinance prohibiting these practices, but the ordinance has not been implemented.

The new refugee law does not provide for the detention of asylum seekers, and the Aliens Law needs to be revised "in order to establish an effective migration and aliens policy." Vague laws are still on the books that can inhibit freedom of expression. Women "continue to be at greater risk of social exclusion than men," and "no progress has been made concerning equal pay and equal access to employment or health and safety at work."

The EU noted that Roma remain subject to "widespread discrimination throughout Romanian society," the government's "commitment to addressing this situation remains low" and there has been "little substantial progress" in this area. In striking contrast, the demands of the "national minorities" for the use of their languages in schooling and higher education are being largely met. The "national minorities" are people who themselves or whose ancestors originated in a territory that was once part of Romania (like ethnic Ukrainians) or in a country that Romania was part of (like ethnic Hungarians), or whose ancestors settled in Romania at the invitation of Romania's rulers—the Germans. At present, 5 percent of educational units teach in a minority language, most commonly Hungarian, though six other languages of instruction are used. The Romany tongue is not among them; the Roma are not a "national minority."

In December 2001, Romania's seventh government since 1989 came to power, led by the leftist Party of Social Democracy in Romania (PSDR), the ex-Communist party. Ion Iliescu, a former Communist and first president after the collapse of Ceausescu's dictatorship, was president again, and Adrian Nastase, also an ex-communist, was named prime minister. CEME participants were told by several experts that to accomplish privatization, modernization, and reform there must be more foreign investment and help from the

EU, but that such commitments are held back by the lack of a secure legal foundation and clear property rights. The political system has not delivered the framework that is necessary, they said.

Economy and Labor

The economy is Romania's most pressing problem. Its course since the collapse of Communism can be divided into three periods: rethinking the economy (1990–1993), economic recovery and growth (1994–1996), and the economic crash (1996–1999). Both the left (ex-Communists) and the center-right failed to reform the economy when they were in power. At the start of the post-Communist period, Romania had the most distorted economic structure of all the Eastern European countries. It was marked by overstaffed heavy industries that are not internationally competitive. State-owned industries remain overstaffed in 2001, even though many older workers were retired early, causing the number of Romanian pensioners to double in the 1990s.

During the 1980s, Romania pursued a relentless policy of paying off its foreign debts, which left it with old equipment and few foreign markets for Romanian products. Successive governments have been reluctant to privatize and reduce overstaffing because when the factories that are often the only enterprise in an area close down, the result is long-term unemployment and depopulation.[12]

At the time of the site visit, the unemployment rate was 10 percent, and 40 percent of Romanians lived on less than $1 per day. Loss-making state enterprises have often received government loans and used them to give wage increases, which have increased pressure to keep the factories open and fueled inflation. The government fears strikes and unrest of the sort that occurred in the early 1990s, and has consequently promised extra social spending to alleviate unemployment and poverty, saying it must balance "market concerns" with "social goals." The government provides workers with health and pension benefits, and other perquisites like lunch meal tickets.

Romania's minimum wage is 1.4 million lei, $50, per month. In April 2001, the average gross monthly wage was 4.2 million lei, $145. The average net monthly wage (i.e., after employee-paid taxes) was 3 million lei, $103. Employers pay an additional 51 percent of gross wages in employment taxes, 2.1 million lei, $72, on this average wage, making the total labor cost to the employer of an average worker 6.3 million lei, $217.

The distortions of the labor market lead to an unusual result, epitomized in the saying that people with jobs in state owned factories do not work, while those with private sector jobs cannot survive. There are still many Romanians employed by loss-making state-owned companies whose poor work habits make private employers reluctant to hire them, even though they pay lower wages than the state-owned enterprises. Further privatization would lead to layoffs and perhaps to more corruption, judging by the past, since previous managers have sometimes bought out the companies they once managed.

Agriculture is a major employer, but only a minor contributor to GDP—some 40 to 45 percent of Romania's 9–10 million workers are employed on farms, usually on large state farms that have not yet been privatized, but agriculture contributes only about 15 percent of GDP.[13] Uniquely in post-Communist Europe, agricultural employment has been rising as the jobless poor abandon the cities and return to their villages to till small plots.

The World Bank, using a different measure, says agriculture's share of unemployment has risen from 28 percent to 36 percent in the 1990s. Romania was providing direct subsidies of one million lei ($35) per hectare of arable land to farmers in 2001, and providing large subsidies on purchases of Romanian-made equipment by larger farms (at least 110 hectares). FDI directed to helping peasants to improve agricultural productivity with modern machinery, and perhaps help switching to higher value crops that could be exported, could go a long way toward slowing what might otherwise be rapid rural-urban migration, especially among young people who see no future in agriculture.

The private sector of the economy accounts for about 60 percent of GDP, but private businesses complain of corruption, red tape, and inconsistent regulation and taxes. Romania has very high payroll taxes, so that there is a significant wedge between what an employer pays for labor and what workers receive. Employers also complain that tax and other regulations change frequently, generating uncertainty and extra costs of doing business.[14]

EU Investment and Migration in Western Romania

We visited Timisoara (pop. 350,000), the main city of the historic Banat region, a rich agricultural plain today shared by Hungary, Serbia, and Romania.[15] As the westernmost city in Romania, Timisoara is located on what was the fault line between Christianity and Islam for a thousand years, and it is the place where the revolution that toppled dictator Nicolae Ceausescu began in December 1989. In the eighteenth and nineteenth centuries it enjoyed the favor of its Habsburg rulers, which is visible today in its town plan and baroque, classical, and Secessionist buildings. Today it is still a cultural crossroads and Romania's window on the West.

Timisoara is one of the two centers of FDI in Romania, the other being Bucharest. FDI has been running at about $1 billion a year, as firms take advantage of a relatively well-educated labor force and low wages.[16] Most foreign investors are permitted to import equipment free of customs duties and value added tax (VAT) (20 percent), and can repatriate profits free of Romanian tax. Foreign firms taking advantage of these investment incentives are obliged, however, to remain employers in Romania for twice the time that they enjoyed the tax breaks.

Foreign investors include Germany's Siemens and Continental Tire, Alcatel of France, and thousands of Italian companies that make garments, shoes, and furniture for export. FDI in Timisoara has created jobs directly and also indirectly, as accounting and personnel agencies spring up to assist foreign investors. Foreign managers living in Timisoara are creating a demand for better housing and services.

Most of the jobs created by FDI in Romania are in manufacturing; 90 percent of Romania's manufacturing exports are products that are assembled in the country from elements made elsewhere. The Continental tire plant accounted for $50 million of the $350 million in FDI in Timisoara, according to the local chamber of commerce. (Continental expects its investment to be $100 million by the end of 2001). Continental employs 460 workers (shortly to be 1,000) whose average age is thirty-three. They assemble imported raw materials to make modular units that are then re-exported to other Conti plants to have tread and sidewalls added. Twenty-two percent of the staff are university-graduate engineers; they earn 6 to 10 million lei per month (gross) while production workers earn 4 million lei per month—about the Romanian workers' average wage.

The Continental plant is capital intensive, using the same machines that would be found in a German plant. Why, then, did Continental locate the plant in Timisoara? Three reasons are evident: (1) Continental wanted a location in Eastern Europe for what it hopes will be a future market, (2) it was faster to get permits and clearances to build the large plant in a space previously occupied by a state-owned Romanian firm than it would have been to build a "greenfield" plant in the EU, and (3) wages, which will eventually be about 25 percent of production costs, are significantly lower, for both engineers and production workers.

Italy is a major investor in Romania. Germany accounts for 35 percent of the $350 million FDI in Timisoara, but Italian FDI, 32 percent of the regional total, probably accounts for more FDI-created jobs, since Italian firms tend to produce labor-intensive shoes and garments.[17] Italy is Romania's number-one trading partner—about 23 percent of Romania's exports go to Italy, and 21 percent of imports come from Italy. Business Week has commented "Romania is Italy's Mexico. . . . Italian manufacturers can expect to save 60 percent making the same product with the same material in Romania. Italy's mom-and-pop businesses are well-suited to Romania's unpredictable business climate."

Many of the Italian-owned firms are from northeast Italy, the Verona-Vicenza-Treviso area (Italy's Veneto region), and their Romanian operations are in the Timisoara-Arad-Oradea area of western Romania.[18] The 1998 wage difference was reported to be about 17 to 1, that is, a wage of $2,000 per month in Italy, compared to $120 per month[19] in Romania (including taxes and benefits). Italian FDI has increased the number of Romanian textile and footwear firms, from 544 in 1989 to 8,500 in 2000 when they employed 422,000 employees, 20 percent of Romania's industrial workers. Most of the new textile and footwear firms are private enterprises, and many of the jobs they offer are associated with Italian investment.

For example Geox, a maker of shoes with "breathable soles" that retail for about $100 per pair, invested $15 million in a footwear factory near Timisoara, hired 800 workers (85 percent women) and produced 200,000 pairs of shoes in 1998. Geox had three major reasons for putting a plant in Timisoara: (1) low cost labor (gross wages average 2.5 million lei or $88 month,[20] (2) transportation across Austria and Hungary is relatively fast, and (3) since Romanian is a romance language, it is possible for Italian skilled workers and managers to learn enough Romanian in three or four months to instruct the workers in the Timisoara plant.

Geox tends to hire women of all ages, but the men it hires are mostly young. The managers say that older men who were previously employed by state-owned enterprises do not have good work attitudes. Most employees are local residents and special Geox buses are provided to take them from the downtown area to the plant. Some of the workers are internal migrants from the region bordering with Moldova, one of the poorest regions of Romania. Since benefits are provided by the state, those who leave for vacation and do not return lose nothing by quitting and coming back later, or switching companies.

Immigration and FDI appear to be complementary in the Italian-Romanian case. Italian firms are pressing the Italian government to make it easier to admit Romanians for work and training, and some Italian investors hope that Italy's "industrial district" model that often leads to cooperation between small and medium sized enterprises can be exported to Romania. An Italian pilot program aims to use recruitment, remittances, and returns to accelerate development in Romania and to ensure that migration is temporary or circular, i.e., that the migrants who come to Italy for training return.

EU entry is, naturally enough, more important to Romania than to foreign investors in Romania. In the interchanges between CEME participants and the managers of foreign-owned firms, the investors mentioned low labor costs and the speed of getting approval to construct their facilities, not Romania's potential EU accession, as reasons for investing in Romania. Nevertheless, EU entry would reduce a major complaint of foreign-owned firms—lengthy delays getting machinery and parts into Romania and goods out across the border.

In looking at the relationship of FDI and migration, an important question is whether the FDI-led assembly model can increase wages and opportunities enough to reduce emigration pressure, and by how much. FDI is creating jobs, but at low wages. Can wages rise with workers' experience, and economic multipliers increase with more local production of inputs? A second question is whether the benefits of FDI will spread throughout the Romanian economy. With FDI concentrated around Timisoara and Bucharest, will FDI increase internal migration from poorer to richer areas of Romania, thus increasing regional disparities?

Hungarians and Roma

Romania's biggest "national minority" is a legacy of the dismemberment of Hungary that followed the First World War. When Romania was awarded Transylvania and the Hungarian part of the Banat in 1920, it acquired 5 million people, of whom 1.7 million were Magyar-speakers. Their descendants are the ethnic Hungarians of today's Romania, who, despite emigration, still number 1.5 million. Polls suggest that about 30 percent of them would emigrate if they could.

Romania actively protects Hungarians and other national minorities. They are guaranteed representation in Parliament. Article 6 of Romania's 1991 constitution lays out extensive minority rights, which were improved in 1999 with amendments to the education law, which created the legal basis for the use of minority languages, upon request, in K–12 publicly funded education as well as in local government meetings when at least one-third of the elected officials request a non-Romanian language. About 5 percent of education in Romanian is in minority languages (2,700 schools teach in Hungarian), with the history and traditions of each minority group incorporated into the curricula and free textbooks. In the old "Saxon" cities of Transylvania there are German *Gymnasia* that teach to a high standard in German, and are attended by pupils whose family language is Romanian as well as children from German-speaking families. There will soon be a "multicultural" university in Cluj, a center of Hungarian culture, at which lectures and examinations will be conducted in Hungarian and to a lesser degree in other minority languages.

In May 2000, Romania and Hungary signed an agreement that permits 8,000 Romanians, mostly ethnic Hungarians, to work seasonally in Hungary each year; the guest worker program was reciprocal, but few Hungarians work in Romania. This was an effort to substitute legal guest workers for the 5,000 to 10,000 Romanians believed to be employed illegally in Hungary during the summer tourism and harvest season; wages in Hungary are at least twice as high as wages in Romania.[21]

In April 2000, the Hungarian government proposed to give ethnic Hungarians in neighboring countries ID cards that would provide them with basic subsidies and preferential treatment while traveling or working in Hungary. Eligible people would be identified by the organizations of ethnic Hungarians in the countries where they live. Since Hungary would join the EU before Romania, this would mean that ethnic Romanian Hungarians would get visa-free access to Hungary and thus, perhaps, to the EU, while ordinary Romanians would not be so privileged. The government of Romania has objected to the proposal.

The Roma are not a "national minority," but may well be as large a group as the ethnic Hungarians. Instead of having special rights, they are widely discriminated against. (The word "Rom," plural "Roma," has nothing to do with "Romania;" it originates in Indian words for "man" and "people.") Their history of migration, enslavement, and the hostility of the Eastern European peoples among whom they now live have made them some of the poorest and most pitiable of Romanians, and at the same time some of the most troublesome. Their dark skin and their tendency to live apart from the rest of society perpetuate their marginal status. Most speak the Romanian language, but they possess their own language, Romany, which is of Indian origin.

Most Roma are Christian; perhaps half speak Romany. Unemployment is very high, sometimes over 50 percent. Few Roma children graduate from secondary school and university, in part because many Roma children, especially those who come to school without speaking Romanian, are placed in schools for the disabled. Roma have far higher fertility than do other citizens, and their share of the population is rising in Central and Eastern Europe.[22]

Romanians complain that the Roma have an alternative society, that few pay taxes, that many marry below the age of consent, and that many parents do not send their children to school. Petty crime such as theft is often attributed to Roma, including Roma children. The economic status of Roma, organized into about 25 clans in Romania, is quite variable. Some are successful business people, while others live in abject poverty. Some Roma have reportedly become smugglers, taking other Roma as well as non-Roma migrants to Western Europe.

The European Roma Rights Center (ERRC) (www.errc.org) argues that the key to reducing discrimination against Roma lies in the schools and calls for an end to the practice of putting Roma children in schools for the mentally handicapped. Others point out that poor families with several children cannot afford to buy the books and uniforms needed to attend school, which goes a long way to explaining low Roma enrollment rates.

The ERRC uses U.S. civil rights techniques to try to reduce discrimination against Roma, including sending matched Roma and non-Roma testers to apply for jobs and housing, and then charging with discrimination employers and landlords who do not treat the applicants equally. In September 2000, a Romanian government ordinance was approved that prohibited discrimination by public and private companies on the grounds of nationality, race, ethnicity, age, gender, or sexual orientation, and set out a schedule of heavy fines for violations. There is not yet enough experience to know if this approach will reduce discrimination.

Emigration and Transit Migration

There are about 30,000 more deaths (118 per 10,000) than births (105 per 10,000) each year in Romania, and according to the government, there was a net emigration of 2,500 in 2000. The country's population fell by about 750,000 between 1990 and 2000, and the number of children younger than fifteen in 2000 was only 50,000 higher than the number of people sixty years old and over.

Many of those emigrating are young and well educated, so that Romania is experiencing a brain drain. About half of the 5,000 graduates in computer science from Romanian universities each year emigrate, and a March 2001 poll found that 66 percent of Romanian students would emigrate if they could. The Romanian winner of the International Computer Olympics in 2000 said he wanted "to study in the United States—and stay."

The government says that 80,000 Romanian professionals have emigrated since 1989, a result, it has been said, of "a good education system and a lousy economy." Dan Nica, Romania's Communication and IT Minister, says "The brain drain is a reality, and for the foreseeable future there do not seem to be any solutions . . . we must [instead] talk about the free circulation of Romania's elite, which brings us closer to the West."

Romanian observers see little general benefit coming from migrants abroad. Remittances are spent on building housing and buying consumer durables. Little economic advantage in the form of economic multipliers for local economies has been seen from this spending. There seemed to be some resentment of Romanian judges brought back from abroad with extra salary payments from foreign benefactors, since this leaves judges on the same bench with unequal salaries.

Romania has been a major transit route for migrants traveling from the Middle East and Asia to Western Europe, and at the time of the site visit, was under pressure to improve border controls and reduce trafficking in migrants, prostitutes, and drugs. Many women from Moldavia and Ukraine are trafficked through Romania. Romania would like EU assistance to improve its ability to monitor its borders. There is a sharp contrast at the Hungarian-Romanian border crossing at Nagylak-Nadlac. The Hungarian side has been modernized with EU support, so that heat-seeking devices can scan vehicles and computers can read passports. We saw none of this technology on the Romanian side.

On January 1, 2002, the EU dropped the requirement that nationals of Bulgaria and Romania have visas to enter Schengen countries, so that only Turks among candidate countries need entry visas for Schengen. However, both the Bulgarian and Romanian governments check those exiting. For example, Romanians need medical insurance, a return ticket or equivalent, and either an invitation or Euro 100 per day in order to visit the Schengen area for up to 90 days, the same requirements that were required to get a Schengen visa, but Romanians rather than Germans or French authorities are enforcing the rules. Bulgaria has a similar exit control system.

In turn, Romania agreed to increase expenditures to police its borders to prevent trafficking and cooperate to readmit Romanians who are refused asylum in Western Europe. The EU noted that Romania approved a new Aliens Law, a new type of passport and a Framework Agreement on Readmission. The Romanian Border Police was reorganized, and new, modern equipment to combat irregular immigration was purchased. As the number of Romanian asylum-seekers increased in the 1990s, many EU countries signed readmission agreements with Romania under which Romania promised to accept the return of its nationals who were refused asylum abroad. Between 1992 and 2000, Ireland received about 5,500 asylum applications from Romanians (mainly Roma), most of which were refused.

Yugoslavia

Several CEME members visited the Federal Republic of Yugoslavia (FRY) in early June 2001 to examine the new government's approach to migration issues and found that both the federal government and the Serb republic were faced with three principal issues related to immigration and refugees: creating a migration and asylum infrastructure, dealing with refugees and internally displaced persons, and building bridges to the Diaspora. The government was very aware that it needed to cooperate with the North American and European countries that are donors of international aid as well as recipients of Yugoslav migrants.

The FRY comprises the republics of Serbia and Montenegro.[23] The election of Vojislav Kostunica as president of the FRY in September 2000 and the subsequent removal of Slobodan Milosevic from power marked a major shift away from a repressive Communist regime and toward a democratic republic governed by a coalition, with the reformist Democratic Opposition of Serbia (DOS), itself a coalition of eighteen parties, holding fifty-eight seats in the Parliament and the Socialist People's Party (SPP) from Montenegro holding twenty-eight seats. The SPP was formerly allied with Milosevic and held a disproportionate capacity to block legislation it opposes.

The Republic of Serbia is the larger and more populous of the two entities forming the FRY. In January 2001, the DOS-led coalition elected Zoran Djindjic prime minister of a reformist government in Serbia, and the new government, cooperating with NATO, appears to have put down a guerrilla uprising on the border with Kosovo. At the same time, the status of Kosovo remains unsettled, with the United Nations continuing to govern the province and NATO peacekeepers maintaining a fragile peace between ethnic Albanians and the smaller number of ethnic Serbs and Roma who remained in Kosovo. The political situation in Montenegro is also unsettled. A minority government was formed in May after protracted negotiations following highly fragmented Parliamentary elections, and the republic appears evenly split between those who want to pursue independence and those who wish to remain within the FRY.

The FRY's willingness to cooperate with the International Criminal Tribunal in The Hague was an uncertain issue at the time of the site visit. The DOS withdrew legislation from the federal parliament that would have permitted the extradition of indicted war criminals, including Milosevic, when it became clear that the SPP would block passage. The legislation may instead go to the Serbian parliament for passage or, alternatively, President Kostunica could re-interpret existing law to permit extradition to an international body, saying that the law only prohibits extradition to a national authority.

The economic outlook for FRY depended heavily on the willingness of western countries and the IMF and World Bank to provide needed assistance and loans. A donor's conference in June 2001 depended on resolution of the extradition issue (Milosevic was extradited). In the meantime, high unemployment and high inflation make future economic recovery unlikely without outside assistance.

In assessing the situation in the FRY, it is important to keep in mind that the new government was less than a year old and faced formidable challenges. Many of the officials representing the new governments in both FRY and Serbia were new to their jobs, in some cases having been in office for less than six months. The holdover civil servants from the old regime continue in place, often creating an awkward situation in which the most knowledgeable officials are those with the least commitment to reform. With the situation in Montenegro in flux, the competencies of the federal government relative to the republican governments were also unclear. If Montenegro were to leave the federation, it was assumed that the responsibilities of the federal government could be incorporated into the republics.

Migration and Refugee Issues

Three principal migration and refugee issues required immediate attention in the FRY. First was the issue of managing migration into and through the FRY, particularly related to border control, smuggling, and trafficking, and the development of an aliens law that includes new asylum procedures. Second was the need to find durable solutions for the thousands of refugees and internally displaced persons on the territory of the FRY. Third was the need to tap the human and financial resources of the millions of Yugoslavs living abroad to help in the reconstruction and future development of the country.

Yugoslavia borders seven countries, making it a major transit route to the West. Its neighbors include Hungary to the north and west, Croatia and Bosnia-Herzegovina to the west, Albania and Macedonia to the south, and Bulgaria and Romania to the east. Once inside FRY, borders are fairly porous to the neighboring countries of Eastern Europe, which are used as a gateway to Western Europe and North America. Yugoslavs emigrated because of the conflicts in the former Yugoslav republics as well as the economic decline due to economic sanctions. Transit migration has been aided by smugglers and traffickers who saw that the FRY did not require visas from nationals of many countries of origin—including China, Romania, Moldova, and Ukraine—and had few incentives to stop migrants from moving through its territory to western destinations. One informant noted that there were frequent charter flights from Belgrade to Banja Luka in the Serb republic of Bosnia-Herzegovina, from which the migrants could continue their journeys.

A first priority was to reduce smuggling and trafficking through Yugoslavia, a major migration and humanitarian problem. An International Organization for Migration (IOM) project that interviewed trafficked women determined that most European women trafficked to the Balkans are from Moldova, Romania, Ukraine, and Bulgaria.[24] Although most are destined for other European countries, Serbian law allows escort businesses to be registered and to advertise their work publicly,[25] creating a market in Yugoslavia for the women. In addition to trafficked women, children are also kidnapped and trafficked for prostitution, begging, stealing, and sold for adoption.[26] The main migrant routes from the Balkans to Western Europe seem to be from Yugoslavia to Hungary and Austria, and other routes are from Yugoslavia to Greece, passing through the Former Yugoslav Republic of Macedonia (FY-ROM).[27] Serbian women are mainly trafficked to Italy, Greece, Cyprus, the Netherlands, and Germany.[28] Roma women and children are also trafficked from FRY. The British journal *Independent* estimates that 7,000 Roma went from Serbia to Italy in a few weeks in the summer of 1999.[29]

The Chinese who came to Serbia usually entered in Belgrade, which has a large Chinese community. Predrag Milojevic, who runs a consulting agency for Chinese who want to remain in FRY said, "About 80,000 Chinese have used Yugoslavia as a first step for their clandestine journeys to the West since the early 1990s. . . . They are using Serbia as a gateway to the West at the rate of 400 people a week."[30] They then illegally cross the border into East European countries. For example, in early 2000 the Hungarian Interior Minister confirmed that an average of 100 to 150 Chinese a month were trying illegally to enter Hungary from Yugoslavia.[31] In addition, the Croatian press reports apprehensions of irregular migrants from Serbia, and most of the migrants into Macedonia are from Yugoslavia.[32]

FRY has signed the Palermo Protocols on Smuggling and Trafficking of the UN Convention against Organized Crime, but Yugoslavia has insufficient legal mechanisms to punish trafficking and smuggling.[33] Yugoslavia's Criminal Code did not contain any specific criminal offense relating to trafficking of women and children, although various provisions relate to aspects of trafficking. Several NGOs are currently working on a draft law to submit to the government.

Even with an improved legal framework, there will continue to be enforcement problems according to our respondents. The police and prosecutors are not familiar with the trafficking-smuggling problem, have no experience dealing with it, and have no means of intervening. Even if they did, the insecurity in the country would place this problem low on the state's priority list. When a trafficking crime is reported, the victims are often treated as criminals. Some observers note that the police are often complicit with the traffickers, requiring more extensive efforts to combat corruption as well as the trafficking itself.

There are also problems arising from a lack of protection for the victims. Since the trafficked and smuggled foreigners are illegal in the FRY, they are afraid of their pimps and smugglers. In addition the migrants avoid contact with the police for fear of being caught and sent home. Thus, the women usually do not report crimes perpetrated against them, and the smuggled foreigners usually do not report mistreatment by smugglers, especially since there are no institutionalized prevention programs or policies to deal with victims.

A second priority relates to border management. The border police had been highly militarized and they required substantial retraining to ensure that they are able to deter irregular crossings in a manner that respects human rights. At the time of the site visit, there was not a clear division of responsibility between the FRY border police and the Serb border police, making it difficult to accomplish some of the necessary reforms and retraining.

The drafting of a new aliens law, with policies and procedures to adjudicate asylum claims, appeared to be a higher priority for the European Union than for the new FRY government. One ministry official said that if cooperation with the EU requires Yugoslavia to be the EU's southern border for asylum purposes, FRY would do its part. At the time of the site visit, asylum seekers were referred to UNHCR for adjudication of their claims, and UNHCR often requested third country resettlement for those found to be refugees. Under a new aliens law, Yugoslavia would adjudicate refugee claims itself, and was preparing for this day examining the policies and procedures of other central and eastern European countries with particular reference to candidate countries for EU enlargement, with Slovenia appearing to be the best model for FRY.

There were more than 400,000 refugees in the republic of Serbia. Most are ethnic Serbs displaced from Croatia (primarily the Krajina region and eastern Slavonia) and Bosnia. Displacement into Serbia began as early as 1992, and continued with large influxes from Croatia in 1995 and again in 1998. In addition, about 200,000 people were internally displaced, mostly ethnic Serbs and Roma from the province of Kosovo. Smaller populations of both refugees and internally displaced persons are in the republic of Montenegro.[34] Some of the refugees and internally displaced moved because of conflict, whereas others were forced to relocate as part of ethnic cleansing campaigns. Most refugees and internally displaced persons rented their own housing or lived with relatives and friends, but about 35,000 refugees and 13,000 internally displaced still lived in collective centers.

The challenge for the FRY and republican governments with the support of the international community is to find durable solutions for the refugees and internally displaced persons. The UNHCR generally favors three durable solutions: voluntary repatriation, local integration, and third country resettlement. All three options are in place in Yugoslavia, but there is debate about the relative balance to be given to each solution, particularly repatriation versus integration.

Agreements in place permit voluntary repatriation to both Bosnia and Croatia. Most returns to Bosnia are spontaneous and appear to be to Republica Srpska, the Serb section of Bosnia. The U.S. Committee for Refugees estimated that about 30,000 ethnic Serbs had returned to Bosnia since the signing of the Dayton Accord, but UNHCR did not have an exact number of returns to Bosnia, noting that the porous borders between FRY and Republica Srpska permit refugees to go back and forth at will. Reclamation of property remains a major barrier to repatriation, however, particularly for those whose property was occupied by others displaced by the conflict and ethnic cleansing in Bosnia.

Under the bilateral agreement between Yugoslavia and Croatia, the Croatian consulate issues travel documents to those in Yugoslavia who wish to return, and UNHCR estimated that 90,000 Croatian refugees had applied for the documents. Far fewer have returned permanently, however; only 8,000 by UNHCR estimate between 1998 and the time of the site visit. Refugees must show that they resided in Croatia for five years prior to their departure to qualify for repatriation and must also demonstrate that they will have accommodations upon return. Since many of the refugees lost their houses, or have seen their public housing privatized, the lack of accommodation is a real barrier to return. An even greater barrier is fear about their future safety once back in Croatia. During several interviews, we heard about refugees arrested upon coming back to Croatia for visits, which has had a chilling effect on the willingness of refugees to repatriate, even if the arrests were for well-documented war crimes. A recent survey by UNHCR showed that a majority of the Croatian refugees do not believe that repatriation is a feasible solution for them.

A number of programs had been established to encourage and facilitate returns to Croatia, but they are small in scale. For example, the Norwegian Refugee Council provides legal counseling to refugees who are finding their return blocked by Croatian authorities. The International Rescue Committee (IRC) works with local organizations to identify potential returnees and prepare them for repatriation, with the few hundred planning a return referred to IRC's Croatia programs to help them reintegrate. A number of respondents thought that more pressure could be placed on Croatia to lift barriers to return, but an equal number also felt that the majority of refugees would prefer to stay in Serbia where many have been for years and have integrated. There is little expectation of return of internally displaced persons to Kosovo.

In contrast to the pessimism about repatriation, there was optimism that large numbers of refugees and internally displaced persons would be able to achieve local integration. First steps toward this goal occurred when FRY passed legislation permitting dual citizenship. Since 1997, refugees have been eligible for FRY citizenship, but, until the new legislation, they had to renounce their previous citizenship. Croatia already accepts dual citizenship, at least in principle, and there are discussions underway with Bosnia, which requires a bilateral agreement to recognize dual citizenship with FRY. Dual citizenship permits refugees who settle permanently in FRY to retain rights to property and eventually return to Croatia, which provides both psychological and practical safeguards to those who are unwilling to renounce their homeland even if they are doubtful that return will take place.

Refugees who did not take on FRY citizenship were afforded most of the rights of citizens, including indefinite permission to remain in FRY, access to the labor market, education, and health care on the same basis as nationals, and passports for foreign travel. Some received small grants from the government in lieu of the pensions that they would have received had they not emigrated.

The barriers to full integration appeared to be economic rather than legal. Hence, the prospects for successful integration depended principally on recovery of the economy, which would affect economic opportunities for refugees and internally displaced persons along with others in FRY. Formal employment was difficult to find in Serbia, and many of the refugees who worked were employed on the gray economy, trading items in street stalls, and similar activities. The refugees and internally displaced persons who remained in collective centers needed their own housing, as do many of those who have been living with family and friends.

The FRY and Serb governments, along with the international organizations and nongovernmental organizations that work with forced migrants, placed great hopes on donors to provide the funds for general economic recovery and refugee-specific programs. The government ministries provided us few concrete examples, however, of the types of refugee and displaced person programs that they would propose to the donors. Even when pressed for examples, the ministries tended to be very general and often referred to the UN agencies and NGOs as the better source of information about specific program needs, suggesting a need for capacity building within the government to be full partners in refugee integration.

The United States, Canada, and Australia operated refugee resettlement programs in FRY, and there were 10,000 Croatian and Bosnian refugees in the pipeline for relocation in mid-2001. Priority for resettlement was given to refugees referred by UNHCR, generally because there are concerns about their immediate protection, but others that get priority include Croatian refugees from the Krajina and eastern Slavonia, some of whom were displaced first from their home country and then from their initial settlement site in Kosovo. The United States also resettled refugees from the former Yugoslavia if they or their spouses had been detained because of their religion, race, or ethnicity; if they or their spouses had suffered torture; if they were members of an ethnically mixed marriage; or if they have close relatives in the United States. The number of UNHCR referrals had diminished since the change in government.

Yugoslav Diaspora

The FRY government estimated there were some 1.5 million Yugoslav citizens and another 1.5 to 1.8 million former nationals working abroad. Many of the expatriates have university degrees, especially Yugoslavs who left during the Milosevic era. On an annual basis, the Foreign Ministry and Ministry of Social Affairs co-hosts a conference to which members of the Diaspora are invited, and this process has led to contributions from the Diaspora towards humanitarian assistance.

There is general recognition that the expatriate community is a source of both human and financial capital for the economic development of Yugoslavia. The government would like to stimulate the return of qualified nationals in the hope that they would bring capital to invest in productive enterprises. The hopes to tap the Diaspora appear very ambitious, focusing on a few wealthy expatriates who could buy entire companies, and the new government was not looking at models used in other countries that permit large numbers of expatriates to contribute small amounts to infrastructure or business development. Officials generally dismissed remittances as an important economic input, saying that the amounts are small and are used for consumption and, once again, were not familiar with the experiences of other countries.

The Federal Republic of Yugoslavia was clearly in a state of early transition from dictatorship to democracy, with the future dependent on both internal reforms and the willingness of the international community to support needed changes with financial and political aid. Issues such as smuggling, trafficking, and durable solutions for refugees and internally displaced persons received welcome attention during the transition, but cooperation between FRY and the donor governments who are recipients of irregular migrants from or transiting Yugoslavia is essential to progress being made on these fronts.

Albania

Albania is a country of 3.1 million people with a GDP of $4.1 billion that switched in the early 1990s, after 45 years of Communism, from economic autarky to a peculiar form of market economy. Albania experienced some of the world's highest emigration rates in the 1990s—some 600,000 to 700,000 Albanians, or almost one-quarter of Albanians, and one-half of Albanian professionals, emigrated, and the effects of their departure was a major focus of the June 2002 visit.

The major destinations of Albanian migrants in the 1990s were Greece, which had 400,000 to 600,000 Albanians in 2002, and Italy, which had 144,000 legal residents and probably some tens of thousands of irregulars at the end of 2001.[35] Many Albanians have become legal residents of Greece and Italy as a result of regularization-legalization programs. Albania is also a transit point for third country nationals attempting to reach the rest of Europe. Of particular interest to the CEME members were efforts by the Italian and Albanian governments to cooperate in managing the flows of Albanian and transit migrants.

In June 2002 Albania was experiencing rapid although unbalanced economic growth as a result of $615 million in remittances from Albanians abroad[36] as well as aid from the European Union (EU) and other sources. The spending of remittances and aid has fueled a building boom, but there was no clear sense of how Albania would use the window of opportunity opened by remittances and aid to develop a viable economy. The optimistic scenario was that remittances and investments from Albanians abroad will produce an economic takeoff based on value-added food production and tourism in the "Switzerland of the Balkans." The pessimistic scenario was that corruption and divided government would prevent the development of a successful economic strategy, and that low wages, high unemployment, and inadequate services such as health care and education would prompt the continued emigration of young and educated Albanians.

History, Politics, and Economics

Albania, or Shqiptarë (land of eagles), is a mountainous and traditionally isolated Balkan country between Kosovo and Greece, and fifty miles east of Italy across the Adriatic Sea at its narrowest point. The 2001 census reported 3.1 million residents, including almost 350,000 in Tirana and 100,000 in Dürres. Albania is the most rural and agricultural country in Europe—1.8 million Albanians live in rural areas, and agriculture accounts for more than half of GDP. About 70 percent of Albanians are Muslims, 20 percent are Greek Orthodox and 10 percent are Roman Catholic.[37]

Albania became an independent nation on November 28, 1912. When Albania's present borders were fixed in 1921, about one-third of Albanians were outside the country, mostly in Kosovo. Enver Hoxha led the Communist resistance to the occupying Axis powers during World War II, and his Albanian Workers' Party (AWP) ruled Albania between 1946 and 1985. Hoxha first allied Albania with Stalin to offset the efforts of Tito's Yugoslavia to include Albania, then switched to China as chief supporter, and finally led Albania into ever-deeper isolation. Albania is physically isolated by mountains from its neighbors: Kosovo and Serbia to the north, Macedonia to the east, and Greece to the southeast, which—associated with the strong cultural and psychological impact of Italian TV—helps to explain why many Albanians look across the Adriatic to Italy.[38]

After Hoxha's death in 1985, Albania began to liberalize, but too slowly for students and others, whose protests led to the downfall of Communism in 1990. However, in March 1991 elections, the AWP, renamed the Socialist Party of Albania (SPA), took power and denounced Hoxha's isolationist rule. Political squabbling dashed hopes for quick economic improvement, leading to mass emigration. In March 1991 Italy accepted a first group of 23,000 Albanian migrants; in August another group of 20,000 people were treated in the opposite way and repatriated without exceptions. In the same period around 30,000 migrants arrived in Greece. In March 1992, the opposition Democratic Party of Albania (DPA) came to power and generated some initial optimism, but in the long run, it produced more economic chaos, a breakdown of law and order, and more emigration.

Between 1992 and 1995, there was an economic recovery and rising imports of consumer goods to which Albanians were obtaining access for the first time; many families' incomes came from remittances and smuggling goods and fuel into Yugoslavia during UN sanctions.[39] However, near the end of 1996, a new wave of political instability was created by the collapse of "pyramid" or Ponzi investment schemes, in which unregulated institutions accepted deposits and paid high interest rates to early investors with deposits made by later investors. When the scheme collapsed, there was rioting, including looting of military arsenals, and mass emigration in early 1997, as many people lost their life savings and crime rose sharply.[40] Also thanks to an Italy-led multinational mission (Mission "Alba") order was restored and emigration slowed; later on, joint Italian-Albanian patrols (*Missione di Polizia Interforze*) contributed to the reduction of the number of migrants. The numbers detected as they arrived in Italy reduced from a peak of 46,000 in 1999 to 7,500 in 2001.[41]

In subsequent elections, the SPA returned to power and has been the dominant political party in the past five years.[42] However, there was a dispute between the dominant SPA leaders in 2001–2002, and the opposition DPA refused to take seats in Parliament to protest what it said were unfair elections, continuing a pattern of unstable politics. There is an important north-south divide in Albania with political consequences. The Geg highlanders in the north, who are closely related to the ethnic Albanians of Kosovo, have relatively poor land and a more tribal, traditional culture. The Tosks in the south developed a village based in coastal areas, and were more open to the outside world. The Northern regions have long been the largest, although certainly not the only emigration basin.

Albania's most important bilateral relationships are with Italy and Greece; they are its leading trade partners and places with large numbers of Albanian migrants. On the regional and international level, Albania has benefited from its cooperation during NATO's air war against Yugoslavia (Serbia-Montenegro) in March–June 1999. The EU, the United States, and Russia in June 1999 launched a Stability Pact for Southeastern Europe with three "working tables": democratization and human rights; economic reconstruction, development, and co-operation; and security—including a special emphasis placed on migration and asylum.

Corruption remains a problem, with police, customs, prosecutors, and judges accused of being susceptible to bribes.[43] Italy has taken the lead in equipping and retraining Albanian police. There has been an attempt to make continued EU aid contingent on reduced crime and corruption. The EU is committed to turning Albania into a crossroads for the Balkans, with highway Corridor 8 running east-west from Durres to Macedonia, and Corridor 4 running north-south from Montenegro to Greece. Albania hopes to join both the EU and NATO, and the EU and the United States are involved in Albania's development. In 1999, the EU launched a new Stabilization and Association Process (SAP) with five Southeastern European countries, including Albania, and it has provided Albania with about $900 million in assistance between 1991 and 2001. The United States is building defense facilities in Albania, aiming to prevent Albania from becoming a Balkans base for Islamic terrorism.

The effort to achieve a self-sufficient economy for four million people in a small and mountainous country left Albania further behind most other transition economies in the 1990s. The first signs were positive, as privatized agriculture in the early 1990s increased its output to compensate for the collapse of state industry. However, the gains from agriculture soon stalled, and emigration and remittances have accompanied slow and partial privatization as an engine of growth.[44]

Agriculture is the most important economic sector, accounting for 50 to 55 percent of GDP, but it remains backward—animal power is still used to plough about one-third of the land. Albania opened to the world in 1990–1991, when its industry was based on antiquated Soviet and Chinese machinery, much of which was looted during unrest in 1991–1992 and 1997–1998, so that manufacturing contributes only 12 percent of GDP. Many of the most promising enterprises operating today are joint ventures with foreign firms in forestry and furniture, or assembly of footwear and garment operations based on low Albanian wages. Construction is 15 percent of GDP, as remittances fuel house building, both to house rural-urban migrants around major cities and to build new or remodel the homes of migrants and their relatives. Typical Albanian wages are $100 per month, and employers and employees contribute an additional 34 percent of wages for health care and social insurance.

Almost 60 percent of Albanians live in rural areas, and the rural areas have the worst poverty. About two-thirds of school age children are in rural areas, and a combination of poor schools, emigrating teachers, and pressure to work on now private farms has led to declining school attendance. Tirana University, which admits about one-third of university students, reports that about half of its graduates emigrate. The Albanian government's Strategy for Economic and Social Development estimates that 60 percent of residents are poor, defined as an income of US$4.30 or less (at 1995 purchasing power parity) per person per day.[45]

Remittances and aid explain why Albania can sustain a large trade deficit: exports were $300 million in 2001, imports were $1.2 billion, and the trade deficit financed in part by remittances from Albanians abroad. According to a survey cited by one respondent, 44 percent of Albanians deliver remittances personally, 36 percent entrust them to friends, and 19 percent remit via banks.

Emigration
Albania has had many waves of emigration, with 25 percent of residents emigrating after the Ottoman takeover in 1478, followed by another wave of emigration from 1912 until the end of World War II, when emigration was prohibited, and then two main waves of emigration in the 1990s, in 1991 and again in 1997. Greece and Italy are the major destinations for Albanian migrants. An estimated 400,000 to 600,000 Albanians reside in Greece and probably somewhat fewer than 200,000 in Italy. Some entered clandestinely, others overstayed visitor visas, and still others participated in temporary work

programs. Some of those who entered or remained illegally in Italy and Greece obtained legal status through amnesty programs.

Recently, movements to the more traditional immigration countries of the United States and Canada have increased, particularly higher skilled migrants. In fact, Albanian respondents referred to the "Canadian phenomenon" when discussing the issue of brain drain, in reference to Albanians admitted under the Canadian point system for their educational and other skills. Most Albanians who obtain permanent residence in the United States enter through the Diversity Program, a lottery open to residents of countries with relatively low levels of admission to the United States.

Albania has also become a country of refuge and transit. In 1999 during the NATO intervention in Kosovo, some 450,000 ethnic Albanian Kosovars fled to Albania. They were largely welcomed by Albanians. Their presence had mixed short- and medium-term effects. On the one hand, international aid arrived to help care for the Kosovars, and aid has continued to flow since. On the other hand, the presence of Kosovars depressed wages and encouraged some Albanians to emigrate or to move from the poorer northeastern regions bordering Kosovo to Tirana and other urban areas. Almost all of the Kosovar refugees returned home after the cessation of conflict, but Albania has since seen the arrival of migrants, in particular from the Middle East and South Asia, who are transiting Albania in the hopes of reaching Europe.

Emigration to Italy

Italy is a country of 57 million with 1.7 million or 3 percent foreign residents; the number of foreigners rose by about 150,000 per year in the past three years, with two-thirds arriving to join settled family members. At the time of our site visit, Italy was enacting a new immigration law aimed at tightening restrictions on foreigners in Italy. The law would also make Italian aid to emigration countries conditional on their cooperating with Italy to accept the return of their nationals and to prevent unauthorized migration to Italy.

The new Italian law increases patrols of Italy's coastlines and requires non-EU citizens to be fingerprinted in order to remain in Italy. Residence permits are to be linked to work permits, so that non-EU foreigners without jobs would have to leave within six months, down from twelve months—some 15,000 non-EU foreigners were admitted to Italy to seek jobs in 2001. Italian employers sponsoring foreign workers have to ensure housing and also provide a bond to cover the cost of removing the worker if necessary.

The new law increases the power of the Ministry of Interior and decreases the power of the Ministry of Labor to manage non-EU foreign workers. Work permits for non-EU foreigners are to be reduced from a maximum of four to a maximum of two years, and requests for renewals must be made ninety days in advance, up from thirty days. In order to become a permanent resident, non-EU foreigners must live six years in Italy, up from five years, so that two renewals are necessary for immigrant status. When leaving Italy, non-EU foreigners will no longer be able to claim immediate refunds of the social security taxes they paid to the pension agency, INPS—pension contributions are 25 to 30 percent of gross wages.[46]

In 2000 and 2001, Italy established quotas for foreigners from particular countries to reward them for cooperation to reduce smuggling and to provide legal channels for migrant arrivals; e.g., the 2001 quotas were for 6,000 Albanians, 3,000 Tunisians, and 1,500 Moroccans. The quotas for 2002 had not been announced at the time of the site visit although respondents expected they would be after the new law was enacted.

Under the new law, bars to legal re-entry are increased. After being detected in Italy, non-EU foreigners are barred from legal entry for ten years, up from the current five years. Penalties for re-entering Italy illegally are increased, with six to twelve months of detention for a first illegal re-entry, and then one to four years in prison for subsequent re-entries. Illegal migrants can be detained sixty days before removal, up from the current thirty days, and foreigners who apply for asylum after being detained are to remain in detention.

About 10 percent of the foreigners in Italy, 150,000 to 200,000, are Albanians, most having arrived in the 1990s. There is an apparent paradox with Albanian migration to Italy: Italian-Albanian government relations are described as the best ever, reflecting Italian-Albanian cooperation to prevent smuggling and trafficking; in spite of this, the anti-Albanian prejudice has grown steadily, fueled by the concentration of the media on a marginal but quite visible criminal minority. There were two major waves of Albanian migrants to Italy, and their reception was very different. The Albanians arriving in 1991, after the fall of Communism, were initially welcomed; those arriving in 1997, after the collapse of the pyramid investment schemes, were not.

Albanian migration to Italy seems to have reached an equilibrium level, which raises the question of what would happen if current requirements that Albanians have visas to enter Italy were dropped, as the EU has done for Bulgaria and Romania. Even were Italy able to drop visa requirements unilaterally (which is impossible under the Schengen Agreement), the government would not be inclined to take that step. Note that 60 to 70 percent of Albanian requests for visas are rejected in Tirana (around 40,000 visas were issued by Italy's three consulates in Albania in 2001).[47] As government officials also point out, despite a drop in unauthorized Albanian migration, there are still about 5,000 unauthorized Albanians apprehended in Italy each month.[48] Italy allows unaccompanied minors to remain until they are eighteen, and there appears to be a surge of under-eighteen unaccompanied minors arriving in Italy. There are also lingering doubts about the commitment of the Albanian government to ending smuggling operations.[49]

Italian-Albanian Cooperation

A significant level of bilateral cooperation was present in Albania at the time of the site visit. One of the most significant Italian-Albanian cooperation efforts is that between Italian and Albanian police, which began in 1997 to restore order after the Ponzi investment schemes collapsed. Five years later, there were token Italian police forces present along the coast to prevent smuggling, and radar, telephones, and backup generators have been installed to detect and report on smuggling boats. The smuggling boats are 35- to 40-foot long rubber dinghies with four 250 hp motors, which enables them to launch from very shallow water, and to travel very fast. Smuggling activities have evolved, and today are as likely to involve drugs as migrants. The Italians report that 90 percent of the boats detected are forced back to Albania, but it is often difficult to apprehend them, since they remain in shallow water.[50]

Much of this bilateral cooperation was focused on the problem of transit migration rather than on stopping irregular Albanian migration.[51] By some estimates, 80 percent of the migrants leaving Albania for Italy are not Albanians. Much of the anti-trafficking activities discussed above are now focused on third country nationals.

The Italian-Albanian cooperation on migration enforcement had undergone a shift during the year prior to the site visit. Initially, the focus was on training and technical assistance. More recently, the Italian presence has been reduced, but the new cooperation takes the form of joint operations against smugglers. The need for action against smuggling is evident. All respondents agreed that the smuggling operations were ruthless, putting migrants at high risk. For example, smugglers may have several boats en route to Italy when spotted; they are likely to push the migrants overboard as a diversion in order to escape with more valuable drug shipments.

Even though the enforcement efforts are now focused primarily on transit migration, all respondents agreed that there was need for additional legal channels through which Albanians in search of employment could find jobs. At the request of the Italian government, the International Organization for Migration (IOM) operated in Tirana a Migrant Assistance Center (MAC) whose goal is to provide Albanians considering emigration with information and advice about jobs abroad. Italy reserved 6,000 slots for Albanians in 2000 and 2001. Since 2000, some 54,000 Albanians wrote to IOM-MAC for information; 34,000 completed applications to work abroad. MAC staff interviewed 17,000 to assess their Italian language work skills. Some 2,000 were sent to Italy, with half reporting that they found jobs during their one-year stays in Italy. The original aim of this $300,000, two-year project was to have Albanian job seekers vetted by MAC, and to have Italian employers view Albanian job seekers on line.[52] However, most Italian employers prefer to request workers by name, suggesting that the Albanian workers requested are known to the employer or recommended by a current Albanian employee, not IOM-MAC.[53]

Albanian migration crises as well as the arrival of refugees from neighboring Kosovo meant that both the International Organization for Migration and the UN High Commissioner for Refugees were present. Their mission had evolved from dealing with irregular Albanian migration to more recently dealing with the transit of non-Albanians through Albania. The international organizations are also helping the Albanian government to draft its own legislation for handling the arrival of asylum seekers and other migrants.

With the help of international organizations, Albania was developing governmental capacity to deal with foreigners seeking asylum. The Albanian government signed the 1951 Geneva Convention in 1992, and began developing the appropriate domestic law and institutions with the aim of having asylum laws that would speed integration into the EU. As with other aspects of Albania, the law on the books seems adequate, but there were many gaps in practice. For example, a 2000 report based on trips to various border police posts found information on detained foreigners mostly entered into logs by hand and no budgets for food or shelter for detained persons.

Foreigners apprehended or detained inside Albania were "pre-screened" by representatives of international organizations to determine if they were trafficked, were potential refugees, or were voluntary economic migrants. Police were to notify the pre-screening team when they detained a foreigner who might have been trafficked or a refugee, and the team was to arrive within twenty-four hours to interview the foreigner. Between March 2001 and March 2002, some 367 foreigners, mostly Kurds, were referred to pre-screeners, 93 requested asylum in Albania, and 7 were granted asylum in Albania—another 72 left Albania voluntarily or disappeared from the shelter.

The CEME team heard varied views as to the overall effectiveness of these efforts at international and bilateral cooperation in managing migration. Both Italian and Albanian police officials expressed satisfaction with the cooperation, but they also voiced concern that the reduction in Italian forces would impede some of their efforts to interdict and apprehend the smugglers. Of equal concern was the failure of the Italian government to announce the year's quota of labor visas for Albanians. Respondents noted that part of the unofficial quid pro quo—cooperation on enforcement in exchange for work visas and other assistance—was now missing. One knowledgeable respondent questioned whether the Albanian authorities had indeed made a long-term commitment to stop the lucrative traffic in humans and drugs, pointing out that some of the police trained in marine interception were quickly relocated to patrolling land borders. Unless work visas or other incentives were provided, there would be little reason for the Albanian authorities to continue working with Italian police officials to control these movements.

Develop or Emigrate?

There are no clear models for stay-at-home development in Albania. Some experts point to organic agriculture (Albania could not afford pesticides or chemical fertilizers during its years of autarky) and tourism. A viable export-oriented agricultural sector requires consolidation of land—there were 467,000 owners of farmland in 1999, and they had an average of less than two hectares each. Tourism is the other hope, since isolation means that Albania has a pristine coastline as well as mountains.

The 1990s did not produce the political stability needed for investment in Albania, either of remittances or Foreign Direct Investment (FDI). Furthermore, the 1997 collapse of the pyramid investment schemes has made many Albanians leery of banks. This reluctance to use official banks affects the transfer of remittances; less than 20 percent of Albanian remittances are believed to be transferred via banks. The absence of credible banking institutions also affected the ability of entrepreneurs to obtain credit for new economic activities.[54]

Respondents differed in their views regarding the current and longer-term impact of remittances on economic development. As in many countries, experts do not necessarily trust the official statistics on remittance flows, leading to some disagreement about the amounts transferred. Those who view remittances negatively pointed out that they were used primarily for consumption, particularly of food imported from other European countries, and hence do little to stimulate growth in agriculture or other business activities. Others countered that remittances have promoted a great deal of construction as well, providing jobs and economic stimulus. Members of the CEME team also noted that increased access to food was itself a contribution

to development; well-fed children are more likely to do well in school, helping with long-term economic growth.

Most respondents agreed, though, that more could be done to encourage
investment of remittances in productive, job-producing activities. Some Albanians project declining remittances as Albanians integrate abroad. This
adds an aura of urgency to the quest for efforts to turn remittances into investments that can accelerate development. Emigration pressure remains significant, even though Albanians are now far more realistic about opportunities abroad—a January-February 2002 poll found that 42 percent of young
Albanians would emigrate if they could. Albanian experts did not appear familiar with the efforts of other countries to increase the development-payoff
of remittances, even though some of this experience would be useful.

The Slovak Republic and Austria

In April 2004, we examined migration in the heart of Europe, specifically the
impacts of EU enlargement, recent changes in Austrian immigration and integration policy, and migration issues in the Slovak Republic. There is a 6:1
difference in per capita income between Austria and the Slovak Republic,
but relatively little labor migration.[55] After May 1, 2004, borders between
these formerly distant neighbors became more permeable, as Slovaks are able
to travel to Austria without passports, but they cannot work unless their employers obtain work permits on their behalf.

There was discussion of three major issues. First, how to deal with growing fears of too much migration and incomplete integration of foreigners,
concerns that are manifested in significant support for anti-migration political parties, new laws that require non-EU immigrants to sign "integration
contracts" that require them to learn the local language or risk expulsion,
and streamlined asylum procedures to deal with the fact that less than a quarter of foreigners seeking asylum are deemed in need of refuge.

Second, about 9 percent of the 8 million residents of Austria are foreigners, most from ex-Yugoslavia and Turkey, countries from which guest
workers were recruited during the 1960s and early 1970s. Their integration
can be seen as a glass half full or half empty. On the one hand, many second and third generation children of guest workers are becoming indistin-
guishable from Austrians on the labor market, including becoming naturalized Austrian citizens. Yet the unemployment rate among foreign
workers is 1.5 times the Austrian rate, prompting efforts to require non-EU
foreigners to take active steps, such as learning German, to make themselves more employable.

Third, the Slovak Republic, which dates from the break-up of Czechoslovakia in 1993, has an economy based on heavy industry such as steel but an unemployment rate of 15 percent. However, the western part of the country near Vienna has emerged as a favorite place for foreign automakers, promising economic improvement. Members of the longstanding minority group, the Roma, are concentrated in the economically lagging eastern regions of the country and have very high unemployment rates; in January 2004 there were violent protests about changes to the unemployment insurance system that reduced payments.

Migration Issues in Austria

Austria has about 9 percent foreign residents, a result as in many other European countries of earlier policies that recruited guest workers that settled. Success at integration of these "foreigners," mostly Turks and Yugoslavs and their children, has been mixed. The Austrian government reacted to high unemployment rates by requiring non-EU foreigners to sign contracts to learn German, which should make them more employable on the labor market. In recent years, Austria has experienced Europe's highest per capita intake of asylum applicants, and in 2004 implemented new policies aimed at making quick decisions and removing foreigners not in need of protection.

Austria recruited guest workers from Yugoslavia and Turkey after reaching full employment in 1962. Like other European states with guest worker policies then, Austria halted guest worker recruitment in the 1970s, and dealt with family unification among settled guest workers, asylum seekers, and east-west migration in the 1980s and 1990s. Austria's economic recovery lagged behind its neighbors, so that even in the 1960s, there were almost as many emigrants from Austria to neighboring Germany and Switzerland, and Austria was a major transit country for migrants and refugees headed west.

The net migration of foreigners into Austria peaked at 90,000 a year in the early 1990s, and was 24,000 in 2001.[56] Austria has about 7.4 million Austrian citizens and 760,000 foreigners, and 20 percent of the foreigners were born in Austria.[57] Both the Austrian citizen and foreign populations are growing slowly. There are about 7,500 more deaths than births among Austrians each year, and 6,000 Austrians emigrate, but 35,000 foreigners a year naturalize, of which 60 percent are from ex-Yugoslavia and Turkey.

The 330,000 foreigners employed in Austria in 2001 represented 10.5 percent of total employment. Half of the foreign workers were from ex-Yugoslavia, 20 percent were Turks and 11 percent were EU nationals, mostly Germans. Some 111,000 work permits were issued to foreigners in 2001. In mid-2002, Austria expanded options for non-EU nationals from new accession countries such as the Slovak Republic to be employed for up to twelve months in non-seasonal industries in Austria, after which the worker is to return home for at least two months. Foreign students were also given permission to work part time. Austria also exports workers; 75,000 Austrians were employed in Germany in 2002 (about 85 percent of total Austrians working outside Austria).

Immigration is subject to an annual quota, 8,050 in 2004, and the two major streams of newcomers are further categorized into key employees (2,200) and family reunification (5,500), with sub-quotas for each of Austria's nine provinces. There are no numerical limits on asylum, and the number of asylum-seekers has risen sharply; in 2003, Austria received more asylum applications per capita than any other country. There were 30,100 applications in 2001, 39,400 in 2002, and 32,400 in 2003. After applying, applicants are sent to centers, where they receive accommodation and food. One of the largest centers is in Traiskirchen, and it has been operated by the German firm European Homecare (www.eu-homecare.com/) since mid-2003 at a cost of € 12.90 per person per day. Many of the center's current residents are from Chechnya, and their complaints center on the activities of foreigners who are not camp residents but would like to be—these non-residents sometimes "buy" food and beds from camp guards and cooks.

Foreigners apply for asylum at federal asylum offices, which make a first decision; if it is negative, as 80 percent of first decisions are, the applicant can appeal to the independent federal asylum board. Many denials of asylum are so appealed, sometimes by NGOs that do not show the appeal to the applicant—the applicant gives the NGO power of attorney, and the NGO files the appeal on his or her behalf. When the oral appeal is heard, a judge, transcriber, and interpreter are present, as is the applicant. Concerns have been expressed that in at least some cases, the applicant is simply seeking to extend his stay in Austria by appealing.[58]

Asylum laws were changed effective May 1, 2004, to require an initial interview with asylum applicants within seventy-two hours of their application in order to determine if the applicant is ineligible for asylum, as would be the case if he/she transited a safe third country en route to Austria or applied previously in Austria or another EU country. If there are such grounds for denying asylum, a denial is to be made within 20 days to facilitate an appeal and removal, and to reduce a common practice of applying for asylum in Austria and then continuing further west, abandoning their Austrian applications.

Immigration and integration have been controversial in Austria, with Joerg Haider and the Freedom Party leading the campaign against more foreigners. National support for the Freedom Party dropped from 30 percent in

2002 to 10 percent in 2004, but Haider was re-elected governor of Carinthia in March 2004. Vienna, a city of 1.6 million, has about half of Austria's foreigners, and has a city government that welcomes immigrants with a letter in their own language and offers German language courses paid for by the city government.[59]

Slovak Migration, Roma, and Economic Issues

The Slovak Republic is primarily a country through which migrants from other countries transit, and this is not expected to change as a result of it joining the EU on May 1, 2004. Western areas of the Slovak Republic are the richest, and the destination of foreign investment that is creating relatively high-wage jobs in the Detroit of central Europe. More problematic is the eastern part of the country, where the Roma are concentrated, and the Slovak government intends to tackle their problems with new assistance programs.

The Slovak Republic has recently experienced robust economic growth, but the unemployment rate remained at 16 percent in 2004. There is relatively little emigration and immigration; most of the movement that occurs is between the Czech and Slovak Republics, where there is free movement. Some 64,000 Slovak workers were registered as employed in the Czech Republic in 2001, 17,000 in Germany, and 5,000 in Austria.[60]

About 400,000 or 8 percent of Slovaks are Roma, and they are considered a poor and non-integrated minority in the eastern and poorer part of the country. In 1999–2000, the government announced new measures aimed at reducing discrimination and promoting economic development in areas with Roma, including easing access to education for Roma children (who are often sent to special schools), improving living conditions by building one thousand new apartments, and reducing long-term unemployment.[61]

In January 2004, Slovak Roma protested cuts in welfare benefits that reduced payments from about the minimum wage of $400 per month to $200 per month. The overall unemployment rate is 30 percent in some eastern districts and even higher in Roma settlements, and there was looting of stores. The center-right government of Prime Minister Mikulas Dzurinda said the looting was organized by Roma loan sharks who had made a profitable business of lending money to Roma families loans that were repaid when they received welfare payments.[62]

The Slovak Republic had a closely watched election in April 2004 in which moderate Ivan Gasparovic defeated Vladimir Meciar, the former prime minister who had led Slovakia to insist upon separation from the Czech Republic in 1993. The current Czech president, Vaclav Klaus, was the prime minister with whom Meciar negotiated the Czechoslovakian divorce.

Slovakia has attracted major inflows of foreign investment, in part because it reduced its corporate and personal income tax rates to 19 percent. Western Slovakia is sometimes called the Detroit of Eastern Europe, with Peugeot and the Hyundai's Kia Motors unit building auto assembly plants near Bratislava. Volkswagen already has a plant employing 10,000 workers to produce 300,000 cars a year, and when all three firms are operating at capacity, Slovakia could assemble 850,000 cars per year. Slovakian wages and benefits are only 25 to 35 percent of those in western Europe (labor represents 10 to 15 percent of the cost of auto manufacturing), and the incentives offered to foreign investors include free land, worker training, and reduced taxes.

The Slovak Republic received 8,100 asylum applications in 2001; 5,000 were administratively terminated rather than refused, and 18 foreigners received asylum—most asylum applications are "defensive," i.e., filed after the foreigner has been apprehended.[63] New asylum laws in 2002 brought Slovak law and procedures into conformity with EU laws.

Illegal migrants tend to enter the Slovak Republic over the Ukrainian border in the east of the country, and to exit via the Czech and Austrian borders, making the Slovak Republic largely a transit country. Of the 12,500 migrants apprehended for illegally crossing the Slovak border in 2003, 5,500 were apprehended upon entering the country from Ukraine and 4,000 and 2,000 for leaving the country in the direction of Austria and the Czech Republic, respectively.

In 2002, new migration laws defined three types of foreigners: "tolerated" residents for up to six months, temporary residents for one to three years for work or study, and permanent residents for three years followed by unlimited residence. There are about 30,000 foreign residents of the Slovak Republic. In a remarkable decade-long change, border controls in new EU member states such as the Slovak Republic have been transformed from keeping citizens in to keeping foreigners out, helped by massive infusions of aid and technical expertise from the EU-15 member countries.

Conclusion

The EU continues to move toward a common immigration policy, but the impetus for coordination has changed from the asylum crisis of the early 1990s to EU enlargement early in the twenty-first century. There is an apparent split between some EU leaders and voters. EU leaders often argue that immigration is necessary and inevitable to stabilize populations and the economy of the welfare state, while voters seem to prefer less rather than more immigration. Asylum remains a flashpoint even though the number of applicants has been reduced in most countries. Migration policies have been an important component of the move towards enlargement, with the fifteen original member states urging migration and asylum reforms onto the would-be members while making limited concessions in the form of work visas and economic aid to help new members develop their immigration systems.

Notes

1. Stephen Castles and Mark Miller, *The Age of Migration: International Population Movements in the Modern World* (New York: Guilford Press, 1998).

2. Philip Martin and Jonas Widgren, *International Migration: Facing the Challenge* (Washington, DC: Population Reference Bureau, 2002).

3. Ireland and the UK are not Schengen members—they maintain their own border checks (europa.eu.int/scadplus/leg/en/lvb/l33020.htm).

4. Speech by EU Commissioner for Justice and Home Affairs, Antonio Vitorino on July 12, 2000.

5. Wayne Cornelius, et.al., *Controlling Immigration: A Global Perspective*, 2nd edition (Stanford, CA: Stanford University Press, 2004).

6. Turkish politicians reportedly tell Turkish migrants abroad that the Turkish government is fighting to reduce the discrimination they experience in Europe, while telling European politicians that they sympathize with efforts to bring Anatolian peasants into the modern world. Mexican politicians, by contrast, call migrants heroes in both the United States and Mexico.

7. These data are from a Household Labor-Work Force survey in April and October each year in which the respondent determines his labor force status.

8. There are large family-run conglomerates, such as Koc Holding, with 108 companies producing, for example, cars and appliances, as well as owning one of Turkey's largest supermarket chains. Sabanci Holdings has 50 companies in chemicals, textiles, cars, banking, and supermarkets, while Cukorova produces commercial vehicles and paper and has finance and telecom companies. Some of these conglomerates have close ties to leading politicians, which leads to charges of corruption. Observers such as Can Paker, chair of the Turkish Economic and Social Studies Foundation, said, "Our economy can no longer finance corruption and hope to compete in the world." Ten of Turkey's 36 private banks were taken over by the government after they were allegedly mismanaged; when healthy banks cut credit lines to the banks in December 2000, there was a financial crisis.

9. Turkey is the largest producer of hazelnuts, accounting for 70 percent of world production and employing three million Turks.

10. FDI plans are reviewed annually at www.atkearney.com. The 2001 survey ranked Mexico fifth in attractiveness for FDI, and Turkey twenty-third, after Malaysia.

11. Comparable "definitely go abroad" percentages were, for Poland, 13 percent; Hungary, 7 percent; and Czech Republic, 4 percent.

12. Sidex, a steel maker in eastern Romania with 28,000 employees, down from 45,000 in 1989, the largest factory employer in the country, was to be privatized in 2001. When miners marched in Bucharest in 1999, the government abandoned plans to close money-losing coal mines in the Jiu Valley in western Romania. Sidex has debts of $900 million, and lost about $250 million in 2000 producing 3.8 million tons of steel. Private buyers of Sidex must commit to maintaining employment for five years.

13. Romania's labor force is about 10 million, and included in January 2001, about 4.4 million employed in the nonfarm sector and 1 million unemployed, suggesting that 45 percent of Romanians are employed in agriculture.

14. For example, tax inspectors may demand additional payments that have to be paid immediately, the firm contests the payments in court, and the courts agree with the firm, which then gets the original payment back in two to three years without interest in an economy with a 40 percent inflation rate.

15. Romania's major cities are: Bucharest (2.4 million), Constanta (350,476), Iasi (342,994), Timisoara (334,278), Cluj-Napoca (328,008), Galati (325,788), Brasov (323,8350), and Craiova (303,520).

16. In 1999, the DAEWOO Group of companies was the largest foreign investor in Romania, with $1 billion invested.

17. Some have well-known brand names, including Benetton, Stefanel, Luxottica, Diadora, Geox, and De Longhi.

18. To highlight the Romanian-Italian links, Tarom, the Romanian airline, flies to Milan, Rome, Parma, Ancona, Bologna, and Verona.

19. Workers reportedly receive only half this wage because of a variety of taxes: wage tax is at 26 percent, Social Security Contribution (CAS) at 31 percent, unemployment fund at 5 percent, and the health-care fund takes up 12 to 13 percent.

20. Geox reported that wages for comparable workers in Hungary were twice Romanian wages.

21. A separate program permits seven hundred youth from each country to gain work experience in the other for twelve to eighteen months.

22. For example, Roma are about six percent of Hungary's population, but one-third of children beginning school in 2000 were Roma.

23. Since the time of the site visit, the country has changed its name to Serbia and Montenegro. Since it was the Federal Republic of Yugoslavia at the time of the site visit, this chapter uses that designation throughout.

24. International Organization for Migration (IOM) Sarajevo, IOM Trafficking in Migrants-Quarterly Bulletin 22, Autumn 2000.

25. IOM Sarajevo, IOM Trafficking.

26. International Helsinki Federation for Human Rights (IHF-HR), Women 2000: An Investigation into the Status of Women's Rights in the former Soviet Union and Central and South-Eastern Europe (Vienna: IHF-HR, 2000)

27. IOM Sarajevo, IOM Trafficking.

28. IHF-HR, Women 2000.

29. IHF-HR, Women 2000.

30. Dragana Jovanovic, " Gateway to Opportunity," July 13, 2000, moreabcnews .go.com/sections/world/DailyNews/yugo_chinese000710.html, accessed on 4/18/2001.

31. IOM Sarajevo, IOM Trafficking.

32. IOM Sarajevo, IOM Trafficking.

33. IOM Sarajevo, IOM Trafficking.

34. U.S. Committee for Refugees, World Refugee Survey: 2001 (Washington DC: U.S. Committee for Refugees, 2001), pp. 274–75.

35. The Albanian government estimates that about one-half of the Albanians in Greece are legal residents. There are also about 100,000 Albanians in Switzerland, the UK, Germany, and other western European countries.

36. As estimated by the Bank of Albania, Annual Report, 2001.

37. R. Morozzo della Rocca, *Albania: le radici della crisi* (Milan: Guerini e Associati, 1997), and Ferruccio Pastore, Conflicts and Migration. A Case Study on Albania, CeSPI Occasional Papers (Rome: Italy, 1998).

38. About 77 percent of Albania is comprised of mountains.

39. Unemployment peaked in 1993 at 30 percent.

40. Between December 1996 and April 1997 some 30,000 migrants landed in Italy and some 40,000 in Greece, but the majority of them were repatriated. Many commentators noted that Italy was far less receptive to Albanians in 1997 than it had been in 1991.

41. The Italian-Albanian MOU was signed in September 1997, and has been renewed annually. Italy provided equipment and training for the Albanian police, and established a radio network so that Albanian police could communicate with each other. In 1999, when 46,000 clandestine migrants arrived from Albania in Italy, 7,156 (15 percent of the total) were Albanians. In 2001, when 7,500 arrived, 4,017 (53 percent) were Albanians.

42. In 1998, a new constitution was adopted, and it included article 8A, which asserts Albania's right to protect 2.3 million ethnic Albanians outside the country, although Albania has not taken concrete steps to protect Albanians abroad.

43. Blood feuds continue to affect thousands of men and boys, especially in northern Albania and Kosovo. The kanun of Leke Dukagjini (1410–1481), who succeeded Skanderbeg as Albanian leader against the invading Turks, codified customary law and helped to maintain the Albanian identity under occupation between the fifteenth and nineteenth centuries. The kanun attempted to regulate the tradition of prolonged family vengeance against perceived injury, under notions of honor (besa). In 1999 there were a reported 2,200 families in Albania who were in feud, keeping some 1,250 adult males and 950 schoolboys at home for fear of assassination. In November 2000 a policy of "no tolerance" was initiated by an amendment to the Penal Code that provided for penalties up to life imprisonment for feud murder undertaken under the kanun.

44. World Bank, Albania. *Interim Poverty Reduction Strategy Paper* (Tirana: World Bank, 2000).

45. In neighboring Macedonia, an estimated 44 percent of residents are poor. Economist Intelligence Unit, *Albania: Country Profile* (London: The Economist, 2001).

46. F. Pastore and G. Sciortino, *Tutori lontani, Il ruolo degli stati d'origine nel processo di integrazione degli immigrati. Ricerca svolta dalla commissione per le politiche di integrazione degli immigrati* (Rome: CeSPI, 2001).

47. In 2000, 35,889 visas were granted altogether by Italian consulates in Albania.

48. A. Silj, "Albanian immigration to Italy: a criminal invasion?," *Ethno Barometer*, CCS-ERCOMER, working paper n.1, 1997; Ministero degli Affari Esteri, *Il ministero degli esteri in cifre. Annuario statistico*, 2001.

49. Most Albania-Italy smuggling uses dinghy boats that are 35–40 feet long, and equipped with four 125 horsepower motors, to pick up and drop cargoes in shallow water. When joint Italian-Albanian patrols see the dinghies set out for Italy, they force them to return, but the dinghies are not normally confiscated in Albania, so they can try again. We were told that Italian police trained Albanians to pursue and capture dinghies in shallow Albanian waters, but the trained Albanians were transferred to jobs in the mountains. In 2002, many of the dinghies were used to smuggle drugs, especially hashish, from the southern Albanian port of Vlore to Italy.

50. One reason that non-Albanian migrants continue to transit Albania is that Greece releases apprehended Kurds and other foreigners, granting them fifteen days to leave Greece.

51. International Centre for Migration Policy Development, *Report from the Evaluation Mission to Albania 2–5 July 2000, Undertaken in the Framework of the Budapest Process, to Examine the Albanian-Italian Co-operation to Stem Illegal Migration* (Vienna: ICMPD, 2000); Council of the European Union, High Level Working Group on Asylum and Migration. *Action Plan for Albania and the Neighboring Region*, June 2000.

52. International Organization for Migration, "L'inserimento lavorativo e l'integrazione sociale degli albanesi in Italia, Research Report," unpublished, 2000.

53. IOM's MAC labor broker role includes providing those sent to Italy a return ticket, a bond to ensure return to Albania after one year, and guaranteed participation in social security—in effect, the MAC is a pre-screener for the Italian consulate.

54. *Albania, Status/Progress Report, Working Table III*, Stability Pact for South Eastern Project, 2001; N. Sokoli and S. Axhemi, "Emigration in the period of transition in Albania," Studi di Emigrazione, XXXVII, n.139, 2000.

55. Austria in 2003 had 8.1 million residents with a $24,000 per capita GDP; the Slovak Republic had 5.4 million residents and a $4,000 per capita GDP.

56. Organization for Economic Cooperation and Development, Trends in International Migration (Paris: OCED, 2001).

57. There are perhaps 70,000 unauthorized foreigners in Austria.

58. For example, we observed the appeal of a Nigerian environmental activist from the Niger Delta oil-producing region who said he organized a demonstration in March 2003 to stop Chevron-Shell workers from going to work, that was attacked by police, causing him to flee. He applied for asylum in Austria March 15,

2003; the appeal of his denial was before a judge who was openly skeptical of the Nigerian's need for protection.

59. Vienna has 17 percent foreign residents and 35 percent foreign-born residents; Austria has 9 percent foreign residents and 12 percent foreign-born residents.

60. In May 2004, several Austria border guards estimated that 35,000 to 60,000 Slovaks were working in Austria, many on a seasonal basis or in an irregular status.

61. There are an estimated 6 million to 8 million Roma in central Europe, a third in Romania. Slovak Roma often have families of six or more.

62. In 2004, several hundred Slovak Romas traveled by bus to Prague, flew to Helsinki, and applied for asylum. Even though almost all had their applications rejected, including 20 percent who applied and were rejected previously in Finland, the 135 Euro they received per week while waiting for decisions on their applications apparently made the trip worthwhile.

63. In 2003, there were 11,400 applications, which resulted in 11 foreigners receiving asylum and 420 having their applications rejected. For 9,800 applications, the process was halted when the applicants disappeared.

CHAPTER SIX

ϑψ

Migration and
European-African Relations

Fostering cooperation between European countries and African countries in managing migration has generally been more difficult than has been the case within Europe itself. Without the lure of European Union membership, there are fewer incentives that Europe can offer to African states whose populations seek to migrate. Yet, Cooperative Efforts to Manage Migration (CEME) identified a number of initiatives, often done under the rubric of "co-development" to promote cooperation. Three components of cooperation were identified: cooperation in managing flows of people, including through guestworker or other visa programs; cooperation in promoting investment by Diaspora communities through remittances and other inputs; and cooperation in targeting assistance to promote development in source regions and to facilitate return of migrants. In some cases, the impetus for cooperation stemmed from the proximity of the source and destination country, as demonstrated in the discussion of Morocco and Spain and in others from a longer standing colonial relationship, as demonstrated in the discussion of Mali and France. In each case, however, tensions over migration continue, requiring constant—though not always present—efforts towards cooperation.

Morocco-Spain

In April 2003, CEME organized a site visit to southern Morocco and Spain. Morocco is a major country of emigration, sending workers to France, Spain, and other European countries. Spain is a "new" European country of immigration, making a migration transition in the mid-1980s when Spain joined the EU. The visit focused on southern Spain, one of the least prosperous areas of Spain, with a high unemployment rate.

Morocco

Morocco is a country of 30 million in North Africa whose population is growing by 1.9 percent or 570,000 per year.[1] There are 1.5 to 2 million Moroccans abroad, primarily in France and Spain, but also in Belgium, Italy, the Netherlands, and other European countries. A third of Moroccans and most of the Moroccans abroad are Berbers, who are concentrated in the mountainous Rif and Atlas regions and have their own language, Amazigh. About 20 percent of Moroccans live in the northern provinces, which generate only 6 percent of Moroccan gross domestic product (GDP).[2]

Morocco has been an independent constitutional monarchy since 1956, with Islam as the state religion and Arabic as the official language. It is currently led by King Mohammed VI, who promised liberalization when he came to power in 1999 to succeed his father, but he has been slow to give up his enormous constitutional powers to the elected Parliament. The Moroccan king has a dual role as temporal leader and spiritual guide; he appoints the government and prime minister and heads the armed forces. Parliament, which has limited power, has been dominated by conservative parties, but in 1997, leftist opposition parties formed a coalition government that included forty ministers from seven parties; the number of ministers was reduced to thirty-three in 2000.[3]

Morocco was ruled by the Alawi dynasty from the mid-seventeenth century until 1912, when the kingdom became a Franco-Spanish "protectorate," with France dominating the south and Spain the north. In 1956, Morocco became independent and the Alawi monarchy was restored under King Mohammed V, whose son, King Hassan II (1961–1999), was succeeded by his son, the current King Mohammed VI. Restrictions include discussing the role of the king in Morocco, the disputed phosphate-rich Western Sahara,[4] and the role of Islam in the country.

Morocco is growing. There are about 20 million Moroccans ages fifteen and older, including 12 million in urban areas and 8 million in rural areas. The labor force is 10.5 million, including 5.5 million in urban areas and 5 million in rural areas. Unemployment is estimated to be at least 1.5 million or 14 percent, but the unemployment rate is much higher in cities, 20 to 25 percent for women and 30 percent or more for university graduates. Economic growth in the 1990s averaged less than 2 percent a year, but 6 to 8 percent growth is needed to provide jobs for the 200,000 to 300,000 labor force entrants each year. Since the population rose by 2 percent a year in the 1990s, poverty also rose, to about 20 percent of residents, with the highest poverty rates in rural areas in the central and north-central regions. Adult literacy is low in Morocco—only 48 percent of adults are literate, and only 52 percent of children are enrolled in school, below, for example, Algeria's 67 and 72 percent school enrollment rates.

Agriculture employs 45 percent of the Moroccan labor force (60 percent of the female labor force) but accounted for only 11 to 18 percent of GDP in the 1990s. Agriculture's contribution to GDP varies with rainfall—farm output rose 10 percent with heavy rains in 1994, fell 7 percent with drought in 1995, and rose 12 percent in 1996 with heavy rains. There are 8.7 million hectares of cultivated land, including 1.2 million irrigated hectares, much of which is controlled by large and export-oriented farms around Fes-Meknes and Casablanca. These irrigated areas, said to be controlled by the king's extended family in cooperation with foreign firms, produce 80 percent of Morocco's citrus and wine grapes and 33 percent of its vegetables.

Manufacturing employs 18 percent of the Moroccan work force. There are export-oriented sewing factories, but observers blame low productivity and high labor costs for the failure of export-oriented manufacturing to expand. Foreigners and Moroccans have been slow to invest in Morocco because of bureaucracy and uncertainty over the country's future. For example, some foreign investors are concerned that the government protects inefficient local businesses at the expense of foreign-owned firms that are not connected to the king. It is estimated that half of Morocco's current firms would fail if there were free trade with the EU.

Morocco runs a trade deficit, which is offset by tourism receipts and remittances—remittances are about $2 billion a year, half from France. Tourism is also a major source of foreign exchange. Morocco attracts visitors from France, Germany, and Spain, some 2.6 million foreign visitors, as well as 1.6 million Moroccans living abroad who returned for visits in 2000, spending $2 billion. Most of the returning Moroccans travel by car through Spain and take ferries to Ceuta or Tangier.

Morocco: Bridge to Europe?

Morocco sees itself as a bridge between Europe and the Arab states. Morocco applied for EU membership in 1987, and signed an Association Accord with the EU in February 1996 that is expected to lead to free trade between Morocco and the EU by 2012. France and Spain are Morocco's most important trading partners—France takes a third of exports and Spain an eighth, and France provides a fourth of imports and Spain 10 percent.

During the guest worker era of the 1960s, Moroccans were recruited to work in France, Belgium, the Netherlands, and other countries. Many stayed abroad, especially in France. More Moroccans would like to emigrate. A 1998 survey done for Casablanca's *Le Journal* found that 54 percent of Moroccans would "certainly" leave if they could, and another 17 percent would "probably" emigrate. Children as young as ten, so-called mice, are reportedly leaving Morocco because they are most likely to receive social services and be allowed to stay abroad. One Moroccan said, "The country (Morocco) is between two fires. On the one hand, [Spanish] television [received in Morocco] describes a paradise [in Europe] with money, power to consume and well-being. Here life is hard and they [people] are deprived of even the basics."

Spanish-Moroccan tensions persist over migration, drugs, fishing, and Moroccan claims on the Spanish enclaves of Ceuta and Melilla. Nevertheless, some forms of economic cooperation remain. The Spanish and Moroccan governments have a joint program, called PAIDAR, that aims to develop Morocco's northern region, where there are about 70,000 hectares planted with cannabis, most of which is smuggled to Europe, but with limited impacts to date. In addition to Spain's own efforts, it works through the European Union to foster development in Morocco. Through the Barcelona Process of the Euro-Mediterranean Partnership, the EU hopes to increase Moroccan cooperation to prevent the smuggling of migrants and drugs. The Barcelona Process ties the EU to non-EU states in the Mediterranean basin.[5]

Spain's enclaves on the Morocco coast, Ceuta and Melilla, have been surrounded since 1995 by barbed wire fences, and in 1999 the fences were raised from seven to ten feet and topped with razor wire. Spain estimates that fifteen to twenty unauthorized migrants slip into Ceuta every day, but it is hard to assess the level of unauthorized migration because residents of Tetouan in northern Morocco have the right to enter Ceuta with border crossing cards rather than visas. Many do so, buying goods that are carried by porters back to Morocco. There is duty free entry for as much as porters can carry on their backs, so there is a line of porters handling refrigerators and other appliances, as well as people in Ceuta throwing bags of goods over the fence into Morocco to waiting porters.

Spain

Spain is a country of 43 million in Southern Europe whose population is rising slightly because of immigration. Spain has one of the highest unemployment rates in the EU and also some of the most rapid job growth, especially in the Madrid and Barcelona areas.[6] Unemployment is over 30 percent in some of Spain's 52 provinces, but residents there say they cannot afford to move to areas with jobs.

Instead, immigrants are arriving to fill jobs in Spain. Moroccans are 17 percent of the nearly 3 million foreigners in Spain, according to the National Statistical Office (INE), but Latin Americans (Ecuadorians, Colombians, and Argentineans) as well as Eastern Europeans (Romanians, Ukrainians, Poles, and Bulgarians) are Spain's fastest growing immigrant groups. Morocco applied for EU entry in 1987, but it is not yet on the list of candidate countries, making freedom of movement unlikely. Spanish-Moroccan relations have improved after several turbulent years in which Spain alleged that the Moroccan government did not do enough to prevent illegal emigration and drug smuggling, and Morocco pursued claims to the Spanish enclaves of Ceuta and Melilla.

The Organization for Economic Cooperation and Development (OECD) says that immigration in the 1990s has been associated with increased employment, as migrants preserve or expand low-wage services and allow Spanish women to work.[7] However, migration's impact on "labor productivity are less clear," and immigration has not reduced regional differences in unemployment rates.[8] The Spanish paradox is that immigration rose sharply in the 1990s despite persisting high unemployment rates—22 to 23 percent in the mid-1990s, and 15 percent in 2000, with young Spaniards entering the labor force often having trouble getting jobs. Most of the one million workers hired in Spain in the past decade received temporary rather than permanent contracts.

One explanation for the immigration and persisting high unemployment paradox is that rigid labor laws allow many Spanish workers to collect unemployment insurance benefits while working for cash wages. Labor force participation rates among Spanish women, youths, and older males are low, and many Spanish workers have reportedly become accustomed to accepting a short-term work contract, collecting Unemployment Insurance (UI) benefits when the job ends, and then accepting another short-term work contract that is followed by UI benefits.

Agriculture provides an example of the paradox. There are about 100,000 migrant farm workers in Spain. Many traditionally followed a route that took them to the vineyards of the Rioja region when fruit picking in Catalunia was completed, then to the orange orchards in Valencia, and finally to the horticultural centers of Almeria and Murcia. Most migrants in 2000 worked nine-hour days for about $37 a day, but deductions were made for food, social security, and lodging. These seasonal earnings were supplemented by UI benefits: in Andalucia and Extremadura, seasonal farm workers can collect up to 75 percent of the minimum wage in UI benefits for six months after working 35 days under a special UI system. In the past five years, foreigners have become the core of the migrant work force in agriculture.

The government has been slow to reform the labor market. In 2002, employers could reduce their UI costs if they agreed that their layoffs were "unfair," but the OECD says that much more must be done to increase labor market flexibility. The OECD recommends that the Employment Service (INEM) should do more to place workers into jobs, that wage indexes that cover 75 percent of permanent workers be eliminated to reduce inflationary pressures, and that education be improved to increase female labor force participation and productivity.

Spain was a country of emigration until the mid-1970s, and two million Spanish citizens remain abroad. Between 1846 and 1932, some five million Spaniards emigrated, mostly to South America. Between 1962 and 1976 some two to three million Spaniards migrated to other European countries, usually as guest workers to France, Germany, Switzerland, and other northern European countries. There was also significant internal migration within Spain, as six million Spaniards moved from one province to another in the 1960s and early 1970s.[9]

Spain experienced guest worker and internal migration during the Spanish economic miracle between 1960 and 1974, when GDP growth averaged 6.6 percent a year, in part because of foreign investment, tourism, and remittances from migrants abroad. Between 1973 and 1980, many of the guest workers returned, so that when Spain entered the EU in 1986, it was a net immigration country, attracting more returning Spaniards and foreigners each year than were leaving. There was a second Spanish economic boom in the second half of the 1980s, as foreign investment and EU aid poured into the country. Spain's relatively small population of foreign residents began to grow and change from mostly retirees from the UK, Germany, and other EU countries to foreign workers, many from Morocco, Latin America (especially from the Dominican Republic and Peru), and the Philippines. During the late 1990s, the foreign worker population continued to increase, as workers arrived from Ecuador and Colombia as well as Eastern Europe and China.

In January 2003, there were 1.6 million legal foreign residents in Spain, including a quarter from OECD countries and three-quarters from less developed countries in Africa, Latin America, Asia and Eastern Europe. The most important source country is Morocco (334,000 residence-permit holders), followed by Ecuador, Colombia, China, Romania, and Peru. Over 40 percent of the foreigners live in Madrid and Barcelona, and another third are in eight provinces in the Mediterranean coast and the Canary and Balearic Islands. Spain is a destination for migrants as well as a transit country for migrants from Africa and Latin America headed to other European countries, and migrants coming from or through other EU countries on their way home transit Spain.

The number of legal foreigners in Spain has increased rapidly, from 430,000 in 1993 to 539,000 in 1996, 800,000 in 1999, and 1.6 million in 2003, with the doubling in four years due to large-scale regularization. The number of non-EU foreigners affiliated with the Spanish Social Security system increased from 212,000 to 448,000 between 1999 and 2002 and reached two million by the end of 2004.

Modern Spanish migration policy began with the Ley de Extranjeria of 1985, which was enacted so that the Spanish government gained more power to regulate non-EU migration on the eve of Spain's accession to the EU. The 1985 law included fines but not criminal penalties on employers who knowingly hired irregular immigrants.[10] However, with many Spanish as well as migrant workers employed in the underground economy, enforcement of the sanctions law has been limited.[11] As a tourist destination, Spain has been liberal in allowing foreigners to enter with tourist visas. Visas were required of Moroccans only in 1991, followed by a visa requirement for some Latin American countries since 1992.

Spanish migration policy is evolving, with Wayne Cornelius summarizing the dilemma as how to allow enough migrants to sustain the sectors of the economy that depend on them while maintaining enough control to prevent tensions between foreigners and immigrants.[12] Asserting that migration is under control is difficult because a high percentage of migrants in Spain are unauthorized—at least 600,000 by most estimates—and some Spaniards associate immigration with rising crime.

President José María Aznar and the center-right Partido Popular, in power between 1996 and 2004, made deterring irregular immigration a top priority. An immigration law passed in February 2000, over the objections of Aznar, offered all migrant children K-12 education and emergency medical care, and gave migrants the right to hold demonstrations and to join unions. However, the Aznar government amended the law in December 2000, tightening the law in several ways, including the assertion that the only way to gain legal status today is to receive a work permit before arrival in Spain, and that there would be no more regularizations—the only way to gain legal status today is to receive a work permit before arrival in Spain.

There is a potential for local incidents to lead to tensions that can be exploited by anti-immigrant groups. In February 2000, a Moroccan migrant killed a local woman in the 50,000-resident city of El Ejido, twenty-five miles west of the port city of Almeria and near the popular beach resorts of the

Costa del Sol. This prompted several days of attacks on some of the 10,000 Moroccan workers in the area who worked on farms that produce fruits and vegetables under plastic sheeting using drip irrigation.[13] Andalusia's Socialist leader Manuel Chaves sympathized with the migrants, saying, "If they left, El Ejido's economic activity would collapse." In El Ejido, authorities promised to rebuild the destroyed worker housing and to provide work permits to some of the 5,000 illegal workers, but the situation had not changed much by 2003.

In July 1999, an anti-immigrant protest in a working-class neighborhood of Terrassa, a city of 175,000 near Barcelona with a 10-percent Moroccan population, turned violent. A Moroccan youth was attacked and the protesters shouted "Moroccans out" and "No more Moroccans." It should be emphasized that most Moroccans do not commit crimes in Spain, but the minority that do have made Moroccan and criminal a common link in the minds of many people. However, the overall assessment is that Spaniards have accepted a sharp increase in immigration with few tensions, even after the March 11, 2004, train bombings in Madrid.

Illegal Migration and Guest Workers

Illegal immigration to Spain is rising. In 2004 there were an estimated 800,000 illegal migrants despite several regularization programs.[14] The census of October 2001 counted 1,572,000 foreigners in Spain, while municipal registers in January 2002 had 1,620,000 foreigners. However, there were only 1,109,000 residence permit holders, suggesting at least 500,000 unauthorized foreigners, and perhaps 1 million in 2004.

Since 1986 Spain has had four legalizations, in 1986, 1991, 1996, and 2000–2002, that legalized a total of 600,000 foreigners. Additionally, in 1994, 1995, 1997, 1998, and 1999 labor entry quotas (*contingentes*) granted 20,000 to 30,000 unauthorized workers per year *de facto* legal status.[15] These data suggest that most currently legal foreigners from Africa, Latin America, Asia, and Eastern Europe were previously illegal at some point, and that some came legally and become illegal, while others may have been legalized several times. Legal status is a fluid concept in Spain, due in part to the past system of separate short-term work and residence permits, so that migrants could move into and out of legal status. For example, each time a migrant changes employers, he had to get a new work permit under the old system, which required a social security card, but few Spanish employers enrolled especially illegal workers in Social Security, so a legal worker could become illegal by changing employers.[16]

Illegal migrants arrive in several ways. Many Latin Americans come with tourist visas, often through other EU countries (Amsterdam was a frequently mentioned entry point), and go to work, while most Africans cross the 14-km (8.7 mile) wide Strait of Gibraltar in small boats called pateras.[17] Spanish police arrested over 18,000 migrants in pateras in 2002, up from the 3,600 in 1999. Moroccan authorities arrested an additional 15,000. Spanish police boats patrol the Strait, and estimate that they catch one in four migrants attempting entry into Spain. Those caught are taken to detention centers in Spain, and the Moroccans among them are deported by ferry back to Morocco. Those who succeed usually head toward the intensive-agriculture areas of Almeria, Murcia, and Huelva. Asians arrive via many routes, including via Schengen visas issued by Greece or other Schengen-member countries.

The small boats traveling between Spain and Morocco have been the focus of recent control efforts under SIVE, an integrated system of surveillance. In the Strait of Gibraltar, the Mediterranean mixes with the Atlantic, producing turbulent waters and leading to frequent boat sinkings that drowned an estimated 200 migrants in 2001.

As Spain cracks down on smuggling across the Strait of Gibraltar, many smugglers have re-directed migrants to the eastern provinces of Granada and Almeria and to the Canary Islands, which are sixty miles from the Morocco coast. Authorities on Fuerteventura, an island of 42,000 residents, in 1999 reported that boats carrying illegal migrants were landing on tourist-packed beaches almost every day. In 1999, the island police arrested 1,000 immigrants, three times the figure in 1998, and over 4,000 in 2000; two-thirds were Moroccans. Migrants can see the Canary Islands' El Roque lighthouse from the African coast; the boat ride takes about twelve hours and smugglers charge $500 to $2,500.[18] Some worry that continued illegal migration will detract from tourism; the Canary Islands receive about 10 million visitors per year.

Spain allows the entry of legal foreign workers under a quota or *contingente* system introduced in 1993[19] and last modified by the Immigration Act of 2000. It distinguishes between temporary permits for jobs that last less than one year and permanent or stable permits for longer-term jobs. Current policy requires foreign workers to have work permits before arrival. They receive these permits under a system in which Spanish employers seeking guest workers prepare generic job offers and make their requests to INEM. Each provincial INEM committee sends a recommended number of work permits for foreigners to the Ministry of Labor (MOL), which transmits them to Spanish embassies in Morocco, Dominican Republic, Colombia, Ecuador, Romania, and Poland,[20] where workers are recruited primarily by local governments under bilateral labor agreements that include a proviso that these countries accept the readmission of their nationals.

In 2002, employers requested 31,000 temporary and 80,000 stable permits, and the MOL approved 21,200 temporary (75 percent for agriculture and 15 percent for construction) and 10,900 stable permits; in 2003, 30,000 permits were made available, including 20,000 temporary.[21] Under the *contingente* system, seasonal foreign workers may enter Spain for up to nine months and, after completing three years of seasonal work, can become immigrants. Legal migrant workers in Spain are protected by minimum wage and other laws, accrue Social Security and retirement benefits, and earn vacation benefits; Spanish employers are responsible for providing their transportation and lodging. However, many of the *contingente* permits are not used. For example, in 2002, only 9,100 seasonal work permits were issued, compared with 3,600 in 2001, 508 in 2000, and 34 in 1999. Catalonia and Andalusia each received a third of these 2002 seasonal permits, and 60 percent went to Poles and 20 percent to Moroccans.

In June 2002, Moroccan and Algerian migrants staged a hunger strike near the EU summit in Seville to protest what they said was their displacement by Eastern Europeans to pick strawberries. The protesting migrants said they earned $25 a day in 2001, and were not hired in 2002 because Huelva-area employers hired Eastern Europeans; the employers said that they had been fined for hiring unauthorized Moroccan workers, and thus switched to legal Eastern Europeans. Many of the Eastern Europeans are young women who live in cabins that were once rented for summer holidays before tourists moved into beachside hotels. Employers paid the Euro 2 a day charge for housing for their migrants, and many of the Eastern Europeans shared the cars in which they had driven to Spain for local transportation.

Spain's two principal labor union confederations, the Comisiones Obreras (CCOO) and the Union General de Trabajadores (UGT), welcome migrants, legal or illegal, as members.[22] The Confederacion Espanola de Organizaciones Empresariales (CEOE), the nation's largest employer association, has expressed concern about labor shortages in some sectors and favors the admission of additional foreign workers.

Morocco-Spain Cooperation?

Emigration pressures remain very high in the north of Morocco closest to Spain, where the Berber minority is rapidly urbanizing. Many Spanish NGOs are helping especially Berber women who migrated from rural to urban areas to achieve literacy, skills in sewing garments, and empowerment. These NGO activities help individuals, but it is not clear that they are successfully transforming northern Morocco in a way that promises stay-at-home development. This is worrisome, since current trends suggest that fast-growing Morocco and slow-growing Spain will have similar populations by 2025.

Spain and Italy are EU's chief frontline states that deal with attempted illegal entries by boat from Africa. Smuggling operations based in Tangier and other Moroccan ports attempt to move Moroccans and others across the Strait of Gibraltar and to the Canary Islands, and Spain advocates EU cooperation to patrol the Strait of Gibraltar to deter such clandestine migration. One source of tension between Spain and Morocco is the sense that Morocco is not cooperating enough with Spanish and EU efforts to deter unauthorized migration.

In southern Spain, labor-intensive agriculture expanded significantly in the 1990s, and the seasonal work force employed seasonally in fruit and vegetable operations that sell their produce to northern EU nations changed from Moroccans to Eastern Europeans and Latin Americans. This has led to tensions in some places, as jobless Moroccan men protest that employers prefer "fellow Catholics," often women from Eastern Europe.

Spain has had the fastest growth in foreigners among EU nations, with the number of foreigners tripling between 1995 and 2003. Spain appears set to repeat the mistakes of other European countries, accepting guest workers from many countries and developing networks that can send more migrants legally and illegally to Spain. The paradox of fewer legal guest workers than there are slots available for them and persisting illegal immigration as well as high unemployment suggest that many employers and migrants prefer to operate outside the guest worker and formal economic system. Until interior enforcement becomes more effective, foreigners who succeed in entering Spain are likely to be able to continue to find jobs, which will lead to pressures for future legalizations.

Mali-France

CEME visited Mali and Senegal in January 2002 to examine co-development, linking official development assistance and migration management. Mali, a poor country that embraced democracy in 1991, is considered a democratic role model for francophone Africa. It is grappling with several migration issues, including well-established networks that move thousands of Malians abroad, often with false documents, for $2,000 to $3,000 each; the dependence of the Kayes region, with 1.5 million residents, on emigration, particularly the remittances sent by its workers abroad—several innovative projects aim to help returning migrants become economically independent and create jobs for non-migrants; and the migration of especially Mali and Burkina Faso children to work on cocoa and coffee plantations in the Ivory Coast and other neighboring countries.

Mali is considered one of the most promising democracies in west Africa. We learned that the Kayes region of Mali is extraordinarily dependent on remittances, which have improved the lives of residents and added schools and clinics, but do not seem to have led to the establishment of large numbers of businesses that promise stay-at-home development. The Mali government cooperates with assisted return programs for unauthorized Malians in France, and works with international organizations to attract educated Malians back to Mali. Finally, Mali is open to donor suggestions for economic development, so that most residents will not have to depend on agriculture and cattle raising in a water-scarce region. However, there was little evidence that Mali and its donors have found the country's comparative advantage for sustained economic growth. For example, even though Mali is a cotton producer, its cotton is mostly exported raw, and the cloth is re-imported to be turned into clothing.

Mali is a large country (the size of California and Texas combined) in central western Africa whose name comes from the Mali empire of the upper and middle Niger River.[23] Because the Niger River makes an arc through Mali from southwest to north to southeast, it has long been a crossroads between northern and western Africa.[24] Mali became a French colony in the 1890s and gained its independence from French colonial rule in 1960. The country immediately adopted a socialist economic model, with rural cooperatives organized to produce cotton and groundnuts (peanuts) for export. Military leader Moussa Traore became president after a 1968 coup and enacted a new constitution in 1974. The democratic uprising led by students March 22, 1991, resulted in the election of Alpha Oumar Konare, the candidate of the Association for Democracy in Mali (ADEMA), and a new constitution in 1992. Konaré was re-elected in 1997; new elections were scheduled in 2002. At the time of the site visit, experts noted that Konare was not expected to run, marking Mali's first democratic power transition.[25] Mali has a free press and a vibrant multi-party system of governance. During our visit, respondents overwhelmingly affirmed their belief that the presidential transition will be peaceful.

Bamako is Mali's major city, with about 1 million residents, followed by Segou, Mopti, and Sikasso, about 100,000 each. Mali is divided into eight regions: Kayes, Koulikoro, Sikasso, Ségou, Mopti, Gao, Timbuktu, and Bamako and, since September 1999, there has been a decentralization of power, with governing authority shared by elected mayors in the 701 communes (including the 19 cities) and appointed officials ("commissaires du gouvernement") who are the representatives of the central government in the regions, and the cercles (districts roughly equivalent to counties).

Mali's 11 million residents are among the poorest in the world. The World Bank put per capita income at $240 in 2000; GDP was $2.3 billion in 2000—equivalent to about two hours of U.S. GDP.[26] Mali has a human development index score of 0.38 and a per capita GDP at PPP of $740; neighbors Ivory Coast and Senegal have HDIs of 0.42, and per capita GDP-PPPs of $1,300 and $1,600, that is, more than twice as much per person buying power.

Mali's population, 4 million at independence in 1960, is growing rapidly, up 3.1 percent or 300,000 a year, which means that 45 percent of residents are under 15. Mali has a projected population of 21 million in 2025. Women average six to seven children, and half have their first child before age twenty. About 60 percent of those fifteen and older are illiterate, and life expectancy is about fifty years. The richest 10 percent of residents have about 56 percent of income and wealth.

Although Mali is mostly an emigration country, it has seen small in-flows of refugees. According to both UN High Commissioner for Refugees (UNHCR) and government estimates, there were approximately 11,000 Mauritanian refugees, mostly Fulani herders, living in the Kayes region of western Mali in 1999, and another 1,900 refugees, 80 percent from Sierra Leone, in Bamako.

About 75 percent of Malians live in rural areas, and 75 percent of Mali's four million economically active workers are subsistence farmers, many located along the Niger river between Bamako and Mopti. Most farmers live in villages that have 150 to 600 residents, and most grow rice, wheat, and corn (maize), as well as potatoes, yams, and cassava for their own consumption. The Office du Niger irrigates about 60,000 hectares of land for rice and sugarcane production.

Mali's major exports are gold and cotton—a massive mine in the Kayes area is the new hope for export earnings, and gold surpassed cotton as the major export in 2001. Gold production more than doubled between 2000 and 2001, as new mines were opened, but cotton production in 2000–2001 was only half 1999–2000 and expected 2001–2002 levels The new gold mine is operated by a South African–Canadian consortium.

One reason for smaller cotton harvests is that the Compagnie malienne pour le developpement des textiles (CMDT), a legacy of socialism, controls all aspects of cotton production—it is the only supplier of seed and fertilizer and the only buyer, ginner, and exporter of cotton. The CMDT is to be privatized, but its unions are resisting plans to reduce current employment of 2,400 by up to half.[27] Despite offering lower-than-world prices to farmers, only CFA107 or $0.15 per kg in 2000–2001, versus CFA200 or $0.28 per kg in 2000–2001, CMDT loses money. Chinese firms participate in the textile industry and in large-scale construction projects, including building a bridge across the Niger, a conference center, an expressway in Bamako, and some of the new stadiums.

Mali also produces millet, sorghum, and rice (in the inland Niger delta), and exports livestock. The quality of most Mali farm products is low, limiting export markets. Some 40 to 60 percent of Mali's imports are food, and Mali pays more for imported food than other developing countries because, as a landlocked country, imports must travel through other countries to reach Mali. Extremely poor road infrastructure within Mali further limits the capacity of producers to reach either internal or external markets.

Mali's economic and democratic reforms have been rewarded with foreign aid—an average $33 per resident in 2000. France, the United States, UK, and the Netherlands are prominent among donors. In September 2000, donors agreed to provide Mali with US$870 million in debt relief under the Heavily Indebted Poor Countries (HICPC) initiative, a sum equivalent to almost half of Mali's GDP. In the late 1990s, the government spent $100 million over five years on five stadiums around the country in order to host the African Soccer Cup January 19–February 10, 2002.

Increasing access to education, and thereby reducing illiteracy, is a major goal of the government. Progress has been seen in recent years to reverse the traditionally very low levels of primary school attendance. An estimated 60 percent of age-eligible Malian children are enrolled in primary schools, 18 to 20 percent in secondary, and 1.5 to 2 percent in universities. At present, the enrollment of girls lags behind that of boys.

Mali's education system needs major reforms, including reducing the CFA 26,000 ($37) per month stipends or salaries paid to university students and increasing the spending and training for K–12 education—the university does not do teacher training. However, with students receiving a stipend that is more than the minimum wage, there is little incentive to finish studies quickly. Disruptions in 2000–2001 meant that there were no university exams, and this may have contributed to more Malian students applying to study abroad—800 received visas to study in France in 2001.

Co-development and Migration

Mali is one of several countries that are targets of "co-development" (other countries are Morocco, Senegal, and Comoros). Mali and France have established the Mali-France Consultation on Migration, an annual binational consultation on migration between the two countries. In an official agreement signed on December 21, 2000, the representatives of the two countries agreed to meet at least once a year at the ministerial level to deal with three issues: the integration of Malians who want to remain in France; co-management of migration flows; and cooperative development. Malian minister Soumaila Cisse defined "cooperative development" as a policy in which industrial nations allow migrants to circulate between their home countries and abroad. The principal focus of our visit was co-management of migration and cooperative development.

Co-management has focused on a number of issues regarding both unauthorized and legal movements. The return of unauthorized Malians from France has long been an irritant in relations between the two countries. Malians figured prominently in mid-1990s protests in France in which migrants trying to avoid deportation occupied churches.[28] When France sent a charter plane with deported Malians to Bamako on August 25, 1996, President Alpha Omar Konare complained that "Some people have been expelled with absolutely nothing . . . [but added] We can't encourage our citizens to breach the laws of their host country." As discussed below, encouraging voluntary assisted returns—rather than relying on mandatory deportation— would better meet the interests of both countries.

Access to legal admissions has been a further area of concern. Traditionally, visa policies seriously restricted family reunification and visits as well as business travel and study abroad. Since 1997, a new visa policy was implemented that includes the obligation for the French consulates to justify some denials of visas (to parents of French citizens, students, etc.). France issued about 25,000 visas to Malians in 2001 compared to 7,000 in 1997 (the United States issues about 5,000 a year, representing about half of the 10,000 Malian applications).

In exchange for facilitating free circulation of bona fide travelers, French authorities urged Malian authorities to cooperate in reducing corruption. In October 2001, a former minister (of sports) was indicted and sent to jail for trafficking in visas.

It is said that 1.5 to 2 million Malians live abroad, usually in nearby African countries such as Ivory Coast (1 million) or other west African countries, including Gabon. Several hundred thousand Malians live in the industrial democracies, including 60,000 to 80,000 in France.[29]

Can some of the Malians abroad be induced to return and contribute to Mali's development? We looked at two types of return programs: a French-funded program of voluntary assisted return, generally of Malians living illegally in France; and a United Nations program that assists temporary return of university professors.

France's assisted return program is part of its co-development strategy. About 500 unauthorized Malians in France agreed to return voluntarily in exchange for CFA 2.5 million ($3,600) and open businesses, most related to agriculture but including hairdressing, importing used auto parts, sewing traditional dresses, and sand dredging.[30] They receive weekly visits for one year from the program's offices in Mali, and it was reported that 80 percent of those who participate are still in business after two years. This French model clearly helps to re-integrate migrants who "failed" in France, but its potential for expansion may be limited. Many of the small businesses begun by returnees had difficulty obtaining bank loans for expansion, in part because they did not have Malian track records and guarantees.

Assisted return is not a new concept to Mali. An early example is a multifunction agricultural cooperative in the Kayes region established in the 1980s. A group of migrants from four West African countries requested help from the French government and nongovernmental organizations to obtain land in the Senegal River basin to begin a farming enterprise. Prior to return, they received training from French agricultural experts and explored innovative farming techniques used in such other countries as Israel. Mali responded positively to their request for land. The cooperative has experimented with various different crops, finding that bananas offer a particularly good investment. They sell their produce to traders throughout the Kayes region, often to women who walk for miles to buy the fruit and vegetables. Poor roads, particularly in the rainy season, hinder their ability to expand.

Regardless of its economic contribution, assisted return programs provide public affairs value to both the French and Malian governments. French officials noted that the cost of deportation is about $3,500 per return because an immigration official accompanies each deportee. The same funds not only encourage voluntary return, which is more humane, but they provide a livelihood for the returnee.

The French program generally focuses on unskilled migrants. Mali suffers as well from a brain drain resulting from the departure of its educated population. For most of the past 40 years, the Mali government provided scholarships for study abroad, and guaranteed government jobs to all university graduates. Some of those who graduated remained abroad, while others returned and swelled government payrolls.

Remittances and Development
Remittances are a major source of income in Mali. The International Monetary Fund (IMF) yearbook shows that global remittances reached $95 billion in 1998, including $61 billion from workers' remittances and $33 billion in com-

pensation of employees.[31] IMF data likely underestimate remittances, since many are transferred outside the banking system. One indicator of the importance of remittances is that France provides about $50 million a year in aid to Mali, and France-Mali remittances are estimated to be at least $50 million.

Most Malian migrants in France come from the Kayes region that borders on Senegal. As elsewhere in Mali, people live near the river—in this case the Senegal river. The Kayes region has about 1.5 million people, including 80,000 in the city of Kayes, and about 150,000 Kayes residents are believed to have emigrated. Migrants left the Kayes region during droughts in the early 1970s, and the region now has a migrant-remittance based economy, with an estimated 80–90 percent of remittances spent on current consumption.

The overall impression of rural Mali is extreme poverty. Cattle and sheep are the mainstays of the economy, with millet, peanuts, and other crops planted and harvested for subsistence. Some cash is earned from the sale of animals, but it appears that most cash must come from outside the village.

The high levels of emigration have produced important financial ties between migrants and their home communities. A typical community is Marena, which has 16,000 residents, many of whom had been in France. Marena migrants in France have an association, and they contribute to the village's budget. Some of the migrants stay in France, but others return with their savings to Marena. Many of the returned migrants complained about the delinquency of Malian children brought up in France and the changing family and gender relationships brought on by life in western society. It appeared that we were hearing from relatively conservative returned migrants who accumulated savings in France, but who preferred to live in Mali—at least one man returned without his wife and family, who preferred to stay in France.

Marena and similar villages are very isolated—although only 50 km from Kayes, the trip can take one to two hours over dirt roads that are not passable in the rainy season, from July to October. The local economy is based on corn, millet, and peanuts, and sheep (worth CFA 15,000 to 25,000) and cows (worth CFA 100,000 to 150,000). There seem to be little evidence of stores or other types of businesses that could be expanded with remittances.

Migrant remittances help to pay for schools and teachers in the Marena area (there were also several Islamic schools). Most people in one village did not have electricity, for example, three families shared a compound fenced with sticks—the mud-brick houses had pantries with meal, etc., and sleeping quarters, but there were no windows or lights. The three families shared a round kitchen, which seemed to have a fire going all day. Water was brought from a well near the clinic. During the dry season, dust permeated the houses. Yet, migrants helped to establish a health clinic, and they were going to send money to cover the cost of medical emergencies. The clinic was built, but coverage is provided under an insurance-type program to fifty-three families paid by families in France. This insurance type program can be an example of best practice that can be expanded to many villages of Mali and other countries.

Kayes, like most of Mali, is wracked by desertification, deforestation, and soil degradation. There has long been significant internal migration within Mali, as farmers left their homes after the harvest for nearby cities, where they worked in a variety of jobs before returning to their villages to plant. A mid-1990s study of migrants emphasized that circular internal migration has a long history, and that some migrants stay away as long as five to seven years. However, some of the migrants who were interviewed had been away from "home" forty-plus years; even if they refused to call their moves "permanent," growing cities mean some circular migrants do not return to their villages of origin.

Within the new Franco-Malian co-development framework, a fund of Euro 2.6 million will finance in 2002–2004 the mobilization of Malians abroad for the service of the Malian education system, economy, and small business development. The skills of Malians in France will be systematically registered and the information co-managed by a Franco-Malian committee. The fund will supplement financing by the Malian Diaspora of local projects. Also a contract will be signed with a Malian bank to guarantee loans to small businesses that require additional funding for expansion of their activities.

At present, the TOKTEN Project (Transfer Of Knowledge Through Expatriate Nationals) aims to persuade Malians established abroad to return at least temporarily and contribute to Mali's development by, for example, teaching at Mali's 25,000-student university, which was established in 1996 and expanded rapidly. The UN Development Program has paid for 133 Malians to return as consultants to help teach and do research.

Throughout the site visit, the solid movement of Mali toward greater democratization and respect for human rights proved to be a positive counterpoint to the country's economic problems. A number of respondents observed that international migration has helped spur the democratic reforms. Malians living in Europe and North America have brought back home some of the lessons learned in western democracies. At a village meeting in Marena, a number of return migrants observed that they expected to participate in community meetings and decision-making.

Even those who expressed concerns about what they considered to be decadent western social values supported the increased democratization in Mali. Often, the reference to western values focused on the greater freedom given to women and children. In fact, the role of women and children remains an area of substantial difference between Mali and the receiving countries in Europe and North America. One European official noted that Malian officials often express concern that two traditional practices in Mali—polygamy and female genital mutilation—are illegal in the receiving state. Questions about North American rejection of these practices also arose at a public conference in which members of the CEME group spoke. Some of the return migrants appeared particularly reluctant to expose Malian women and girls to western values if it meant the undermining of cultural traditions, observing vehemently that they would never allow their wives or daughters to migrate with them to Europe or North America. In some cases, the return migrants appear to have become more socially and religiously conservative as a result of their own migration experience.

Malian Migration to Cote d'Ivoire (Ivory Coast)

An estimated one million Malians live in Ivory Coast, which accounts for 40 percent of total GDP produced in the Union economique et monetaire ouest-africaine (UEMOA).[32] The Ivory Coast is a major source of remittances to Burkina Faso and Mali. According to the IMF, Mali was receiving about $100 million a year in remittances in the mid-1990s, although remittances were trending downward in both Mali and Burkina Faso.

Migration from Mali (and Burkina Faso) to the Ivory Coast involves adults and children migrating to work on coffee and cocoa plantations. The problem area is children—an estimated 15,000 Malian children between the ages of twelve and eighteen have been "sold into forced labor" on the cotton, coffee, and cocoa plantations of northern Cote d'Ivoire over the past few years; an even greater number have been pressed into domestic service. The migrants have contracts, most of which offer CFA95,000 to CFA125,000 ($135 to $189) for a year's work—some reports discuss annual wages of $200 to $300.

Most reports emphasize that migrants go voluntarily, but they often do not know that hard work and low pay await them, since the middlemen recruiters who visit Malian villages exaggerate the pay and understate the work. The recruiters pay parents $30 to $40, and then take the children away for "work

Table 6.1.   Workers' Remittances: Selected Countries

	Credits ($ million)		
	1995	1996	1997
Burkina Faso	128	117	80
Mali	112	107	90
Senegal	86	82	92
Ivory Coast (debits)	457	510	517

Burkina Faso data is for 1992–94.

and training." In Ivory Coast, work conditions are variable—the worst employers make migrants work for ten to twelve hours a day.

According to the International Labor Organization (ILO), the best defense against the sale of child migrants is to have local NGOs educate villagers about what really happens to their children, and to step up enforcement of laws that make recruiting and enslaving children a crime. The ILO defines a slave as someone "forced to work under physical or mental threat, and where the owner or employer controls the person completely—where a person is bought or sold."

The fifteen-member Economic Community of West African States (ECOWAS), including Benin, Burkina Faso, Cape Verde, Gambia, Ghana, Guinea, Guinea-Bissau, Ivory Coast, Liberia, Mali, Niger, Nigeria, Senegal, Sierra Leone, and Togo, called on member countries in October 2001 "to adopt laws criminalizing trafficking in human beings and to build the necessary administrative structures."

Mali is a traditional country of emigration, with a growing number of its migrants heading to Europe and North America. Migration occurs for work, family reunification, and education. Remittances from migrants abroad are essential to subsistence in many of the emigration communities. They also support infrastructure development and social services, including health clinics, schools, and roads. As long as too few economic opportunities exist in Mali, migration will continue to follow the long-entrenched networks that help Malians go abroad.

The French program of co-development may help pave the way toward reducing emigration pressures. Targeted aid in high emigration regions could help build infrastructure, establish more viable markets, stimulate job creation, and support education and health care. Remittances will likely continue to be an important support for individual families and communities, and local efforts to channel remittances toward infrastructure development and income generation should be encouraged. Assisted return programs have less far-reaching economic impact, but in helping some migrants return voluntarily and become self-supporting, they provide incentives for further cooperation in managing migration to the benefit of both countries. In our opinion, transportation and education should be the two top priorities for the development of Mali.[33]

Conclusion

The efforts at cooperation between European countries and African countries are based on unequal economic relationships. Unlike the EU enlarge-

ment context discussed in the previous chapter, there is little prospect for reducing the differences in income and wealth in the short to medium term.
The basis of cooperation in migration management is a common interest in
promoting economic development of the source countries, with migration
recognized as an essential component of the development process. Only with
economic development will emigration pressures reduce in the long-term,
though as discussed above, the countries may go through the migration hump
to get there. We will return to this theme in the final chapter of the book.

Notes

1. Over 10 percent of Moroccan residents, or 3.3 million individuals, live in
Casablanca and another 1.4 million in Rabat-Sale; Tangier has about 500,000 residents.

2. Morocco's GDP is about $33 billion, or $1,100 per person, lower than the
$1,800 in Algeria and the $2,000 in Tunisia.

3. Elections were held in Morocco in 1977, 1984, 1993, and 1997, and September 2002.

4. The Algerian-supported Polisario Front, which operates from a base at Tin-
douf, Algeria, began a guerrilla war in support of independence for the self-proclaimed
Sahrawi Arab Democratic Republic (SADR) in 1975. There has been a cease-fire in
place since 1991. Western Sahara occupies 35 percent of Morocco's 710,850 sq. km.

5. An Arab Maghreb Union (UMA in its French acronym) was set up in 1989
to link Morocco, Algeria, Tunisia, Libya, and Mauritania, but the dispute over the
Western Sahara has prevented implementation.

6. In 1998, about three million workers, or 18 percent of the Spanish labor force,
were jobless, but employment rose by 400,000 to a record 13.3 million.

7. OECD, *Trends in International Migration*, 2003.

8. OECD, *Trends in International Migration*, 2003, p. 13.

9. Half of all Spaniards lived in cities of 50,000 or more by the mid-1970s.

10. Employer sanctions, implemented in 1988, are enforced by the Labor Ministry.

11. However, in June 1990, when an employer with a textile factory in the Cat-
alonian city of Vic was fined for employing unauthorized migrants, replacement
workers from Andalucia soon quit, and the company moved to Morocco, the source
of its workers.

12. Wayne A. Cornelius, "Spain: The Uneasy Transition From Labor Exporter to
Labor Importer," in Wayne A. Cornelius, Philip L. Martin, and James F. Hollifield,
eds., *Controlling Immigration: A Global Perspective* (Stanford, CA: Stanford University
Press, 2003).

13. There are 10,000 plastic-covered greenhouses in the area that grow fruits and
vegetables on 24,000 hectares (60,000 acres). Most of these greenhouse farmers, who
can achieve gross revenues of $50,000 an acre, do not provide housing for farm work-
ers, so most workers build their housing from plastic or live in derelict buildings

called *cortijos*. Many of the workers are hired in day-labor markets, with legal workers in 2000 reportedly earning $30 per day or $312 per month. The illegal workers, perhaps half of the total, earn less.

14. In 1985–1986, there were 40,000 applications for regularization, and 23, 000 approvals; between June 10 and December 10, 1991, there were 128,000 applications. Among the 110,000 workers legalized in 1991, 21 percent were in domestic services, 15 percent in construction, and 14 percent in agriculture; the sectoral shares were similar for the 43,000 workers legalized in 1996.

15. Joaquín Arango, "Becoming a Country of Immigration at the End of the Twentieth Century: The Case of Spain," in Russell King, Gabriella Lazaridis, and Charalambos Tsardanidis, eds., *Eldorado or Fortress?—Migration in Southern Europe* (London: Macmillan, 2000), p. 259

16. Arango, "Becoming a Country of Immigration," p. 264 reported that in 1995, a third of migrant workers had long-term work permits, a quarter had less-than-one-year permits, and the rest had other types of permits.

17. Most of the Moroccans and other Africans paid $1,000 or more in 2001–2002 to be taken by smugglers in groups of thirty to forty across the Strait of Gibraltar. As soon as they arrive, most African migrants head for major cities such as Madrid and Barcelona—44 percent of the illegal migrants who were legalized in 2000 were in the Madrid and Barcelona areas.

18. Some pregnant women believe that if they give birth in the Canary Islands or Spain, they will be allowed to stay. However, Spanish law requires babies to have at least one Spanish parent to obtain automatic Spanish citizenship.

19. The *contingente* system expanded an existing program that allowed the entry of such people as English-language teachers and farm workers.

20. The first guest worker agreement was signed with Morocco on September 30, 1999. Morocco's minister of labor, Khalid Alioua, said the agreement was "the first agreement of this type. It is an important agreement . . . it was signed with a country that is a member of the Schengen area [and] introduces a new approach in managing migration into Europe. . . . [Spain] admits workers into the European space, even on the temporary basis. Therefore, it is responsible toward other European nations." Morocco hoped to conclude similar agreements with Italy, Belgium, the Netherlands, and France.

21. Only 3,900 of the 10,000 stable permits were granted, but over 100,000 permits were granted to foreigners, suggesting that most are granted outside the *contingente* system.

22. Cornelius, "Spain: The Uneasy Transition," 2003.

23. The empire of Mali in the 1300s stretched from present-day Senegal to Nigeria, with Timbuktu as its center of commerce and Islamic culture. Mali means "hippopotamus"; Bamako means "crocodile pond."

24. The Niger River begins in the southwest of Guinea and makes an arc through Mali before flowing into Niger and Nigeria—near Mopti, Mali, the Niger River creates an inland delta, which is an important source of fish.

25. Konare has won praise for promoting women to senior public positions, speaking on national television about the HIV/AIDS crisis and the need to use condoms, and pressing for laws that would grant women equal inheritance rights with men, who are strongly favored under current law. After stepping down from the presidency, he assumed leadership of the African Union.

26. U.S. GDP is $10 trillion, or about $27 billion a day.

27. About 90 percent of manufacturing is accounted for by state enterprises, and most state enterprise workers belong to unions. The national minimum wage rate, set in 1994, is approximately $40 (CFA26,000 francs—CFA700 = $1) per month; the normal legal workweek is 40 hours (45 hours for agricultural employees).

28. There were an estimated 10,000 sub-Saharan Blacks in France in the 1960s, 80,000 in 1975, and 320,000 in 1992.

29. Sally E. Findley, Dieudonne Ouedraogo, and Nassour Ouaidou, "From Seasonal Migration to International Migration: An Analysis of the Factors Affecting the Choices Made by Families of the Senegal River Valley," in African Population Conference/Congres Africain de Population, Dakar, Senegal, November 7–12, 1988, vol. 2 (Liege, Belgium: International Union for the Scientific Study of Population [IUSSP], 1988), pp. 4.3.39–53.

30. The hairdressing shop was the second business tried, and it employed five people to give haircuts for CFA 1000 ($1.45). The car parts importer buys old cars in Europe for $200 each, sends workers from Mali to remove engines and other components, and ships the parts in containers to Mali at a cost of about $400—he employs twelve people. The dressmaker employs fourteen to twenty employees to stamp imported cloth with traditional designs and make dresses for Malians, especially abroad. The sand dredging involves dugouts moving sand twenty to twenty-five km and then sifting it for sale—the returned migrant had ten boats, and twenty to thirty workers, but needed a truck to expand operations.

31. Total remittances should include both categories. For example, Mexico reported most of its $6.5 billion in 1998 under worker remittances, while the Philippines, which had a total $5.1 billion, reported most of its remittances under compensation of employees. Between 1992 and 1998, remittances rose by 76 percent in Mexico and by 102 percent in the Philippines.

32. Cote d'Ivoire, a country of 15 million, with a GDP per capita of $670, is half urban, and experienced unprecedented instability and uncertainty in the 1990s. Felix Houphouet-Boigny was the president of Cote d'Ivoire from 1960 to 1993, and Ivory Coast became one of Africa's few stable and economically successful countries, exporting cocoa, coffee, timber, and tropical fruits. Houphouet-Boigny provided stability, but also borrowed heavily in the late 1970s, in part to build a capital at Yamoussoukro, in the central part of the country, the village where he was born. It includes the Basilica of Notre Dame de la Paix, one of the largest churches in the world.

Agriculture accounts for 25 percent of GDP and employs 80 percent of the labor force. Immigrants from Burkina Faso, Guinea, Mali, and other neighboring countries are seasonal workers on cocoa and coffee plantations, and some settled in Abidjan, population 2.5 million—an estimated one-third of the Ivory Coast's population are immigrants. Relative harmony between immigrants and local ethnic groups ended after the 1993 death of Houphouet-Boigny, who had encouraged immigration; immigrants are about 15 percent of residents. Houphouet-Boigny's successor, Henri Konan Bedie, adopted the philosophy of "Bviorite or ivoirite" or preferential rights for "pure" Ivorians, which aroused opposition to immigrants. Burkina Faso reported that 300,000 migrants returned from the Ivory Coast in January–February 2001.

Commodity prices fell and political unrest increased in the late 1980s and 1990s. Alassane Dramane Ouattara, a Muslim from the northern part of the country who was prime minister when Houphouet-Boigny died, was accused of having forged national identity papers and blocked from running for president in 1999. Ivory Coast, previously known as the "West African Miracle," has been in a political crisis since the country's first military coup toppled the government of President Henri Konan in December 1999. The subsequent military dictator, General Robert Guei, was himself overthrown by a popular revolt just ten months later, after attempting to rig presidential elections. The winner of the disputed elections, long-time opposition party leader Laurent Gbagbo, was declared president.

Gbagbo's supporters clashed with a rival opposition party called the Rally of Republicans, whose leader, Alassane Ouattara, was prevented from running on the grounds that he might be a foreigner. Ouattara says he is an Ivorian, but admitted using a Burkina Faso passport in some of his travels. A 1994 change in law requires presidential candidates to be born in the Ivory Coast to parents both born there as well.

Christians dominate in the center and south, and Muslims in the north. Most Ivory Coast residents live along the southeastern coastal strip, which is approximately 100 km deep and includes oil palm, coconut, pineapple, banana, and rubber plantations. Further inland and to the west, occupying much of the southern half of the country, is where the most cocoa and coffee are grown, mostly by family farmers, together with the domestic food staples such as rice, cassava, plantain, yams, and maize. In the northern half of the country, cotton, sugar, millet, sorghum, groundnuts, and maize are grown.

Ivory Coast accounts for 43 percent of the world's cocoa supply (1.3 million tons), and is a leading producer of robusta coffee (300,000 tons)—cocoa and coffee accounted for 42 percent of export revenue in 1999. Prices have been freed, and for cocoa were CFAfr325/kg in 2000–2001, CFAfr200–225/kg for coffee, and CFAfr201/kg in 2000–2001 for cotton. After migrants were driven out of the country in January–February 2001, some farmers complained that they could not hire enough seasonal farm workers. One farmer said that he wanted thirty workers on his three hectares of cocoa, six hectares of coffee and eighty hectares of oil palm, but could find only ten. Cocoa is harvested between October and April, with seasonal workers often promised CFA120,000 ($160) for the season.

33. Most of the group traveled to Senegal. About 20 percent of the residents of Senegal, a country of 10 million with a GDP of $5 billion, a per capita income at $500 in 2000, or $800 at PPP, live in Dakar. About 64 percent of those fifteen and older are illiterate, and life expectancy is fifty-two years. Even though 47 percent of

the population lives in urban areas, formal employment is limited—77 percent of the labor force is in agriculture, 16 percent in services, and 7 percent in industry—Senegal is third behind South Africa and Cote D'Ivoire in sub-Saharan Africa in its level of industrial development.

The Parti socialiste (PS) governed Senegal from independence in 1960 until March 2000, when President Abdou Diouf (1981–2000) was defeated by the veteran opposition politician, Abdoulaye Wade, who got a new constitution approved in January 2001 that dissolved the PS-dominated Assemblee nationale (Parliament). In April 2001, the electoral alliance led by President Wade's Parti democratique senegalais (PDS) won a very large majority. In rural areas, *marabouts* (spiritual leaders) of the Islamic brotherhoods (*turuq*) are powerful.

There are Arabic-speaking Mauritanians in Senegal, but 200,000 were deported in 1989 after a border flare-up. There was tension again in 2000, when differences over a controversial water project on the Senegal River almost led to the expulsion of all Senegalese from Mauritania.

The area inland from Dakar, stretching up towards St. Louis, is the traditional groundnut basin and contains around 40 percent of Senegal's cultivated land. The major crop is groundnuts, with almost 1 million tons produced in 2000–2001. The fishing industry is Senegal's largest source of foreign exchange, constituting 30 percent of total merchandise exports in 1998, as well as the second most important source of employment. Gross tourism receipts reached CFAfr101bn (US$164m) in 1999, making the sector Senegal's second biggest foreign exchange earner, after fish.

CHAPTER SEVEN

✑

The Americas

Whereas immigration to and within Europe affects numerous destination countries, the largest recipient by far of migrants in North America is the United States. Canada, by contrast, has fewer absolute numbers of immigrants, but they form a higher proportion of Canada's population. What distinguishes the North American case is the long history of immigration, with both the United States and Canada traditional countries of immigration. In addition, a number of major source countries of migration to the United States are also transit countries for migrants seeking access to the U.S. labor market. Such countries as the Dominican Republic and Mexico also host migrants from within the region, generally neighboring countries. The Regional Migration Conference, also known as the Puebla Process, is one of the most highly developed mechanisms to promote cooperation. It involves all of the countries of North America and Central America, as well as the Dominican Republic (DR). Cooperative Efforts to Manage Migration (CEME) conducted site visits in the Dominican Republic, focusing on U.S.-DR cooperation as well as the DR's response to Haitian migration, and the United States and Mexico, focusing on border relations.

Dominican Republic

The Caribbean island of Hispaniola is divided into two quite different countries, the Dominican Republic and Haiti. Emigration pressures from the Dominican Republic are often described as "structural," suggesting that foreign investment and the creation of factory jobs in export-processing zones or services would not reduce the desire of many Dominicans to emigrate. The Dominican Republic is often described as a transnational society—one in nine residents lives abroad, and many shuttle between New York City or Boston and the Dominican Republic in a lifestyle characterized by work in the United States and vacation or retirement in the Dominican Republic: "Over there (U.S.) is the country of work. This is the country of the heart."

The central issues explored in the March 2002 visit included the economy, Haitian-DR migration, and transnationalism. The DR economy grew rapidly in the 1990s—6 to 8 percent per year—as thousands of especially rural women found sewing jobs in free-trade zones. But why have emigration pressures remained so high despite rapid job creation? Are emigration and remittances substitutes for socio-economic reforms, notably in the education system and the labor market? Do remittances, which account for almost 10 percent of the DR's $20 billion GDP, increase or decrease the desire to emigrate?

Hispaniola is a relatively small island shared by peoples with different origins, histories, and languages. The populations of the DR and Haiti are each 8 to 9 million. Some 500,000 to 800,000 Haitian nationals live in the DR, equivalent to almost 10 percent of Haiti's population. What are the impacts of Haitian immigration on the DR, and on the desire of Dominicans to emigrate? Finally, the DR is simultaneously a country of emigration, transit migration, and immigration. About 1 million Dominican nationals now reside abroad, mostly in the United States. The DR is an important transit country for migrants, with many non-Dominicans entering the DR in an effort to reach the United States or Europe. Finally, the DR is an immigration country, attracting up to 1 million Haitian immigrants. Does the DR represent a new era in which middle-income developing countries become destinations for migrants well before their own economically motivated migration stops?

Population and Economy

The Dominican Republic (population 8 million, projected 12 million in 2025) and Haiti (8 million; projected 11 million in 2025) share the island of Hispaniola, the second largest of the West Indies, comprising 30,000 square miles, about the size of South Carolina, which has 4 million residents. If current population growth continues, about 23 million people, about half the Caribbean population, will live in Hispaniola in 2025.[1]

The DR occupies the eastern two-thirds of the island. Hispaniola is mountainous, with east-west mountains dividing the DR and creating the

Cibao, a 140-mile long, 10- to 25-mile wide valley that is the heart of DR agriculture. Columbus landed at its western end about Christmas in 1492. Santo Domingo, the Dominican capital, is a city of 2.5 million, almost one-third of DR residents, located on the coastal plain in the south central region of the country.

The Caribbean was one of the first areas of the world that was integrated into a global economy, in that, since the late fifteenth century, the Caribbean imported slaves and immigrants to produce tropical crops grown for export. The French and Spanish colonial administrations shared Hispaniola after 1697, and French Haiti became the richest of the West Indies during the eighteenth century. As of 1800, there were about 500,000 slaves and 75,000 French settlers in Haiti, compared to 40,000 slaves and 10,000 Spanish settlers in the DR. Haitian slaves revolted in 1804, defeated the French colonial government, and occupied all of Hispaniola between 1822 and 1844. Haitian occupation in the DR was harsh. The DR is the only Latin American country that won its independence from an occupying neighbor rather than from a distant colonial power. This history has contributed to continuing tension in DR-Haitian relations.

After 1844, the DR experienced a series of strongman dictators, a brief return to Spanish rule, and achieved independence in 1865. However, DR dictators ran up large debts to U.S. lenders and found it necessary to grant the foreign investors economic concessions in exchange for loans to keep them in power. When DR leaders threatened not to repay the loans, the U.S. government intervened between 1916 and 1924 to ensure that the debts to U.S. creditors were paid.

Rafael Trujillo came to power in 1930 and pursued an import-substitution manufacturing strategy. He also controlled two-thirds of DR sugar production, and in 1960, the companies Trujillo and his family controlled employed about 45 percent of DR workers. Trujillo was assassinated in 1961. A leftist, Juan Bosch, was elected president, prompting some emigration by those fearing "communism." Bosch was ousted by the military, and when his friends tried to restore him to power in 1965, the United States intervened militarily, and Joaquin Balaguer, Trujillo's press secretary, was elected president in 1966. Balaguer was president from 1966 to 1978, and he implemented policies favoring his rural supporters and sugar production, which encouraged some urban residents to emigrate. Antonio Guzman's Partido Revolucionario Dominicano (PRD) came to power in 1978, but Balaguer was re-elected in 1986, and this time Balaguer favored the development of export-processing zones (maquiladoras) to provide jobs.

Balaguer was accused of preventing a free election in 1994, and served only two years before a new election was held in 1996. Leonel Fernandez (a U.S. citizen who grew up in New York City) and the Partido de la Liberacion Dominicana (PLD) won it.[2] In 2000, Hipolito Mejia, another U.S. citizen, of the Partido Revolucionario Dominicano (PRD) was elected president. Mejia launched a *paquetazo social* (social package) in Spring 2001 to improve water, sewer, and other services in low-income DR communities— 25 percent of DR residents have below-poverty-level incomes. Mid-term elections were scheduled for May 2002, and presidential elections in 2004.[3] There are fifteen to twenty political parties, with the major parties including the PRD and PLD as well as Balaguer's Partido Reformista Social Cristiano (PRSC) and the Bloque Independiente Pena Gomista (BIPG).

The Dominican Republic had a gross domestic product (GDP) of $16 billion in 2000, for a per capita GDP of $1,900; Haiti is poorer—its GDP was $4 billion, or $500 per capita. DR's economy is based on agriculture (sugar), mining (ferro-nickel), textiles, and tourism. The DR exported goods worth $6 billion in 2000, and imported goods worth $10 billion; the deficit was covered in part by $1.5 billion earned from services (tourism) and $1.7 billion in remittances, making remittances 10 percent of DR GDP. Manufacturing accounts for 17 percent of GDP, construction and agriculture 13 percent each, and tourism—transport and hotels and restaurants— accounts for 13 percent of GDP. Remittances play a large role in the DR economy; they averaged $1.8 billion per year in the late 1990s.

The Caribbean colonial islands were never self-sufficient in food—arable land was used to produce high-value export crops and food was imported. This pattern continues today: The leading crops in the DR are sugar, coffee, and cocoa. Sugar cane, concentrated in the eastern DR, is the leading crop and export—about 375,000 tons of sugar were produced in 1999 from 4.5 million tons of sugarcane, a smaller than usual crop because of Hurricane Georges in 1998. There are three main sugar producers—the state-owned Consejo Estatal de Azucar (CEA) and two private companies, the Central Romana Corporation and the Vicini group. All of the sugar industry is to be privatized. Coffee production (93,000 tons in 1999) is expanding, while cocoa production (34,000 tons in 1999) is declining. Nickel and gold mining was suspended several times in the late 1990s because of low world prices.

Most residents of Caribbean countries were employed in agriculture until the 1960s, when there was a push to industrialize. Urbanization was rapid— about 60 percent of Caribbean residents were urban in 2000, when the percentage of urban dwellers varied from 34 percent in Haiti to 62 percent in DR and 75 percent in Cuba. As Dominicans migrated to cities, many were replaced in agriculture by migrants from Haiti—over 90 percent of DR's sugar workers, and two-thirds of the coffee workers, are now Haitians.

One reason why rural-urban migration was so rapid in Caribbean countries was because many of its political leaders were influenced by economist W. Arthur Lewis, winner of the 1979 Nobel Prize in economics. Lewis, born in St. Lucia, believed that agriculture held a reservoir of non-productive labor that could be used to industrialize without reducing agricultural output. In 1954, he wrote an influential article, "Economic Development with Unlimited Supplies of Labor," that argued that rapid population growth in rural areas held down workers' wages, and that the only solution was rapid industrialization.[4]

The DR has two manufacturing sectors—domestic and free zone—with a total of 500,000 employees in 1999. Domestic manufacturing, with 300,000 workers, is dominated by food-processing operations such as grinding sugar cane and the production of non-tradable goods such as cement. "Free zone" refers to fenced-off manufacturing areas where goods are produced for export, and into which imported raw materials and components of the finished products can be brought free of duty. With 200,000 workers, this sector functions like Mexico's *maquiladoras* and is dominated by garment manufacturing.[5] A 1990 survey of problems encountered by U.S. firms with free-trade zone operations in DR emphasized the following: (1) lack of reliable electricity supplies;[6] (2) absenteeism and turnover of workers, due in part to inadequate public transportation for workers; and (3) slow and sometimes corrupt customs officials (Krämer, 1990).

About 90 percent of free-zone exports, some $4.8 billion in 2000, are destined for the United States; free zone imports were $3.1 billion, for $1.7 billion value-added in the DR in the form of workers' wages and utilities, etc.[7] By contrast, nickel exports were worth $140 million, sugar $88 million, tobacco (cigars) $75 million, and cocoa and coffee about $30 million each. The DR peso was linked to the U.S. dollar until 1985—the current exchange rate is 17 pesos to $1. The Central Bank charges a 5 percent exchange rate commission, generating funds for the government.

The DR shifted from a "breakfast economy"—producing sugar, coffee, and cacao—in the late 1980s when sugar prices slumped. The government promoted tourism, which expanded rapidly, from 11,000 beds in 1987 to 52,000 beds in 2000, but occupancy reached only 67 percent. Tourism employed 141,000 workers in hotels, bars, and restaurants in 1999; the leading resort is Puerto Plata on the north coast. Some 2.1 million foreign tourists arrived in 1999; 57 percent were from Europe, and most stayed in all-inclusive hotels owned by international (Spanish) chains. Another 500,000 Dominicans who live overseas visited the DR in 1999.

The DR government employs 350,000 people in a labor force of four million; 70,000 or 20 percent of government employees were fired when the PRD took power in August 2000. About 30 percent of government revenue comes from tariffs and another 25 percent from a value-added tax (VAT).

The DR minimum wage varies by type of employer: for private businesses with a capital valued at over RD$500,000, it is RD$3,415 (US$200) per month, while the public minimum wage is about RD$1,200 (US$71) per month. There are deductions for social security and health benefits, but wages up to RD$10,438 ($614) per month or RD$125,256 ($7,368) per year are exempt from income taxes.[8]

The DR has an unequal distribution of income. The World Bank reported that 26 percent of residents—about two million—were poor in 1998, defined as having an income of less than $2 per day. The World Bank concluded that remittances "do not significantly impact the poor [since] international migration in the DR . . . is mostly a middle class phenomenon and does not play an important role in providing a safety net for the poor or contribute to improvements in equity."

Migration from Hispaniola

Some 3.5 million Caribbean residents immigrated legally to the United States between 1820 and 1998, but most of this migration was recent—half of all Caribbean immigrants were admitted in the 1980s and 1990s. Two-thirds of Dominican immigrants and three-fourths of Haitian immigrants arrived since 1980. Immigration and Naturalization Service (INS) data show that 810,000 Dominicans and 376,000 Haitians have immigrated legally to the United States; 90 percent of these were admitted since 1970, including 40 percent who were admitted in the 1990s. About 200,000 Dominican and 75,000 Haitian nonimmigrants a year have been admitted; some 2,500 Dominicans and 500 Haitians a year were deported.

One of the leading experts on Caribbean migration, Anthony Maingot, argues that trade, aid, and economic growth will not slow emigration from Haiti and the Dominican Republic because migration from Hispaniola is structural: "the direction of the flow might shift occasionally, and the magnitude might also vary, but [emigration] pressures are constant."[9] Maingot emphasizes that Caribbean people have often associated manual labor on their home island with slavery and were eager to go abroad, for example, to build the Panama Canal early in the twentieth century. West Indians who migrated to the United States have often been very successful, as exemplified by former Secretary of State Colin Powell, who is descended from

Jamaican immigrants. Their success in the United States provided anchors for later Caribbean immigrants who followed migration networks from the Caribbean.

Maingot noted that there was little immigration to the United States from the DR before the 1965 changes to U.S. immigration laws, when the U.S. family unification system permitted chain migration. Working-class Dominicans migrated to New York in the 1960s and early 1970s, getting factory jobs and establishing small businesses such as grocery stores (*bodegas*) and remitting money to the DR. The 2000 Census reported that there were 765,000 Dominican-born residents in the United States, including 407,000 in New York City, up from 520,000 in the United States in 1990, 333,000 in New York City.[10]

Some Dominicans try to migrate to the United States illegally by crossing the 60-mile Mona Channel between the Dominican Republic and Puerto Rico in wooden boats called *yolas* for smuggling fees of about $600. American Airlines is the major airline between the DR and the United States, prompting many in the DR to talk of "going AA" to the United States. Those who go legally, go AA by air; the illegal route is sometimes called the other "AA" route to the United States (*agua por delante, agua por detras*—water in front, water in back). Once in Puerto Rico, Dominicans often find jobs at higher wages than they could earn in the DR. Others try to pass themselves off as Puerto Ricans, who are U.S citizens, and take domestic flights to the mainland United States.

The Dominican Navy and the U.S. Border Patrol cooperate to detect *yolas* being built in rural areas of the DR, engines as they are transported to power the *yolas*, and people being taken by bus or truck to board them. During the first nine months of U.S. fiscal year 2001, almost 4,000 people are believed to have traveled by *yola* between the DR and Puerto Rico; the number fell sharply after September 11, 2001. DR nationals are well known as experienced smugglers; Cubans and Chinese are also smuggled from the DR to Puerto Rico and the U.S. Virgin Islands. This DR Navy–U.S. Border Patrol cooperation is considered very successful—some Dominicans complain that the DR Army is much less successful at preventing unauthorized Haitian immigration into the DR than the Navy is in discouraging illegal migration across the Mona Channel.

In addition to emigration from the DR to the United States, there is Dominican migration to Spain, the Netherlands, and Argentina. In 2000, there were an estimated 40,000 Dominicans in Spain, including 14,000 unauthorized Dominicans.

Dominican Transnationalism

At least 10 percent of the nine million persons born in the DR are living in the United States. Like Cuban immigrants, Dominicans are concentrated in a few places—60 percent live in New York City. Since 1996, Dominicans who become naturalized citizens abroad may retain their DR nationality, and their children born abroad may retain Dominican nationality. In 1997, the DR enacted legislation allowing Dominicans with dual nationality to vote in DR elections, prompting many Dominicans running for office in the DR to include campaign stops in New York City. In 2004, dual national Dominicans abroad will be able to vote in DR elections by absentee ballot.

According to the Central Electoral Board (JCE), for the May 2002 elections, 4.6 million Dominicans were eligible to vote, including one million who live abroad.

The editor of the El Caribe newspaper believes that allowing and encouraging dual nationality and absentee voting is a mistake. His reasoning is that DR elections tend to be very close, so that dual nationals abroad—who may have a limited interest in the DR—could hold the balance of power. The same reasoning has been used to argue against regularizing Haitians in the DR, and granting DR nationality to Haitians born in the DR.

DR migrants are considered a leading example of transnationalism, a concept used by some scholars to describe persons with connections and loyalties to two societies. Instead of moving from the DR, learning English, and integrating into the United States, transnational DR migrants may learn English and integrate but retain very close business and personal ties to the DR. Since most DR migrants are working class, the DR is often described as transnationalism from below.

One of the leading scholars of Dominican transnationalism is Peggy Levitt. Her book, The Transnational Villagers, is "about how ordinary people are incorporated into the countries that receive them while remaining active in the places they come from, and about how life in sending and receiving countries changes as a result."[11] Levitt studied Dominicans in Boston and concluded that migrants from Miraflores, a village near the 100,000-resident city of Bani, had far more impact on the village they left behind than on the city to which they moved. In Boston, they were blue-collar factory and service workers or the owners of small corner grocery stores and other service businesses.

Levitt considers the Dominicans to be transmigrants, and uses transnationalism to describe individuals from one country who maintain ties to two or more countries. Transnationalism has been common for executives and professionals employed by multinationals, governments, and news and other organizations. The new transnationalism is from below, as when unskilled immigrants maintain ties to and participate in life in their villages of origin as well as in their destinations. Levitt emphasizes that transnationalism among unskilled Dominicans from Miraflores

- involves both migrants and non-migrants who are affected by the remittances and new ideas that return to the village because of emigration;
- persists because of remittances and "social remittances," new ideas, including new male-female roles;
- leads to new organizations, including more effective political participation at home because of earnings abroad; and
- increases inequalities or contrasts, pushing some up and others down the socioeconomic ladder, depending on access to remittances.

There is a dispute among immigration researchers about whether transnationalism today differs in degree (same concept, but cheaper communication and transportation) or kind (a new desire to maintain ties to both countries) from that at the beginning of the twentieth century; Levitt concludes there is a difference in kind, that today's transnationalism is different and will persist.

The first Miraflores-to-Boston migrants arrived in the 1950s. Many followed, usually illegally, so that by 1994, 60 percent of households in Miraflores received remittances from the United States. Most Miraflores migrants have not fared well economically in Boston. In 1994, half worked part-time in the United States, and many were janitors, though 75 percent had become legal immigrants. On the one hand, DR migrants told Levitt how hard they worked—many had two jobs—and spoke of the discipline that regular U.S. work schedules imposed on them—many were accustomed to farm work. On the other hand, some DR migrants were able to take advantage of the U.S. workers' compensation system and claim payments for false injuries, while others made money dealing drugs. The migrants change—especially the children of migrants, who learned English and became aware of their rights under U.S. child-abuse laws, enabling them to achieve far more independence from their families in the United States than they would have in the DR. Miraflores-to-Boston migration also affected Miraflores residents who did not migrate, as new ideas were introduced by return visitors.

Levitt emphasizes that when parents leave their children to be raised by relatives in the DR, family life becomes a fluid affair, with "multiple mothers" often leading to confusion among children. She contrasts life in Miraflores, where children and adults often spend the day together, with life in Boston, where children may see immigrant parents with two jobs only rarely. The same pessimistic tone surrounds the discussion of schooling. Migration has accentuated differences and rivalries among children in school in Miraflores, and led many not to study hard because they plan to emigrate. Levitt paints a picture of those in Miraflores living off remittances from Boston, or of dreaming of working in Boston for high wages, and concludes that remittances and hopes of emigrating lie behind the refusal of men to work in DR agriculture—Haitians do the farm work in Miraflores. Parents rank their migrant children by how much and how often they send home remittances, and even those without migrant relatives seem to know who made money in the United States working and who made money dealing drugs.

Levitt reports that Dominican prejudices against Blacks seemed to become stronger after a stint in the United States. While in Boston, migrants had little interaction with U.S. Blacks because the social networks they relied on to find work and housing were dominated by Dominicans. Many Dominicans in Boston equated U.S. Blacks with Haitians, who are generally looked down on in the DR. Returned migrants became much less tolerant of bribes and corruption in the DR, such as police stops that required payment of a bribe or charges for government forms or benefits.

Emigration increased migrant incomes, which strengthened the role of migrants in DR politics and community development. In many cases, migrants were surprised to get benefits from the U.S. government without paying bribes, and some who returned wanted to clean up DR politics and governments but were usually unsuccessful. Migrants who were used to getting social services from the church in Boston had to learn to contribute there, as well as to request benefits. Finally, the migrants in Boston created a Miraflores Development Corporation (MDC) to improve the infrastructure at home, relying on migrant contributions to fully or partially fund bridges, parks, and clinics at home in a process that was "in sharp contrast to the corruption and inefficiencies pervading Dominican life." However, the MDC was not able to create the jobs or economic structure that would make additional migration unnecessary.

Levitt concludes that most of the migrants from Miraflores in Boston are oriented to their village of origin, not to the United States. Their U.S. incomes give them more influence at home, but they remain fairly isolated and invisible in the United States. The decisions of the migrants' children about which society they choose to identify with is likely to shape the course of DR-U.S. migration. Transnationalism is a very mixed blessing in this case—it certainly helped some individuals, but did not set in motion changes in Miraflores that make migration self-stopping. Indeed, many of the changes set in motion by migration are likely to lead to more migration from Miraflores. The structure of the Caribbean family—with many women having children with different fathers, each of whom tries to contribute to the support of his children—made many rural families dependent on an often absentee bread-winner, and thus social mores seemed to support continued emigration.

Economic Development Zones

Some 195,000 workers are employed in DR free trade zone (FTZ) factories, and most sew garments—the DR is well-known for producing pants. The San Pedro de Macoris FTZ is a 25-year-old collection of one hundred factories operated by fifty firms that employ about 15,000 workers—it is the economic lifeblood of San Pedro, which is one hour east of Santo Domingo.[12]

Western International Trading is a 25-year-old, five-hundred-employee sewing operation that makes uniforms for U.S. firms such as McDonalds. Workers are guaranteed at least RD$2,490 per month, but most work for piece rate wages—they are paid according to the number of units they sew—and earnings for a 44-hour week average RD$3,200 to RD$4,000 per month ($188 to $235). In addition, employers must contribute 7.5 percent for social security and workers 2.3 percent, and the DR is gradually adding other benefits, including unemployment insurance. Many FTZs have cafeterias that offer employees subsidized meals, such as lunch for 9 pesos.

The sewing-based FTZs are under threat from increased foreign competition. Since NAFTA went into effect in 1994, Mexico has replaced the DR as the chief source of pants in the U.S. market. However, the real threat in the eyes of FTZ managers is China, which can more cheaply produce many of the garments and shoes now produced in the DR. Several shoe firms have already closed their operations in the DR and moved production to China, and the fear is that more FTZ firms will do so.

Under World Trading Organization (WTO) rules, FTZs that allow the import of machinery and materials and the export of finished goods must be phased out by 2005–2007. The FTZs, facing the threat of Chinese entry into the WTO, are seeking two major paths to protection:

- Make the DR more than a sewing country by upgrading machines and operating them more hours to cover the cost of more expensive capital, and move from sewing garments to more electronics and higher value-added products. The challenge to make such an up-wage move is to find trained workers—the DR has one of the poorest education systems in Latin America, and its teachers are frequently on strike.

- Get the DR included in NAFTA or a possible Central American free-trade agreement with Canada and the United States. One Free Trade Agreement (FTA) association has agreed to spend $200,000 to have a U.S. lobbying firm try to get NAFTA privileges extended to the DR. The United States and thirty-three other Western Hemisphere nations (all except Cuba) were committed to establish a Free Trade Area of the Americas by 2005.

The FTZs have done more than create jobs. One leader said that they have fundamentally changed the role of women in the DR. Most FTZ employees are women from rural areas, and their movement to cities in which they have jobs that pay above average wages has empowered them.[13]

Smuggling and Trafficking

The DR is a major source of trafficked women, generally ranked fourth after Thailand, Brazil, and the Philippines in the number of women working overseas in the sex trade, some 50,000 a year, according to the International Organization for Migration (IOM). The tradition of emigrating for work, and the recruitment of maids for foreign jobs, helped to make going abroad for sex work more acceptable than it would otherwise be. Indeed, many Dominican families and communities reportedly accept emigration for prostitution, and women who return with money earned from prostitution abroad are reportedly considered successes at home.

Most women incur debts of several thousand dollars to go to Argentina or Europe as prostitutes. To combat the trafficking of women, the Dominican Government tries to screen women going abroad. Policies to combat the trafficking of women abroad include a rule that women traveling abroad alone must have at least $1,000. IOM and the Dominican State Secretariat for Women are working on an information campaign to warn women of the dangers of prostitution. However, penalties on convicted traffickers are relatively light. In February 2002, a thirty-year-old DR woman convicted of trafficking young Dominican girls to Costa Rica, taking away their passports, and sexually exploiting them was sentenced to five years in prison in Costa Rica.

The INS cooperates with DR immigration authorities to reduce illegal immigration by air to the United States, while the Coast Guard cooperates with the Dominican Navy to reduce the smuggling of migrants across the Mona Passage to Puerto Rico.

Visas

The U.S. consulate in Santo Domingo is the third busiest American consulate after Mexico and the Philippines. It handles about 45,000 immigrant and 100,000 nonimmigrant visa applications a year, and houses representatives of federal agencies that provide benefits such as Social Security payments to those who earned them while in the United States—some 6,000 Social Security checks are distributed in the DR each month.

About 98 percent of DR immigrants arriving lawfully in the United States to live have obtained visas under family unification criteria. The 1996 immigration reforms added criteria for the granting of such visas, including the criterion that the U.S. sponsor of immigrants must earn at least 125 percent of the U.S. poverty line for the U.S. sponsor and the immigrants being sponsored taken together. Since many Dominicans in the United States have low incomes, it is hard for them to satisfy this 125 percent income criterion. In such cases, the U.S. consulate accepts applications for immigrant visas, but does not grant the visa until the income and other criteria are satisfied. About 35 percent of the applicants receive immigrant visas the first time they apply.

There is also a 60 percent rejection rate for nonimmigrant visas, which are typically requests for tourist visas to visit friends and relatives in the United States. U.S. law requires applicants for nonimmigrant visas to prove that they do not intend to immigrate to the United States, that they plan to return to the DR, which means that they generally need to prove they have employment and/or assets in the DR.

To apply for U.S. visas, applicants pay application fees at local banks and are given appointment times. While standing at windows in front of U.S. consular officers, they are interviewed. Consular officers are expected to conduct four immigrant visa interviews per hour, twenty-five in a six-hour day. During their interviews, applicants are expected to produce the documentation needed to secure the visa for which they are applying.

Consular officers believe there is a great deal of fraud in applications for immigrant and nonimmigrant visas. For example, many U.S. sponsors claim non-existent family ties to the Dominicans they are sponsoring, so the consular officer may require additional information, such as a blood test paid for by the applicant, to prove a family tie. Many applicants present "false proof" of DR employment and assets. Document fraud is common in the DR. The DR is the birthplace of 25 percent of major league baseball players, and many young DR players present fraudulent birth certificates that make them appear to be one to three years younger than they are, and hence more attractive to U.S. teams.

Haiti-DR Migration

Haiti is the poorest country in the Western Hemisphere, with a per capita income of $200 to $500 a year. It was not always so. Haiti was the richest

French colony in the late 1700s, and remained richer than the DR in the nineteenth and early twentieth centuries. Thus, American diplomats in the 1930s posted to the DR lived in Port-au-Prince and traveled periodically to the DR.

Beginning in the 1950s, Haiti launched an industrialization program that appeared to achieve some success. For instance, a number of factories were created to produce manufactured goods for export. Dictatorship and corruption led to a popular revolt and the election of Jean-Bertrand Aristide as president in 1991. Aristide was removed from the presidency by a military coup in 1991 and restored to power as the result of a U.S. military intervention in 1994;[14] his term ended in 1995. In 2000, Aristide was re-elected, even though he did not campaign. He resigned (or was ousted, depending on perspective) in February 2004. Interim President Boniface Alexandre, as Chief of the Supreme Court, constitutionally succeeded Aristide. Interim Prime Minister Gerald Latortue was chosen to be head of state by an extra constitutional Council of Eminent Persons. The future stability of Haiti is still in doubt. The UN Stabilization Mission in Haiti (MINUSTAH), composed of about 8,000 peacekeepers, attempts to maintain civil order in Haiti.

Haiti is the most rural country in the Caribbean. Most rural Haitians live in 300-person lakous, clusters of fifty to sixty houses dominated by extended families. The 30,000 lakous have become progressively poorer as land has been subdivided, and the amount of arable land declined as the number of farms rose—marginal land cleared of trees soon proved too poor to grow crops, and the countryside is undergoing desertification. Desertification in the countryside encouraged many rural residents to move to the capital city, Port-au-Prince, and to emigrate to the DR, the Bahamas,[15] and the United States. Most experts are very pessimistic about a revival of the rural Haitian economy that would lead to stay-at-home development.

Haiti had about 100,000 jobs in *maquiladora*-type light assembly factories in the early 1990s, but the 1991 coup and subsequent embargo reduced the number to 16,000 by 1996–1997. In the early 1980s, *maquiladora* assembly operations had employed 60,000 workers in mostly Haitian-owned operations, while the DR had only 25,000 *maquiladora* jobs.[16] *Maquiladora* employment shrank in Haiti and expanded in the DR, so that DR had 130,000 such jobs in 1990. Haitian politics and its economy are centered in Port-au-Prince, which has 90 percent of government employees.

The Dominican Republic and Haiti share a 186-mile or 330-km border, and the border region is the poorest part of both countries. There has been discussion of joint development projects in the border area. The DR government would like them to be financed by industrial countries that forgive the

DR's external debts, and then the DR would instead divert the interest payments on the forgiven debt to a trust fund for border area development. However, cooperative DR-Haiti development is complicated by a troubled history and unauthorized Haitian-DR migration, which is abetted by corrupt elements of the DR military, responsible for guarding DR borders.

Historical incidents are recalled frequently. Dominicans recall Haiti's invasion of the Dominican Republic to abolish slavery in 1822; February 27, 1844, DR's Independence Day, marks the end of Haitian, not Spanish rule. Haitians recall that, in 1937, Dominican dictator Rafael Trujillo ordered 17,000 to 30,000 Haitians killed all over the DR by the Dominican army, including at the shallow Río Masacre (Massacre River) that separates DR and Haiti.

The massacres of the 1930s slowed Haitian-DR migration, but it soon resumed because, in the words of Haitian writer Jean Price-Mars, "The density of our population impels the Haitian workers, as if driven by a mechanical force, toward the neighboring land."[17] Anthony Maingot noted that Cuba expelled many Haitian workers in the early 1930s, and that Cuba and DR shared a desire to stay "white," which meant that Haitians were accepted as guest workers but not as settlers. DR leaders often talk of a silent invasion from Haiti and assert that Haitian immigration threatens the "three pillars" of DR society: Spanish ancestry, Hispanic culture, and Catholicism. The best estimate is that 10 to 12 percent of Dominicans are Black, 8 to 9 percent are white, and 80 percent are mulatto.

When agriculture in rural Haiti was still viable and when the major employment for Haitians in the DR was sugar harvesting, Haiti-DR migration was a seasonal phenomenon. Between 1952 and 1966, Haitian-DR migration for sugarcane production was regulated by a bilateral agreement that was renewed informally between 1966 and 1983–1984. However, as agriculture declined in Haiti, more Haitians settled in the DR to work in long-season crops such as coffee and rice and for small farmers; many Haitians eventually moved to urban areas for construction and service jobs. The DR seems to be trying to curb the official recruitment of Haitian workers: during the 1999–2000 season, for the first time since 1952, government-owned DR sugar mills hired no Haitian cane cutters. With the privatization of DR sugar, there are expected to be no new Haitian cane workers admitted legally in 2002.

Haiti's embassy in the Dominican Republic estimated in 2001 that there were 1.1 to 1.5 million Haitians in the Dominican Republic; some DR politicians also talk of 1 to 1.5 million Haitians in the DR.[18] The numbers are probably too high—500,000 to 800,000 Haitians in the DR is more likely, and the World Bank estimated there were 800,000 Haitians in the DR in

1998. According to the International Organization for Migration, there are an estimated 600,000 to 800,000 Haitians in the DR, with a like number in the United States, 60,000 in France, 40,000 in Canada, 40,000 in the Bahamas, and another 40,000 in other Caribbean islands.

During the 1990s, as Haiti-DR migration rose, there were more complaints about the treatment of Haitians in the DR from NGOs as well as from the Haitian government. Haiti and the DR established a migration commission, which has met six times between 1996 and 2002 and reached three agreements:

- A June 1998 Memorandum of Understanding that laid out the goals of the bilateral discussions, viz., to reach agreement on the management of migration flows, contracting, repatriation, regularization, and unauthorized migration.
- A December 1999 agreement that called for reforms such as repatriation only during daytime hours, removals of families as groups, and the designation of four specific border cities for repatriations.
- A 2001 agreement on labor contracting includes arrangements for Haitians in the DR to obtain documentation of their nationality from the Haitian embassy. Beginning in 2002, Haiti is to establish mobile centers in the DR to issue Haitian documents at no charge to Haitian adults in the DR who bring along two witnesses to testify that the person seeking the Haitian ID is Haitian. Haiti is also reducing the cost of a Haitian passport from $70 to $35 for Haitians in the DR.

Most Haitian migrants in the DR are men from rural areas whose first Dominican jobs are in agriculture or construction. Traditionally, 15,000 to 25,000 Haitians per year were recruited to work in the DR as sugarcane cutters, but Haitian migrants have spread to other sectors of DR agriculture, including rice and coffee. Most Haitians in the DR live in urban areas, and Haitians dominate among construction workers.

According to the DR government, there are about 2,000 Haitians lawfully resident in the DR, and another 2,000 Haitians have been recognized as refugees. What should be done about the other 500,000 to 800,000 Haitians living in the DR? IOM and many migration experts recommend regularization or legalization followed by a guest worker program. Their hope is that legal status would facilitate the integration of settled Haitians in the DR, and that a guest worker program would divert to governments the fees that now go to smugglers, which would use them to promote development.

There are periodic crackdowns on illegal Haitians in the DR, including the removal of 15,000 Haitians in 1997. Most Dominicans favor the removal of Haitians: a 1998 Gallup poll found that 45 percent of Dominicans favored deporting illegal Haitians and an additional 17 percent favored repatriating all Haitians, legal or illegal. President Mejía asserted that the Dominican Republic "was experiencing a peaceful invasion of Haitians." His spokesperson said: "That statement has nothing to do with racist sentiments. It's a fact. . . . The roundups . . . will continue to be done against illegal immigrants."[19]

In January-February 2000, during such a crackdown, the DR deported 2,000 Haitians a month, and thousands of Haitians reportedly returned voluntarily so that they would not have their possessions taken away by Dominican soldiers. Typically, the Dominican military drives through Haitian settlements when the sugarcane cutting season ends in February–March, and loads onto trucks for deportation all those without birth certificates or work permits. After the 2000 crackdown, Dominican farmers[20] and other employers complained of labor shortages—an estimated 80 percent of DR construction workers are Haitians, earning $5 to $8 a day.

It is very hard for Haitians and those of Haitian descent born in the Dominican Republic (Dominoco-Haitians) to get DR documents. The DR constitution provides citizenship to persons born in DR, but not to children born to parents who are "in transit" in the DR; the DR government considers Haitians to be "in transit." Ivan Pedna, former director of Haitian migration at the Dominican Immigration Department, says, "We are not violating their human rights. The constitution says they are in transit. They aren't Dominicans."[21] The result is confusion, with some Haitians obtaining DR papers, allegedly in exchange for supporting particular political parties and other Haitians unable to obtain them.

The present-day DR government is attempting to relax policy toward Haitians. In July 2001, the DR government announced that it would no longer require students to provide birth certificates to attend school, thus opening both primary and secondary schools to unauthorized Haitian children. This is considered an important step to allow Haitians to help themselves with education, but Vice President and Education Minister Milagros Ortiz Bosch noted that the DR will eventually have to deal properly with Haitians: "Dominican laws already guarantee the right to an education to all children. But if you want to get a job, open a bank account, travel, vote, simply be a citizen, you need a birth certificate."[22]

Thus, there is a debate between those who want to regularize and those who want to remove unauthorized and quasi-authorized Haitians. Many opinion leaders, as well as the World Bank, emphasize that in order to help raise wages for unskilled Dominicans the influx of Haitians must be slowed.

The *El Caribe* newspaper is among those who argue that the DR should do more to prevent illegal Haitian migration. *El Caribe* in January 2002 argued that "those who employ Haitians, primarily sugar cane mills, rice plantations, coffee plantations, construction engineers, and the military, would make less profit if they had to hire Dominican workers, invest in automation or modernize their harvests." The editorial concludes: "The fact that our governments have favored landholders, engineers and the military over unskilled laborers explains why our politicians talk so much of the presence of Haitians, but do little to confront the situation."[23]

In fact, there are some 250,000 residents of *bateys* in the DR, of which 65 to 75 percent are Haitians. *Bateys* were originally company-constructed housing for year-round and seasonal employees of sugarcane plantations. As the work force changed from Dominicans to Haitians and conditions in Haiti deteriorated, more Haitians began to live year-round in the DR in *bateys*. Most *bateys* have some electricity and some have schools to educate the children among the 300–1,000 residents of the *batey*.

The *batey* visited in March 2002 had about 450 residents, half of whom were Dominicans. There was barracks-style housing for solo men who cut cane—five to a room. In addition, there was family housing that consisted of tin-covered shacks. Water was obtained from several fountains, some of the shacks received electricity by tapping into the main lines, and sewage flowed openly between the shacks. There was a school built several years ago with U.S. AID funds, but it has never opened. UNICEF had a small operation dispensing medicines.

The DR economy has traditionally been based on sugar production. A visit to a sugar mill that was built in 1885 and last upgraded in the 1950s showed an abundance of old machinery and overstaffing. Mill jobs were traditionally given to workers who supported the winning political party, and the FTZ managers said that the workers earned less than those employed in FTZ factories, about RD$2,500 per month compared to RD$3,200 to RD$4,000, but the mill workers also worked less.

The mill was privatized in 1999, and leased to Grupo Consuelo, a corporation that operates five other mills, and remains the property of the DR government. Grupo Consuelo, which has pledged to upgrade the mill's technology, grinds about 300,000 tons of sugarcane per year in this mill, produced from 15,000 hectares of cane, so that yields are about 20 tons per hectare, or eight tons per acre—Florida sugarcane yields, by contrast, are 35 to 40 tons per acre. The usual conversion ratio of cane to sugar is 12 percent—this mill had an 8 percent cane to sugar yield, which Grupo Consuelo raised to 10 percent by automating temperature controls in the furnaces and replacing outmoded equipment. The mill's "raw" sugar is refined, and some of it is exported to the United States.

Most sugarcane is cut by hand. The piece rate for cutting cane in March 2002 was RD$45 a ton ($2.60 a ton), and the Haitian migrants who cut most of the cane average two to three tons a day. In addition to cutting the cane, cutters must load it onto field carts that are pulled by tractors to a transfer station where the cane is stacked by hand into rail cars or trucks to be taken to the mill for grinding.

Haiti and the United States

The United States spent $2 to $3 billion on Haiti in the 1990s, or $2,500 to $3,750 per Haitian—$400 million of this cost was incurred in 1994 to interdict and care for or return about 30,000 Haitians who left the country in boats. U.S. government statements on Haiti often lament: "Haiti must deal with challenges more numerous, complex and deep-rooted than any other nation in the Western Hemisphere. . . . Haiti has the lowest annual per capita income and the highest child mortality rate; the highest illiteracy rate and the lowest life expectancy age. Haiti's fledgling democracy is a brave attempt to overcome decades of despotism and dictatorship."[24] The Haitian government's revenue comes from taxes on imports and telephone calls as well as foreign aid and $700 million a year in remittances.

The U.S. national interest in Haiti is frequently expressed in terms of preventing unwanted migration: "our clear national interests with respect to Haiti certainly are driven in significant part by the geography of Haiti, its proximity to the southern coast of the United States, the experience of what happened when there is a brutal, repressive regime and Haitians fled Haiti in huge numbers and we were not on humanitarian grounds able to put them back into Haiti. So that very clearly drives our national interest."[25] On December 4, 1997, the *New York Times* reported that the departing UN troops were: "leaving behind a country nearly as poor, prostrate, and paralyzed as when they stepped in to help."

Between 1991 and 1994, many Haitians fled the country in small boats, aiming for Florida, about 735 miles north, or the Bahamas, about 680 miles north. Some 67,140 Haitian migrants were stopped at sea by the U.S. Coast Guard, including 38,000 in 1992 and 24,000 in 1994. The United States practiced a policy of direct returns, without hearing asylum claims, from 1992 to 1994. As conditions worsened in Haiti in 1994, and efforts to restore Aristide to the presidency grew more serious, the United States reversed course, eventually providing temporary protection to fleeing Haitians at Guantanamo Naval Base. With the return of Aristide to Haiti, the vast majority of Haitians repatriated. Since then, the number of Haitians intercepted in boats leaving for the United States has been about 2,000 per year. With the new political instability and Aristide's departure in 2004, boat departures appeared likely to increase again. However, the Bush administration re-enforced the direct return policy for interdicted boats and mandatory deten-tion for all Haitians who did make it to the United States. These policies were justified as a security measure that would allow the Coast Guard to con-centrate on terrorist movements instead of rescue operations of Haitian boat people, but the same policy was not applied to Cubans coming to the United States by boat.

Mexico-U.S. Migration

CEME met in San Diego in January 2003 to discuss migration between Mex-ico and the United States, countries that were "distant neighbors" for much of the twentieth century. Mexico had an import-substitution economic model until the mid-1980s, and the major economic link between Mexico and the United States was the migration of rural Mexicans to rural America. During this time of limited trade, the treatment of legal Mexican guest work-ers on U.S. farms was often the source of friction between the Mexican and U.S. governments.

Mexico-U.S. relations changed in the mid-1980s, after Mexico suffered a severe economic crisis and reoriented its economic policies, seeking to emu-late the East Asian tiger economies by fostering export-oriented growth. The United States in the mid-1980s sought to reduce illegal immigration by im-posing sanctions on employers who knowingly hired unauthorized workers and by legalizing 2.3 million unauthorized Mexicans in the United States (al-most 3 percent of the Mexican population). As Mexican economic policies changed, they accelerated changes underway in Mexico, including rural-urban migration, and one result was increased legal and illegal Mexico-U.S. migration, since the employer sanctions legislated by the U.S. Congress in the 1980s were not enforced effectively.

During the 1990s, both Mexico-U.S. economic integration and Mexico-U.S. migration increased. Economic integration, symbolized by the North American Free Trade Agreement (NAFTA) that went into effect on January 1, 1994, helped bilateral trade to triple to almost $725 million per day.[26] The Mexican-born U.S. population doubled in the 1990s, from 4.5 million to 9 million, and led to reactions in both countries. The United States launched Operation Gatekeeper in 1994, a border control strategy designed to deter unauthorized migrants with more border patrol agents, physical barriers in the form of fences, and new lights along some otherwise dark border areas near urban areas. In 2000, the newly elected Mexican government of President Vicente Fox declared improvement of the status of Mexicans in the United States its top foreign policy priority.

The purpose of the 2003 seminar was to explore the unfolding process of Mexico-U.S. integration and migration and to ask questions such as whether economic forces are in place to stabilize and eventually reduce Mexico-U.S. migration, whether Mexico can upgrade worker skills and *maquiladora* (foreign-owned assembly plant) technologies fast enough to create jobs in Mexico for young Mexicans entering the labor force, and whether U.S. policies to facilitate legal migration and legitimate flows of goods and reduce unauthorized migration are having their desired effects.

The discussion centered on three themes. First was the difficulty of developing alternative employment in Mexico for people in regions that have been linked for decades to U.S. jobs. Instead of seeking upward mobility at home, many rural Mexicans find it easiest to do what their parents did— migrate to the United States. Second, employment in Mexican *maquiladoras* peaked in 2000 and has since fallen by 15 percent and seems likely to decrease more as *maquiladoras* that compete largely on price are closed and the assembly work moved to even lower-wage countries such as China and Indonesia. Third, there is a political consensus in the United States to try to prevent the entry of unauthorized foreigners, but no consensus on stepping up employer sanctions enforcement.

Evolution of Mexico-U.S. Migration

Spaniards arrived in Mexico in 1519, when there were five million to 25 million Native American (Indian) residents. Many of the Indians died in fighting and from disease, and the population of present-day Mexico was estimated to be one million in 1600. By 1800, Mexico and the United States had similar populations, six million, and Mexico's GDP per capita was about half that of the United States. An 1848 Mexico-U.S. war ended with the Treaty of Guadalupe Hildalgo, under which the United States acquired most of the southwestern states, including California. By 1900, the United States was far more populous than Mexico, with 76 million people compared to 15 million in Mexico, and U.S. per capita income was eight times higher than in Mexico. In 2000, the United States had 282 million residents and a GDP per capita of $34,300, while Mexico had 100 million residents and a GDP per capita of $5,100, a 7 to 1 ratio.

As a result of civil war and disease between 1910 and 1920, Mexico had only 20 million people in 1940, when a population explosion began that increased the number to 70 million by 1980. Mexico in the early 1970s had one of the world's fastest population growth rates, 3.5 percent a year, and the average Mexican woman had 6.2 children, which prompted the World Bank to project a Mexican population of 250 million by 2075. However, in April 1972, Mexico embarked on what became a very successful family planning campaign that sharply reduced fertility and population growth to 2.9 babies per woman and a 2.1 percent population growth rate in 2002.

High Mexican birth rates from the 1940s through the 1970s produced rapid labor force growth and rising emigration pressures, but it was the U.S. government that set Mexico-U.S. migration flows in motion. In 1942, the U.S. government authorized a "temporary wartime emergency" measure known as the Bracero program that allowed U.S. farmers to recruit farm workers from Mexico. After the wartime emergency ended in 1945, U.S. farm employers lobbied for continuation of this program, and succeeded in extending it for nearly twenty years, to 1964. In the 1950s, when 300,000 to 400,000 Mexicans per year arrived to do farm work, the U.S. government made it easy for even illegal Mexicans in the United States to become legal farm workers—the process of legalizing such workers, even in U.S. government publications, was termed "drying out the wetbacks."[27] Between one and two million Mexicans gained U.S. work experience before the Bracero program was terminated as part of the civil rights movement of the early 1960s, after U.S. unions, churches, and Latino groups convinced Congress that the presence of Braceros in the fields held down farm wages and impeded the upward economic mobility of U.S. Hispanics.

Mexico during the Bracero period pursued a capital-intensive, import-substitution economic policy marked by rapid aggregate economic growth, formal sector jobs, and urbanization, but growth had fewer significant poverty-reduction effects outside the three largest cities: Mexico City, Guadalajara, and Monterrey. U.S. farmers employing Braceros had to pay transportation costs from the place of recruitment to their farms, and Mexicans improved their chances of being selected as Braceros if they moved to the Mexico-U.S. border. Many did, which resulted in very rapid growth of then-small border towns and cities such as Tijuana and left thousands of Mexicans living in the border area with few prospects for employment.

In a cooperative effort to provide jobs for these would-be and ex-Braceros, in 1965 the United States and Mexican governments launched the Border Industrialization Program, which sought to stimulate the development of *maquiladoras* by providing special exemptions from both Mexican and U.S. policies. Mexico allowed U.S.-made components to be imported without duties, and the United States facilitated re-importation of goods assembled into finished products by Mexican workers—the United States charged duty only on the value-added by Mexican workers in Mexico, typically 10 to 20 percent of the value of a product such as a television. The *maquiladora* program expanded slowly, and never provided many jobs for ex-Braceros—*maquiladora* operators preferred to hire young women, whereas almost all Braceros were men. In 1965, there were 12 *maquiladoras* employing 3,000 workers, and it took 15 years until *maquiladora* employment surpassed 100,000.

In the late 1970s, large oil and gas deposits were discovered in Mexico, and the Mexican government went on a borrowing spree, with loans from U.S. banks backed by anticipated oil revenues. Much of this borrowed money was squandered or invested in ways that generated low returns, and when the price of oil plunged in the early 1980s, Mexico could not repay its $60 billion foreign debt. The peso was devalued sharply, the Mexican government nationalized the banks, real wages fell, and emigration pressures increased. However, *maquiladora* employment increased in response to lower wages. In the mid-1980s, the Mexican government dramatically changed its economic model as foreign debt approached $100 billion and inflation exceeded 100 percent a year. Mexico switched from import-substitution to export-oriented growth, joined the General Agreement on Tariffs and Trade (GATT) and the Organization for Economic Cooperation and Development (OECD), and in 1990 proposed the North American Free Trade Agreement (NAFTA)—in effect, Mexico decided to integrate its economy with that of the United States.

The process of North American economic integration has been very uneven. Mexico, whose GDP is about the size of Florida, averaged 3.1 percent economic growth in the 1990s, while the United States averaged 3.4 percent—Mexico had years in which GDP rose by 7 percent and years when GDP fell by 7 percent. After NAFTA went into effect on January 1, 1994, real wages fell in Mexico, which expanded foreign investment and *maquiladora* employment in the northern part of the country, raising wages there while leaving southern agricultural states behind. Opening the Mexican economy displaced some workers in agriculture as well as in previously protected manufacturing, as when textile and shoe employment fell over 30 percent in the late 1980s. Mexico-U.S. immigration also increased sharply— the number of Mexican-born persons in the United States doubled in the 1990s, from 4.5 million to 9 million, and most of the 1990s arrivals were unauthorized.[28]

Migration was a central and often troublesome feature of Mexico-U.S. relations during most of the twentieth century. There were incidents during the 1950s when, for example, the Mexican government attempted to block the exit of Braceros to the United States to protest discrimination and poor working conditions, and the U.S. government removed the border patrol to allow the entry of Mexican farm workers. Mexico and the United States today are much closer neighbors, and President George W. Bush asserts frequently that the United States "has no more important relationship in the world than the one we have with Mexico," while President Vicente Fox lays out a vision for a North American community with freedom of movement. NAFTA and economic integration changed Mexico in the eyes of many Americans from a cheap tourist destination to a partner in the integrating North American economy.

Mexican politics changed along with the economy. In 2000, Mexico elected its first president in seventy years from a party other than the Institutional Revolutionary Party (PRI), and President Fox declared improving conditions for Mexican migrants in the United States his government's top foreign priority, and pushed hard for a "whole enchilada" migration policy package in 2001 that included legalization for unauthorized Mexicans in the United States, a new guest-worker program that would reduce deaths and violence along the border, changes in U.S. law that would exempt Mexico from the immigrant visa ceilings that apply to all other countries, and aid for high-emigration regions of Mexico. Just before the September 11, 2001, terrorist attacks, Fox said: "The time has come to give migrants and their communities [in the United States] their proper place in the history of our bilateral relations . . . we must, and we can, reach an agreement on migration before the end of this very year . . . [2001, so that] there are no Mexicans who have not entered this country legally in the United States, and that those Mexicans who come into the country do so with proper documents."[29]

The September 11, 2001, terrorist attacks stopped the momentum for a new Mexico-U.S. migration agreement. As unemployment rose in both countries and job growth was slow, the debate about a new Mexico-U.S. migration arrangement changed. The focus shifted from the "U.S. need" for Mexican workers to sustain the 1990s economic boom to "President Fox's need" for some type of new migration agreement to demonstrate to Mexican critics of his pro-American stance that ever-closer integration with the United States benefited Mexico. Mexican Foreign Minister Jorge Castaneda resigned in January 2003, citing his inability "to achieve faster and more concrete results in implementing new ideas about migration" with the United States.

Mexican and foreign observers point to the unfinished domestic agenda in Mexico. It is generally agreed that Mexico must reform its tax system to increase government revenues (taxes are only 11 percent of GDP, compared to 20 percent in the United States). There are looming crises in the Mexican energy and electricity sectors that can be resolved only with additional investment, which is likely to be forthcoming only if these sectors are deregulated and privatized. Finally, the government is under pressure to ease the adjustments in the countryside by providing more support to farmers. The Fox government must tackle these daunting challenges without a majority in Congress.

The migration issue is still being discussed in Mexico, the United States, and at bilateral forums. Within the United States there are three major U.S. policy options being debated: guest workers, amnesty, and earned legalization. The policy most likely to win approval is earned legalization, which would allow some unauthorized Mexicans in the United States to be granted a temporary legal status that can be converted to an immigrant status within three to six years, with some form of guest worker program for new arrivals. Among the many details to be worked out are whether such a program would apply only to Mexicans or to all unauthorized foreigners in the United States, how much work would be required during the transition to immigrant status, and the status of spouses and dependents of earned-legalization immigrants.

Remittances and Home Town Associations

Reported remittance transfers to Mexico have grown dramatically during the past decade. Just in the period from 1999 to 2004, remittances grew from $5.9 billion to $16.6 billion.[30] The growth is attributed to better reporting as well as real increases in volume. The average transfer has remained highly consistent, at about $330 per transfer throughout this decade. About 90 percent of the remittances are sent through electronic transfers. The cost of transferring remittances has been greatly reduced during the past decade, largely because of increased competition. The cost still takes up about 10 percent of the value of the remittances, however. Remittances compare very favorably to other external sources of income, equal to or surpassing foreign direct investment and international travel flows.

As in other countries, remittances are used primarily for purchase of consumer items. Research on Mexican remittances indicates, however, that consumer use of remittances can have positive impact on economic development, particularly when households spend their remittances locally. The multiplier effects of remittances can be substantial, with each dollar producing additional dollars in economic growth for the businesses that produce and supply the products bought with these resources.[31]

A recent trend has been collective remittances transferred by Hometown Associations (HTAs). HTAs are composed of migrants abroad who meet primarily for social purposes but often send communal resources to the villages from which they emigrated. The Mexican government has registered some seven hundred HTAs in the United States, which probably under-represents the total number of such clubs. Mexican HTAs have evolved from U.S. organizations that sponsor beauty contests and soccer matches involving local residents and migrants to organizations with considerable economic and political significance. Southern California is the capital of the Mexican Diaspora, and organizations such as the Federation of Zacatecan Clubs are playing an increasingly important role in the politics and economics of both Mexico and the United States.

HTAs have been making contributions for the economic development of their areas of origin for decades, and the Zacatecan HTAs pioneered the practice of having first local governments and then the state of Zacatecas match HTA contributions for development. Since 1998, Mexico's fund-matching scheme has been known as the "Citizen Initiative 3 X 1" and is managed by the Federal Ministry for Social Development (SEDESOL). In 2003 the federal government invested $10 million dollars, and with matching contributions from HTAs, state, and local governments, $40 million was invested in nine hundred projects; the federal government raised its contribution to $14 million for 2005.[32]

HTAs submit their project proposals and funding pledge to the state and federal government in the area where the project is to take place, with each state's Development Planning Committee (COPLADE) charged with evaluating proposals (most COPLADE committees have a migrant representative). The state office of SEDESOL provides a technical feasibility of the proposed project, which releases the federal funds to municipal authorities and a local representative of the migrants.

In most cases, 3x1 programs support infrastructure projects such as the expansion or renovation of health clinics, electrical grids, roads, or the town square. However, as the 3x1 program expands, there have been disagreements over priorities. For example, some HTAs want to renovate churches in their hometowns, while local mayors often prefer roads or electricity. In 2002, the federal government sided with mayors, and said that 3x1 matches would be provided only for "productive investments," but HTAs protested, and 3x1 now supports projects to renovate churches.

Although the projects funded by HTAs tend to be small, and only an estimated two percent of Mexican remitters belong to HTAs, their impact can be great on communities with few other resources. One study found "[HTAs] can facilitate projects that would otherwise be impossible for the receiving communities to implement. The contributions are even more striking when compared to the municipal public works budgets. In towns with fewer than 3,000 people, HTA donations are equal to more than 50 percent of the municipal public works budget. For localities with populations less than 1,000, the HTA donations can amount to up to seven times the public works budget."[33]

Migration and Mexican Development

Mexico's population doubled between 1970 and 2000, from 53 million to 100 million, while the number of Mexican-born U.S. residents increased tenfold, from less than 800,000 to about 8.5 to 9 million. Over the past thirty years, Mexicans pioneered what has become the "normal" way to immigrate to the United States—arrive with some temporary status, often unauthorized, and later find a way to adjust to permanent immigrant status.

Both Mexico and the United States want to make mass Mexico-U.S. migration unnecessary for economic reasons by substituting trade in goods for the migration of workers. There is general agreement that the durable solution to unauthorized Mexico-U.S. migration is job and wage growth in Mexico, but there is also a consensus that significant Mexico-U.S. migration will continue for at least another decade. The policy issue is how to manage migration during this period of likely increased pressures for Mexico-U.S. migration during economic restructuring in Mexico, the "migration hump." According to this formulation, once the Mexican economy is restructured so that there are more high-wage manufacturing jobs and fewer poor farmers, Mexico-U.S. migration should decrease.

Increased Mexico-U.S. migration—the hump—began in the 1980s, and the question is whether we are on the upside, at the peak, or on the downside of the migration hump; the position on the hump has important implications for the policy options being debated. If Mexico-U.S. migration pressures are still increasing, then launching a new guest worker or legalization program could further increase Mexico-U.S. migration, as new areas begin sending migrants to the United States as guest workers, or persons in traditional areas become convinced that the best way to benefit from legalization is to migrate illegally to the United States.

It is very difficult to determine the current location on the migration hump, since it depends on both long- and short-term variables. The key long-term variables are Mexican fertility and job creation rates; while key short-term variables are economic conditions in agriculture and the ability of migration networks and smugglers to evade tougher border enforcement. The direction of the fertility variable is clear—the number of persons turning fifteen each year is expected to drop by 50 percent between 1995 and 2010, from about one million a year to 500,000 a year. Declining fertility reduces Mexico-U.S. migration directly as well as indirectly, because households with fewer children tend to keep them in school longer, which reduces the need to create as many jobs for young people. Most U.S.-bound migrants have little education—the probability of migration to the United States is lower among the better educated in Mexico (though quite high among the best educated—those with advanced degrees).

The second key variable is job growth, which depends on economic growth. The ratio between economic and job growth in Mexico is about 2 to 1, so that 5 percent annual economic growth is associated with 2.5 percent job growth, or 750,000 new jobs per year on an employment base of 30 million.[34] However, this ratio also operates in reverse, so that the number of jobs shrinks in recession. This is what happened in 2001: President Fox promised to create 1.3 million new formal sector jobs per year, but employment in 2001 shrank by 400,000. If Mexico could sustain 6 to 7 percent economic growth, as East Asian nations did, economic growth could create enough jobs to absorb new labor force entrants and begin to reduce under-employment among Mexican workers. However, between 1990 and 2003, Mexico averaged 3 percent annual economic growth while the United States averaged 3.2 percent growth. Mexico needs substantial foreign investment to achieve robust economic and job growth.

In the late 1990s, when the Mexican and U.S. economies were booming, it seemed easy to imagine that Mexico-U.S. migration was on the downward side of the migration hump—still high, but falling fast. After the 2001–2002 recession in both countries, the strains evident in agriculture, continued smuggling, and the movement of some plants from Mexico to China, there is less confidence about where Mexico-U.S. migration is on the hump. Thus, a brief review of agriculture, networks, and the China threat is warranted.

Agriculture

Agriculture in Mexico has been in "crisis" for the past fifteen years, as the Mexican government reduced input subsidies, subsidized credit, and output price supports while opening to trade, which brought cheaper foreign farm commodities into Mexico. Some six to eight million Mexicans are employed in agriculture, and farmers and farm workers are 20 to 25 percent of total employment. Yet agriculture generates less than 5 percent of Mexican GDP, which means that most rural Mexicans had per capita incomes that are much less than the $6,200 national average in 2003.

Mexicans were tied to the land for generations by government input subsidies and output price supports as well as a unique land tenure system, known as *Ejidos*. The Mexican revolution was fought in part to provide land for the peasants, and since the 1930s large haciendas have been broken up and land redistributed to peasants in parcels of nine to forty-five acres. *Ejido* farmers could work the land individually or collectively and bequeath it to their heirs, but could not sell it or use it as collateral for loans. Some Mexican migrants in the United States rented out their land, although by so doing they ran a risk of losing their rights to it.

Beginning in the late 1980s, Mexico began to change its farm policies, reducing input subsidies, and then in 1992 amending Article 27 of the Mexican Constitution to allow the sale or rental of *ejido* land. In 1993, the Mexican government replaced output price supports with direct payments to farmers under the Procampo program.[35] The hope was that freeing up the land market would allow Mexicans in the United States to sell or rent their land to more efficient resident producers. They in turn could mechanize and change crops to take advantage of lower wages to produce fruits, vegetables, and flowers, and thereby generate jobs in rural Mexico.[36] States such as Sinaloa have been able to expand their export-oriented agricultural sectors, but it has proven to be very difficult to produce, pack, and export sufficient volumes of high-quality labor-intensive commodities to create large numbers of high-wage jobs in most areas of rural Mexico.

Mexico has been slow to take advantage of its comparative advantage in labor-intensive crops, but the United States' comparative advantage in capital-intensive production of grains and meats is already apparent. On January 1, 2003, Mexican tariffs on all U.S. farm commodities except corn, sugar, and dairy products ended. In anticipation of increased competition, Mexican farmers' organizations, prompted by the opposition PRI party, staged noisy protests in seeking additional Mexican government support, especially for pork and chicken farmers.[37] U.S. farm exports to Mexico have risen, giving the United States an agricultural trade surplus with Mexico in the 1990s, while the United States had an agricultural trade deficit with Canada.

Mexican agricultural policy changes and NAFTA have compressed the period of large-scale rural-urban migration in Mexico. In the United States, the great migration off the land was concentrated in the period from 1945 to 1970—1 million people per year left the farm during this quarter century. In rural Mexico, many young people see that they will not have a prosperous future in farming and have been moving out of rural areas to provincial Mexican capitals, to *maquiladoras* along the border, and to the United States. The Mexican villages these youthful migrants leave behind are dominated, in the words of some observers, by "nurseries and nursing homes," and their lack of both infrastructure and young workers thus becomes a vicious circle that makes it very hard to invest remittances and other jobs in migrant areas of origin.

Networks and Migrant Diffusion

The Bracero program brought Mexicans from west-central Mexico to the southwestern U.S. states because north-south rail lines ran through west-central Mexico, and agriculture in the southwestern U.S. states was expanding in the 1950s when the Bracero program was at its peak. The west-central states of Guanajuato, Jalisco, Michoacan, Nayarit, and Zacatecas remain major places of origin for Mexican migrants. However, migration networks have diffused within Mexico, and Mexicans in the United States are diffusing across states, industries, and occupations.

A modernizing Mexico marked by inequality—more jobs in the north and in urban areas—has been attracting more Mexicans into internal and international migration networks in the 1990s. In the United States, the single most important factor spreading Mexicans around the country was the legalization of 2.3 million Mexicans in 1987–1988. There were two legalization programs, one for foreigners unlawfully resident in the United States for at least five years and another for foreigners who had done at least 90 days of farm work in 1985–1986. The second legalization, called the Special Agricultural Worker (SAW) program, was based on the false premise that rural Mexicans only wanted to work seasonally in the United States, so only unauthorized farm workers and not their families were legalized.

Most SAWs were married men—typical was a 28-year-old with three or four children. The 1990s changes in the Mexican countryside encouraged many SAWs to settle in the United States and send for their families to join them via unauthorized entries, especially because U.S. family fairness and similar policies sent very mixed messages about how tough the United States would be on unauthorized migrants. This provoked political backlash in California, which accounted for half of the SAW applicants and was in its worst recession in fifty years in the early 1990s. The backlash took the form of a 1994 ballot referendum known as Proposition 187, which called for the establishment of a state-funded screening system to prevent unauthorized foreigners from accessing state-funded services, including K–12 schools.[38] Proposition 187 was passed by a large margin in the referendum ballot, but its implementation was blocked by a federal district judge. In 1996, some of its restrictions on non-U.S. citizen access to welfare were implemented in federal laws.

The California economy recovered more slowly than did the rest of the U.S. economy in the 1990s, and very low unemployment rates in the Midwest led to the recruitment by farmers and meatpackers of Mexican workers resident in California. Pioneer migrants recruited friends and relatives to join them in meatpacking, construction, and service jobs outside the southwest, and U.S. employers were happy to turn recruitment, screening, and training over to migrant networks that relied on currently employed workers to obtain additional workers. In less than five years, Mexican migrants became significant fractions of labor forces from Maine to Georgia, and from Delaware to Iowa. Earnings from such low-paid but often year-round jobs in these places, with their low costs of living, enabled many migrants to buy houses and have their families join them.

Within Mexico, migration streams also diversified. Most noticeable was the movement of non-Spanish speaking migrants, such as Mixtecs and Zapotecs from Oaxaca and Chiapas, who began arriving in the United States in the 1990s. In this case, internal Mexican migration eventually became Mexico-U.S. migration, as the Mixtecs and Zapotecs recruited to fill seasonal jobs in export-oriented agriculture in northern Mexico continued on to the United States when they were laid off in April–May.

Today there are migrants from each of Mexico's 31 states in each of the 50 U.S. states. Mexico serves its citizens in the United States with 43 consulates, apparently the most consulates one country has in another. Mexican government attitudes and policies toward migrants in the United States have changed markedly, with President Fox frequently calling the migrants heroes for the remittances they send home. Mexico in the 1990s permitted dual nationality, so that Mexicans who become naturalized U.S. citizens no longer lose rights in Mexico, and promoted the *matricula consular*, a Mexican consulate-issued photo ID that has become increasingly necessary to enter government buildings in the United States or fly on an airplane.[39]

NAFTA, *Maquiladoras*, and Jobs

There were many hoped-for side effects of NAFTA, including reduced Mexico-U.S. migration. NAFTA got off to a rocky start, as Mexico suffered a Zapatista uprising January 1, 1994, the PRI presidential candidate was assassinated in March 1994, and there were cries of fraud after the elections of July 1994 that brought Ernesto Zedillo to power. As Zedillo took office in December 1994, a currency crisis and peso devaluation led to a recession and sharp drop in employment in 1995.

The Mexican economy recovered in 1996, and Mexico enjoyed its best five years of economic and job growth between 1996 and 2000. The economy grew, exports rose, and the labor market became more formal as more jobs were included in the Social Security (IMSS) system. Labor force participation rates fell, reflecting more schooling and less work by teens. However, the late 1990s were also marked by more regional and other inequalities inside Mexico. The north and those involved with the export sector did far better than the south and those involved with the domestic market, and these internal differences accelerated displacement and internal migration, especially from the poorest states such as Oaxaca and Chiapas.

Mexico needs foreign savings—foreign investment—to create jobs. Foreign savers invest where they see opportunities for the highest returns, and during the 1990s, Mexico was seen as one of the most attractive developing countries for foreign investment. Most of the foreign investment was from the United States and Asian countries such as Japan and Korea, and much of it flowed into the auto industry and into *maquiladoras* that assembled electronics and apparel.

Foreign investment that leads to the construction of factories generally creates permanent jobs; portfolio investment seeking high returns, on the other hand, can quickly leave a country if there is a threat of devaluation or the prospect of better returns elsewhere. Some of the foreign investment in Mexico was portfolio investment, and Mexican and foreign investors in the tumultuous year of 1994 began converting pesos to dollars at the fixed 3.45 pesos to $1 rate because they feared a peso devaluation. By December 1994, Mexico ran out of reserves to support the peso at this rate and devalued, leading to the economic crisis. The United States provided financial assistance to stabilize the Mexican economy and as President Clinton said, "to better protect our borders."

Mexico recovered from the 1995 crisis, but wages fell sharply in dollar terms, and have not yet recovered to 1993 levels. These low Mexican wages attracted foreign investors who almost doubled the number of *maquiladora* jobs between 1995 and 2001, from 675,000 to 1.3 million, so that *maquiladora* jobs accounted for a third of Mexican manufacturing jobs. Some 80 to 85 percent of workers in *maquiladoras* are "direct hires" or assembly-line workers—the other 15 to 20 percent are engineers or managers and workers with technical skills. For 48-hour work weeks—often 9.5 hours per day five days a week—gross wages are about $96 per week or $2 per hour, and net wages are $1.50 per hour—similar workers in the United States earn about $8 per hour.

Maquiladoras create jobs, but do they generate stay-at-home development? Most *maquiladora* workers are young women, many of whom finished school at age twelve to fourteen and are in their first jobs in *maquiladoras* at age sixteen to twenty. Most receive subsidized transportation to the factories in which they assemble auto parts, apparel, footwear, and other consumer goods, as well as subsidized meals. However, wages and benefits are similar between *maquiladoras*, and worker turnover is very high—often 5 to 15 percent per month, or 50 to 150 percent per year, so that two workers must be hired during a year to keep one assembly line job filled. Such high worker turnover discourages investment in training to increase worker skills and productivity.

Maquiladoras are controversial, criticized for offering low wages to young women while polluting the environment. Plant managers say they prefer local workers, but internal migrants have become an ever-bigger share of the *maquiladora* work force because many local workers shun the *maquiladoras'* low wages for repetitive work. More men and more highly skilled technical workers have been hired, but most assembly-line workers are still women with a sixth-grade education doing simple hand-assembly tasks. There is also concern about the inadequate storage of hazardous wastes around the plants, which are often on steep hillsides so that rainwater can wash them into shantytowns nearby.

Most *maquiladoras* remain isolated enclaves in the Mexican economy, contributing primarily jobs and wages but little in the way of local procurement; most of the components that are assembled into products continue to be imported. About 40 percent of the *maquiladoras* compete primarily on price, and the 2001–2002 recession showed that *maquiladora* employment can fall just when other jobs also disappear, making them poor economic shock absorbers.

There are a growing number of exceptions to this picture of footloose assembly operations seeking out low-wage workers. Such exceptions are most visible in the auto industry. Auto parts makers such as Delphi have both engineering and production facilities in Mexico and are moving up the value chain from assembly to research and development. Similar efforts are underway among some electronics manufacturers. Yet perhaps half of the *maquiladora* jobs continue to exist primarily because of low wages. There is general agreement that Mexico must upgrade the skills and productivity of its *maquila* and other workers, and the technologies they work with, so that employers can pay them higher wages and still remain competitive. This is a challenge, because Mexico still spends relatively little on K–12 education, and although schooling levels of young people are increasing, many children continue to drop out after primary school.

Maquiladoras are also controversial in the United States, and their growth in the 1990s seemed to vindicate the prediction of 1992 Reform Party presidential candidate Ross Perot, who asserted that NAFTA would lead to a "giant sucking sound" of U.S. jobs moving to Mexico for lower wages. There were periodic announcements of U.S. plants closing and their production shifting to Mexico, but U.S. worker protests were muted by U.S. adjustment assistance and the booming U.S. economy.

Mexican *maquiladora* employment fell by 250,000 in 2001–2002 because of the U.S. recession, a strong peso, and the shift of some jobs to even lower-wage countries, especially China. There is little information on what happened to jobless *maquila* workers, many of whom had migrated to the border regions from the interior of Mexico—did they return to their villages of origin, migrate to the United States, or are they staying in the border area awaiting a rebound? Most observers note that to pay the $1,000+ cost of a smuggler to illegally enter the United States, it is better to have friends or relatives in the United States provide a loan that can be repaid with U.S. wages than try to save the smuggling fee from *maquiladora* wages of $15 a day. However, a year's employment at a *maquiladora* can qualify the worker to obtain a U.S. border crossing card (known as the laser visa) that expedites legal entry.

Plamex, the Mexican subsidiary of Plantronics (PLT), illustrates this challenge at its communications headset facility in Tijuana. Based in Santa Cruz, California, Plantronics reported 2002 sales of $310 million and a workforce of 2,600. Of these 1,700 are employed in a 240,000-square-foot complex in Tijuana that produces over 8,000 variants of headsets and handset products. About 85 percent of the Tijuana employees are assembly workers, usually women who work on 5- to 10-person assembly teams for gross wages of about $105 per 48-hour week, ($2.20 per hour) and net wages of $80 ($1.65). Most of the workers are internal migrants, many from the Mexican states of Sinaloa and Sonora.

Plantronics, which is almost always hiring new workers to replace those who quit, depends largely on current workers who bring family members and relatives to work. Plantronics has lower than average turnover because it makes extra efforts to have its employees (called associates) identify with Plantronics, issuing them business cards and putting their names on their chairs. This loyalty-enhancing strategy seems to reduce turnover, and many of the workers we met had been at the plant for several years.

We were also interested in exploring the *maquiladora* and the emigration to the U.S. linkage. If a family has two earners in *maquiladoras*, are they likely to be satisfied or eager to cross the border to the United States? Workers with families mostly rented housing, although some were building houses in the shantytowns around Tijuana. Very few Plantronics workers were able to build "normal" houses with support from the Workers' Housing Fund (INFONAVIT), which provides low-interest loans from contributions made by employers, workers, and the government. INFONAVIT, begun in 1972, originally depended only on worker and employer contributions, and supported little housing during the 1990s, because real worker wages were falling at a time when INFONAVIT charged market interest rates. Since 2001, INFONAVIT interest rates have been subsidized, and there has been a big increase in house building.

A few Plantronics workers had spouses who commuted daily to U.S. jobs, but the higher U.S. wages were mostly offset by higher transport and meal expenses. Surprisingly, some Plantronics workers had never been to the United States despite having lived several years in Tijuana. Instead, it appears that some *maquiladora* workers "graduate" to the service sector, where incomes can be higher and women have more control over their time.

The San Diego–Tijuana Region

The San Diego–Tijuana region has about 4 million people—2.9 million in San Diego and 1.1 million in Tijuana, making it the most populous area along the Mexico-U.S. border. Tijuana is growing much faster than San Diego. Tijuana in 1900 had perhaps 250 residents and was not connected to the rest of Mexico by road or rail. In 1930, Tijuana had 30,000 residents and in 1980, 462,000—Tijuana has been growing by 70,000 to 80,000 residents a year.

The 2000-mile Mexico-U.S. border area is one of the richest areas of Mexico and one of the poorest areas of the United States. San Diego is an exception, a prosperous U.S. metropolitan area with an economy anchored by the military, tourism, and high-tech industries, including biotechnology, pharmaceuticals, software, and computer services. Many Mexican immigrants enter the United States via San Diego, but only to pass through on the way to their destination of Los Angeles. In the 2000 census, San Diego county had 21 percent foreign-born residents, compared to 26 percent in California, and 33 percent of the immigrants spoke a language other than English at home, compared to 40 percent in California. San Diego County's GDP is estimated to be about $120 billion.

Tijuana accounts for about one half of the residents of the state of Baja California, whose capital is Mexicali.[40] Electronics dominate *maquiladora* assembly operations: the Tijuana Economic Development Corporation reported that there were 740 *maquiladoras* employing 172,000 workers in 2001, led by Sony, 6,500; Sanyo, 5,000; and Panasonic and Samsung, 4,000 each. Toyota has announced plans to build a truck assembly plant in the Tijuana area, and several aerospace firms have announced plans to move to the Tijuana region.

Responsibility for controlling the entry of people across the U.S. border from Mexico is divided between two units of the Immigration and Naturalization Service (INS), an agency that moved in January 2003 from the Department of Justice to the new Department of Homeland Security (www.dhs.gov). INS inspectors monitor entries at legally established ports-of-entry, while the U.S. Border Patrol attempts to prevent entries between the ports-of-entry. The San Diego–Tijuana border crossing is the world's busiest land border crossing, with about 50 million entries per year,[41] 10 percent of the United States total, reflecting the entry of 45,000 vehicles a day with an average two occupants, plus 20,000 to 30,000 pedestrians. Since September 11, 2001, all entrants must show some form of ID, which has led to waits of more than an hour for both pedestrians and vehicles.

About 40,000 of the 150,000 entrants each day at the San Ysidro and Otay Mesa ports-of-entry are frequent border crossers who can pay $129 per year to enroll in the seven-year-old Secure Electronic Network for Travelers' Rapid Inspection (SENTRI) system. SENTRI requires background checks and the placement of a transponder on the commuter's car. As the car enters a special lane and approaches the inspector, details of the pre-cleared traveler flash on the inspector's screen; waits for the 26,000 persons enrolled in California are typically less than 15 minutes.[42]

Border Enforcement

There are two major types of attempted illegal migration at ports-of-entry—people trying to hide in vehicles, and pedestrians trying to cross with false or imposter documents. Suspicious vehicles are sent to secondary inspection, where sniffer dogs and a variety of inspection technologies are used to locate concealed people or drugs. Foreigners sometimes attempt entry by using legitimate documents that belong to someone else, making false claims to U.S. citizenship, or using counterfeit or altered documents. The most common method is to use legitimate border crossing cards (laser visa) issued to Mexicans settled in Mexican border areas. The cards are stolen or rented to similar-looking persons who attempt to use them to enter the United States.

Apprehensions of would-be illegal entrants at the San Diego port of entry peaked at 70,406 in FY2000, were 47,970 in FY2001, and 27,358 in FY2002.[43] Foreigners who have been apprehended many times in the company of different people are sometimes prosecuted as smugglers; 150 were prosecuted in FY2002. However, in most cases, smugglers if convicted are sentenced to time already served pending trial, and are released and returned to Mexico.

In FY2000, the U.S. Border Patrol apprehended a total of 1.8 million persons attempting to enter the United States illegally between all ports-of-entry (the same person caught three times counts as three apprehensions), exceeding the previous peak in FY1986. A large but unknown number of people, thought to number at least several hundred thousand, eluded Border Patrol agents and entered the United States unlawfully, although some number (again unknown) of these unauthorized foreigners are believed to have departed after several months or years.

In 1993, the Border Patrol in El Paso experimented with a new approach to border management: deterrence. To deter migrants from attempting unauthorized entry, agents were stationed within sight of each other along the border separating El Paso and Juarez. Apprehensions fell sharply, as Mexicans were deterred from commuting illegally to jobs in El Paso or going to El Paso to commit petty crimes. However, Mexicans intending to migrate further inland went around El Paso to enter the United States illegally.[44]

In 1994, the INS expanded the deterrence strategy to most urban areas along the 2,000 mile Mexico-U.S. border, adding agents, fencing (including a triple fence along a few miles of the 2,000-mile border), video and thermal imaging surveillance systems, and lights to deter entries in urban areas. These measures clearly deterred entries in the urban areas where most had been occurring and reduced crime in the border area, in effect calming what had been chaos.

The Southwest Border Strategy assumed that migrants forced to attempt entry in desert and mountain areas, would not try, or if they did, they would be easier to apprehend. However, migrants turned to smugglers and continued to try to enter the United States, bolstering the smuggling business—one million migrants paying $1,000 each would make smuggling a $1 billion per year business—and likely increasing deaths of migrants abandoned in mountains and deserts, an average one per day in the past several years.[45] It is not clear when or if deterrence becomes the norm. The GAO concluded: "Although illegal alien apprehensions have shifted, there is no clear indication that overall illegal entry into the United States along the Southwestern border has declined."[46]

It is generally agreed that one effect of these deterrence strategies has been that unauthorized foreigners who enter the United States stay longer, since they know that the costs and risks of unauthorized re-entry with the help of a smuggler have risen. Reduced circular migration may have contributed to more remittances being sent back to Mexico via banks, which might explain the sharp rise in remittances reported by the Bank of Mexico, from $5 billion in 1996 to $10 billion in 2002.

The INS's Border Patrol had a FY2000 budget of $1.2 billion, and 93 percent of its 9,096 agents in September 2000 were on the Mexico-U.S. border, providing 11 million person-hours of border enforcement. The INS estimates it needs seven to ten more years and 3,200 to 5,500 more agents, plus $450–$560 million in spending on additional technology to achieve control over the border.[47]

It is clear that there is more political consensus to step up border patrols to prevent illegal entries, but there is less agreement that employer sanction enforcement should be stepped up. There have been some successful experiments (called Vanguard in Midwestern meatpacking and Tarmac at some U.S. airports) that show that interior enforcement can deter unauthorized worker employment. Nonetheless, while the number of Border Patrol agents increased 2.5 times between 1993 and 2002, the number of interior enforcement agents remained unchanged at 2,000. There is general agreement that unless and until there is an effective interior enforcement strategy, border controls alone are unlikely to prevent unauthorized entries.

When migrants do not succeed in reaching the United States, some turn to Casa de Migrante, a hostel in Tijuana operated by the Scalabrini order of the Catholic Church. This hostel provides free accommodation and food for up to 220 male migrants. Stays are limited to fifteen days, and would-be residents are screened to ensure that they are migrants rather than homeless residents of Tijuana. Begun for men heading north, the home now serves primarily men who are being deported from the United States as criminal aliens—they usually return to Mexico with no money and no means of returning to their homes. There are other such facilities for women and children in Tijuana.

In the aftermath of September 11, Mexico and the United States signed a "Smart Border" initiative aimed at deterring the movement of terrorists and other security threats. The twenty-two-point U.S.-Mexico Border Partnership Agreement, which was signed in March 2002, included provisions for the secure flow of people, goods, and infrastructure. The provisions related to the movements of people included establishing a joint advance passenger information exchange mechanism; exploring methods to facilitate the movement of NAFTA travelers; reaffirming mutual commitment to the Border Safety Initiative; continuing frequent consultations on visa policies; conducting joint training in the areas of investigation and document analysis to enhance abilities to detect fraudulent documents and break up alien smuggling rings; developing systems for exchanging information and sharing intelligence; and enhancing cooperative efforts to detect, screen, and take appropriate measures to deal with potentially dangerous third-country nationals, taking into consideration the threats they may represent to security.[48] Perhaps more significant than the specific proposals, the border agreement represented the resumption of bilateral consultation and discussions that had been abruptly terminated by the terrorist attacks in the United States.

Conclusion

Migration in the Americas follows well-recognized paths from source through transit to destination countries. While policies tend to be made unilaterally by destination countries, there has been growing awareness in the region that cooperation is needed to manage migratory flows. As discussed further in chapter 9, this awareness has led to both bilateral and regional mechanisms for consultation and coordination. In the case of the United States and the Dominican Republic, bilateral cooperation has centered on the deterrence of smuggling and trafficking operations, particularly those bringing third country nationals through the DR to the United States. The U.S.-Mexican bilateral arrangements have focused as well on smuggling of third country nationals, but they have also promoted greater coordination between the two countries in border management, including commuter lanes to facilitate travel and initiatives to increase safety along the shared border.

Notes

1. The Caribbean had about 36 million residents in 2000, including 11 million in Cuba, 4 million in Puerto Rico, 2.6 million in Jamaica, and 1.3 million in Trinidad and Tobago—about 41 percent of Caribbean residents lived in Hispaniola.

2. Some 15,000 Haitians were deported from the DR early in 1997. Fernandez visited Haiti in 1998, the first time a Dominican president made such a trip in sixty-two years.

3. DR has a Senate with 30 members, one for each province and one for the national district, and a 149-member Chamber of Deputies.

4. In Lewis's words, "An 'unlimited supply of labor' will keep wages down [in rural areas], producing cheap coffee . . . and high profits in [steel]. The result is a dual (national or world) economy, where one part is a reservoir of cheap labor for the other. The unlimited supply of labour derives ultimately from population pressure, so it is a phase in the demographic cycle." www.nobel.se/economics/laureates/1979/lewis-autobio.html.

5. Of the 475 free-zone companies that receive fifteen to twenty years of tax exemption and are allowed to import inputs and machines duty-free, 57 percent make garments, followed by footwear, leather goods, electrical and electronic goods, and cigars.

6. The DR is beset by blackouts—privatized generators are accused of deliberately shutting down plants to pressure the government to pay past-due bills. Electricity was privatized in 1999, when $600 million in FDI was invested in DR electricity generation and distribution.

7. Since October 2000, DR exports have had easier access to the U.S. market under the Caribbean Basin Trade Partnership Act (CBTPA)—duty-free and quota-free entry to the U.S. market of apparel sewn and assembled in the Caribbean Basin Initiative from fabric "wholly formed" in the United States.

8. The Código de Trabajo (Dominican Work Code) is at www.set.gov.do. Those who earn RD$125,256 to RD$208,760 per year pay 15 percent in taxes on income above RD$125,256; those who earn RD$208,760 to RD$313,140 pay RD$12,526 in income taxes plus 20 percent of the amount over RD$208,760; and those who earn more than RD$313,140 pay RD$33,402 plus 25 percent of the amount over RD$313,140.

9. Anthony P. Maingot, "Emigration Dynamics in the Caribbean. The Cases of Haiti and the Dominican Republic," in Reginald Appleyard, ed., *Emigration Dynamics in Developing Countries*, vol. 3, *Mexico, Central America and the Caribbean* (Brookfield, VT: Ashgate, 1999), p. 182.

10. Local activists believe that there were 550,000 to 600,000 Dominicans in New York City in 2000, and that imprecise wording on the census form kept Dominicans from being properly enumerated (www.danr.org/).

11. Peggy Levitt, *The Transnational Villagers* (Berkeley, CA: University of California, 2001), p. 4.

12. There is a debate over the role of government in the economy. The Dominican Center for Promotion of Export (CEDOPEX), for example, is funded by fees paid by exporters, and some complain that to export goods they need a certificate from the Ministry of Public Health, two from the Ministry of Agriculture, three forms from CEDOPEX, and approval from customs.

13. The DR's major media are owned by four large business groups. Corripio owns *El Dia*, *Hoy* and *El Nacional*; Bancredito-Tricom owns *Diario Libre*, *Omnimedia* magazines; Baninter owns *Listin Diario*, and several magazines; and Banco Popular owns *El Caribe*.

14. The United States intervened in Haiti with Operation Restore Democracy in 1994 to restore Aristide to power, and has spent $2.3 billion since then trying to help Haiti become a sustainable democracy. The United States says that the aid paid for a new police force, new roads, bridges and other infrastructure, and a higher voter consciousness, which led to an impressive 66 percent turnout in the first election round in May 2000.

15. The Bahamas, a nation of seven hundred islands and 280,000 people, included 20,000 to 40,000 unauthorized Haitians in 2000.

16. There was reportedly an influx of Dominican sex workers to Haiti in the 1980s to service tourists.

17. Quoted in Samuel Martínez, *Peripheral Migrants: Haitians and Dominican Republic Sugar Plantations* (Knoxville: University of Tennessee Press, 1995).

18. The Haitian embassy reported there were 280,000 children born to undocumented Haitians in the Dominican Republic.

19. Quoted in Nancy San Martin, "Haitians Crossing into Dominican Republic Seeking Jobs are Finding Abuse Instead," *Miami Herald*, July 19, 2001.

20. Dominican coffee growers employ about 35,000 Haitians and 15,000 Dominicans to harvest coffee, and they complained in 2001 of labor shortages—coffee pickers earn about $3 for each seventy-pound box of coffee beans they pick.

21. Quoted in David Abel, "Haiti's Poorest Cross Border, Face Backlash," *Boston Herald*, November 28, 1999.

22. Quoted in "Latin America: DR-Haiti, Argentina," *Migration News* 8, no. 8 (August 2001). migration.ucdavis.edu.

23. Found at www.elcaribe.com.do.

24. Statement of David Greenlee, Special Coordinator for Haiti, State Department, Hearing of the House International Relations Committee, December 9, 1997.

25. Statement of David Greenlee, Special Coordinator for Haiti, State Department, Hearing of the House International Relations Committee, December 9, 1997.

26. U.S.-Mexican trade was $95 billion in 1993 and $274 billion in 2000, when the United States exported goods worth $128 billion to Mexico and imported goods worth $136 billion from Mexico.

27. Drying out the wetbacks meant that the INS took unauthorized Mexicans to the Mexico-U.S. border, issued work permits to them, and then allowed them to return to the farms on which they had been found working illegally.

28. Since nine million is the estimate of the settled Mexican population, the gross number of arrivals by Mexicans is considerably larger.

29. Quoted in "Fox Visits Bush," *Migration News* 8, no. 10 (October 2001).

30. Inter American Development Bank, "Remittances and Development: The Case of Mexico" (Washington: IADB, June 8, 2005), available at: idbdocs.iadb.org/wsdocs/getdocument.aspx?docnum=561166.

31. See J. Edward Taylor, "The New Economics of Labour Migration and the Role of Remittances in the Development Process," *International Migration* 37, no. 1 (1999): 63–88.

32. www.sedesol.gob.mx/mexicanosenelexterior/main.htm.

33. Manuel Orozco, B. Lindsay Lowell, et al., *Transnational Engagement, Remittances and their Relationship to Development in Latin America and the Caribbean* (Washington, DC: Institute for the Study of International Migration, 2005), p. 20.

34. Mexican employment is often listed as 40–42 million in 2002, but this includes 11–12 million self-employed, about three-fourths in agriculture. About 15 million Mexicans are enrolled in the IMSS or social security system, and many of the other 15 million are in small establishments with five or fewer workers that do not necessarily pay minimum wages or provide any benefits.

35. Procampo offers fifteen years of cash payments based on production between 1990 and 1993, and does not require farmers to continue producing corn and other supported crops to receive the payments.

36. Fruits, vegetables, and flowers cover 10 percent of Mexico's cultivated land and generate 35 percent of farm sales.

37. U.S. farmers can produce meat more cheaply because animal feed is cheaper in the United States, and transportation costs are lower to ship meat than animal feed. Chickens require about two pounds of feed to produce one pound of meat, pork has a 5 to 1 ratio, and beef a 7 to 1 ratio. Feed for animals is cheaper in the United States than in Mexico, so U.S. producers can ship a pound of meat more cheaply to Mexico than 2, 5, or 7 pounds of feed, which is what threatens Mexican producers. Over time, feed-to-meat conversion ratios may rise in Mexico, new slaughtering facilities may be constructed, and trains that haul autos north may be able to haul animal feed south, but during the next decade, it is likely that U.S. meat will flow south,

displacing Mexican animal producers. In the longer term, Mexico is likely to become a center of manufacturing and to import meat from the United States and Canada, where feed costs are lower.

38. Republican governor Pete Wilson won re-election in part by arguing that expenditures on unauthorized foreigners were 10 percent of state spending in the early 1990s.

39. The *matricula* also enables Mexicans to open U.S. bank accounts and provide ID to police and local authorities.

40. Baja is the state furthest from Mexico City, and was the first to elect a PAN opposition governor.

41. About half of the 500 million entries a year into the United States are returning U.S. citizens.

42. A similar program in Texas enrolls 14,500.

43. The number of foreigners processed for "expedited removal," deportation for attempting to use false documents to enter, similarly fell at the San Diego port of entry from 41,000 in FY2000 to 26,000 in FY2001 to 7,000 in FY2002. Many of those who could be processed for expedited removal accept "voluntary return" to Mexico.

44. Frank R. Bean, R. G. Chanove, R. G. Cushing, et al., *Illegal Mexican Migration and the United States Border: The Effects of Operation-Hold-the Line on El Paso/Juarez* (Austin, TX: Population Research Center, University of Texas–Austin, 1994).

45. Before 1993, the INS did not count the number of deaths of migrants attempting to enter the United States.

46. Government Accunting Office (GAO), INS' Southwest Border Strategy: Resource and Impact Issues Remain After Seven Years. GAO-01-842, August 2, 2001.

47. GAO, INS' Soutwest Border Strategy, pp. 7, 10.

48. The twenty-two–point plan may be accessed at www.thebta.org/keyissues/homelandsecurity/documents/USMex_BorderPartnershipActionPlan.pdf. For an excellent review of its first year implementation, see Deborah Waller Meyers, "Does 'Smarter' Lead To Safer? An Assessment of the Border Accords with Canada and Mexico," in MPI Insight no. 2, June 2003.

CHAPTER EIGHT

✑

The Global Migrants

The previous chapters focused primarily on regional migration patterns between source countries and destination countries with obvious geographic or colonial ties. International migration is also a global phenomenon, as witnessed by migration across vast geographic, cultural, and linguistic divides. Two notable examples of global migration are the Philippines and China—nationals of both countries work in almost all corners of the globe. Managing migration from these countries (or India, another notable example) through bilateral or regional mechanisms requires numerous agreements and negotiations, raising the question, discussed in the next chapter, of the need for global frameworks for addressing the challenges of migration.

Philippines

Cooperative Efforts to Manage Migration (CEME) organized a site visit in February 2004 to the Philippines, a country with 3 million legal overseas foreign workers, perhaps 2 million unauthorized migrants abroad, and an additional 2.4 million Filipinos who are immigrants and naturalized citizens in other countries. These 7.4 million Filipinos abroad remit almost $8 billion a year, equivalent to 10 percent of the Philippines' GDP and as much as the revenue of the agriculture, fishery, and forestry sectors combined, which together employ about 12 million Filipinos. One million Filipinos a year, 2,700 a day, are "deployed"—sent under Philippine government auspices to work abroad. Most are women leaving to be domestic helpers, entertainers, and nurses. The Philippine government is recognized as a leader in promoting and regulating the deployment of migrants and seeking to protect them abroad.

Emigration has become a major element in Filipino society. Over half of Filipinos have been abroad, or have a relative who is or was abroad. The experiences of migrants are reported daily in the press, and their homecomings are depicted in novels and dramatized in movies. Enterprises related to the business of migration are a key part of the Filipino economy: recruiters, travel agents, remittance and insurance services, and businesses that help migrants to invest their remittance savings are common, even in remote rural areas whose major link to the global economy is migration.

The press and the national government treat migrants as national heroes for venturing into strange lands to work and send their earnings to families at home. Returned migrants are viewed with respect in their hometowns for their hard work and achievements abroad. Nevertheless, the impacts of migrants on families, communities, and the economy are mixed. There are many accounts of mothers working abroad so that their children can finish school, but also of relatives who become dependent on remittances and stop trying to improve their lot by their own efforts. Some returned migrants lose their savings in failed business, and then re-migrate.

Labor Secretary Patricia Sto. Tomas says that migrants are a "permanent fixture of Filipinos' socio-economic life." To avoid becoming a society in which young people look only abroad for opportunity, the Philippines needs strategies to more effectively promote stay-at-home economic development.

History and Economy

The 7,100 islands that comprise the Philippines were settled in prehistoric times from the continent of Asia by Malay and Chinese peoples. Their European discovery was made by Ferdinand Magellan, who claimed them for the Spanish crown in 1521. For three centuries Spain ruled, until in December 1898, after an almost successful revolution against Spain, the Philippines were ceded to the United States after Spain lost the Spanish-American War. The United States replaced Spain as colonial ruler until Japan conquered the islands during World War II. American and Philippine troops fought their way back, and after Japan's final defeat, the country was given independence. On July 4, 1946, constitutional government modeled on that of the United States was established, including a 24-seat Senate and a 204-member House. Special privileges for U.S. citizens and corporations and long-term leases for the U.S. military continued until the early 1990s.

During the first three decades of independence, political leadership alternated between the Nacionalistas and Liberals. Near the end of his second term in September 1972, Ferdinand Marcos, who was president between 1965 and 1986, declared martial law and suppressed growing opposition to his rule. The long-time leader of the democratic opposition, Benigno "Ninoy" Aquino, was assassinated by the Philippine military in 1983, but the opposition parties united under his widow, Corazon "Cory" Aquino. They lost the election of 1986 to Marcos because of widespread cheating, prompting a peaceful revolt that led to Aquino becoming president and Marcos going into exile (People Power 1). The Philippine constitution limits presidents to one six-year term, and Aquino was followed by Fidel Ramos (1992–1998) and Joseph Estrada. Vice president Gloria Arroyo replaced Estrada as president in January 2001 with the support of the military after impeachment proceedings against Estrada stalled (People Power 2).

Arroyo ran for a full term as president in May 2004 elections, and trailed a popular actor in the polls. Campaigning was raucous, with opponents of Arroyo alleging that she had done little to end corruption—the Department of Management and Budget estimated that 10 to 50 percent of the value of all government contracts goes to bribes and kickbacks. A 2003 law allows some 1.7 million overseas Filipinos to vote, but only 350,000 had registered by the September 2003 deadline; half were in Asian places such as Hong Kong, and 40 percent were in the Middle East.[1] Arroyo won the election with 40 percent of the vote.

Politics in the Philippines are based largely on personal popularity, but the Catholic Church also plays an important political role. The smallest governmental unit is the *barangay*, a village in rural areas, where local "captains" hold sway. Many studies conclude that the centralization of power in Manila has created a "handout mentality" or "dependency culture" at the local level, with politicians arriving just before elections offering food, drink, and promises of infrastructure improvements in exchange for votes. Low-paid and corrupt police as well as frequent natural disasters such as typhoons contribute to a widespread fatalism and acceptance of things as they are in the rural areas where most Filipinos live.

The Filipino economy is an example of crony capitalism. Especially under Marcos, businessmen with political connections received monopolies to import or export particular commodities, enabling them to amass personal fortunes. The domination of a feudalistic economy by large landowners has given way to the rise of a new economic elite that includes many Filipino Chinese. Risk assessments prepared for foreign investors cite uncertainties that range from armed conflict with Muslim rebels in the south to "people power" civil unrest in Manila, and crime involving drugs and kidnapping for ransom. There is a major pollution problem in urban areas, and corruption is reported at every level of government.

The country has slipped in economic rankings. In 1960, the Philippines had a $300 gross domestic product (GDP) per capita, which was second in Asia only to Japan at $500. Successive governments maintained an import-substitution strategy for much longer than the East Asian "miracle" economies, so that the Philippines did not receive the foreign investment that led to export and job creation booms like those of Taiwan and Thailand. Because of widespread corruption, complicated tax laws and tax evasion, tax revenue remains low, accounting for only 15 percent of GDP. This limits the government's ability to invest and improve infrastructure. Efforts to increase tax collections, end monopolies, liberalize trade, and privatize state-owned businesses have been blocked in Congress by those who would lose privileges. The country has a low savings rate and high levels of domestic and foreign debt.

Economic growth averaged only 1 percent a year during the turbulent 1980s, and real wages declined in the 1990s, especially after the 1997 Asian financial crisis. Average daily wages in Manila were reported to be 170 pesos per day in 2004, and outside Manila 60 to 160 pesos per day. About 40 percent of residents live on less than $2 per day ($1 = 55 pesos in January 2004), and about 75 percent of Filipino poor are in rural areas where they receive little assistance.[2] The Family Income Expenditure Survey found that 34 percent of Filipinos were poor in 2000, up from 32 percent in 1997, under the criterion that a family of six needed at least 9,000 pesos ($180) per month to meet subsistence needs in 2000. Income is distributed more unequally in the Philippines than in any other southeast Asian country. Thus under current conditions it would take extraordinarily high economic growth for significant benefits to reach the poor.[3]

Services account for over half of GDP, industry accounts for one-quarter, and agriculture 15 to 20 percent. The Philippines hopes to compete with India for call-center and other service jobs that are outsourced from industrial countries. Filipino call-center workers earn $300 to $400 a month, and often work overnight for 2 to 3 years before they graduate to daytime work. The 15,000 manufacturing establishments with ten or more workers employed 1.2 million workers in 1997, but informal operations with five or fewer employees employed twice as many workers. Unions are weak—about 4 percent of the 12 million wage and salary workers were union members in the mid-1990s.[4]

Agriculture, which employs one-third of the labor force of 34 million, is dominated by two crops, rice for domestic consumption and coconuts. Rice production rose in the 1990s, while coconut production fell. Other export crops are bananas and pineapples; many sugar producers have switched to other crops and fish farming

Most farms are very small—90 percent were smaller than 5 hectares in the early 1990s, and there are far more landless peasants than farmers with land. Efforts to break up land holdings larger than 5 hectares have floundered as large landowners blocked effective redistribution—some incorporated and gave their workers shares of stock instead of land.[5] Small farmers who received redistributed land often failed because of poor infrastructure and declining prices of coconuts and sugar.

Demography and Migration

The Philippines in 2003 had a population of 81 million, including 10 million in the Manila area, and a relatively rapid population growth rate of 2.3 percent per year—over one-third of Filipinos are under fourteen. About half of Filipinos live in rural areas. Nationally, there is significant permanent emigration—a peak 66,000 registered emigrants in 1993, and an average of 44,000 annually in recent years.

The unemployment rate is about 10 percent, but would be 15 percent without emigration. The 30 million employed include 10 million in agriculture, 14 million in services (including 5.5 million each in government and commerce), and 3 million in manufacturing. Access to education is widespread and of high quality, and 2.6 million students were enrolled in higher education in 2000.

Filipinos have been leaving for overseas employment for decades, including to work in Hawaii and California in the 1920s. In 1974, President Marcos encouraged overseas employment to provide jobs and remittances during the global recession in the wake of oil-price hikes. The U.S. military during the Vietnam War used Filipino contractors to build and operate support facilities, giving both employers and workers experience with overseas employment. Filipino contractors took their own workers to the oil-exporting countries in the mid-1970s.

An average of 700,000 Filipinos per year left with contracts for temporary overseas jobs in the 1990s. About 40 percent of the migrants went to the Middle East, and 40 percent stayed in East and Southeast Asia. About 60 percent of those leaving had been abroad before; 40 percent were first-time migrants. Filipino migrants are often preferred to other foreign workers in

Table 8.1.   Filipino Migrants Deployed: 1985–2002

	2002	2000	1995	1990	1985
Total	891,908	841,628	653,574	446,095	372,784
Land-based	682,315	643,304	488,173	334,883	320,494
Sea-based	209,593	198,324	165,401	111,212	52,290
Saudi Arabia	193,157	184,645	168,604	169,886	185,837
Hong Kong	105,036	121,762	51,701	34,412	22,020
Japan	77,870	63,041	25,032	41,558	16,029
UAE	50,796	43,031	26,235	17,189	15,093
Taiwan	46,371	51,145	50,538	54	9
Kuwait	25,894	21,490	9,852	5,007	21,167
Singapore	27,648	22,873	10,736	4,698	10,047
Italy	20,034	26,386	5,829	3,229	1,413

Source: POEA

their major destinations because of their skills, English fluency, and a talent for adapting to different cultures.

Between 1985 and 1990, deployments of Overseas Foreign Workers (OFWs) rose 4 percent per year, then increased by 9 percent per year between 1990 and 1995 and continued rising by 6 percent per year between 1995 and 2000. Some 891,908 Filipinos were deployed in 2002, as compared to 372,784 in 1985. About 80 percent of the OFWs who leave each year are land-based; the other 20 percent are seamen—the 220,000 Filipinos on ships are almost one-quarter of the world's seamen on commercial ships.

The southern Philippine island of Mindanao is closer to the eastern Malaysian states of Sabah[6] and Sarawak than to Manila, and there has long been migration between the Philippines and Borneo, which includes Brunei. Muslim Filipinos have been commuting between Mindanao and Borneo for centuries without documents. One-quarter of the 20 million residents of Mindanao are Muslims, and there has been a long-running low-level guerrilla war against the central government on the island.

Despite a law that makes many activities relating to mail order brides illegal, there is a thriving marriage market in the Philippines, with women agreeing to marry foreign men after meeting them through brokers. The "bride price" paid to the woman's family is typically $3,000 to $5,000; the groom pays $10,000 or more to the broker. In 1995, for the first time, the number of Filipinas leaving the Philippines to marry Japanese men outnumbered those leaving to marry Americans.

The Philippine government has been a leader in developing policies to protect migrants abroad. The Labor Code of 1974 established a system to regulate the recruitment of Filipinos for work abroad by establishing minimum standards for the work contracts migrants must have and a system to verify these contracts. December 18 is celebrated as the International Day of Solidarity with Migrants; this was the day that the United Nations General Assembly in 1990 approved the International Convention on the Rights of All Migrant Workers and Members of Their Families, and there are "Pamaskong Handog sa OFWs" campaigns to welcome home migrants in December. June 7 is Migrant Workers Day in the Philippines, and 2002 was the "Year of Overseas Employment Providers."

The most common sort of first-time migrant is a 25-year-old female college graduate going abroad to work as a domestic helper on a two-year contract. Women are a majority of the migrants, reflecting the importance of domestic helpers, caregivers, and nurses among the emigrants; many women complete five or more two-year contracts abroad before returning home to stay.[7]

Recruiting migrants for overseas jobs is a big business in the Philippines, and there are almost 1,200 licensed recruitment agencies,[8] including some operated by ex-government employees; the recruitment industry has annual revenues of over $400 million a year.[9] Many recruitment agencies, which must be 70 percent Filipino-owned, belong to the Philippine Association of Service Exporters, Inc. (PASEI) or the Overseas Placement Agencies of the Philippine (OPAP). The government would like to reduce the number of recruiters, and requirements such as doubling the capital required from one to two million pesos and deploying at least one hundred workers per year aim to cut the number in half.[10] The Philippines Overseas Employment Administration (POEA) deployed about 10,000 OFWs directly in 2003, and the largest agencies deployed 3,000 to 5,000 migrants each.

The Philippine government's migrant processing and protection system has three major elements: the Philippine Overseas Employment Administration to regulate recruitment and provide pre-departure orientation; labor attaches stationed at consulates abroad to provide assistance to migrants while they are abroad;[11] and the Overseas Workers Welfare Administration to operate welfare centers in major areas of concentration of Filipino workers abroad, organize and cover the cost of emergency repatriation, and to provide various services to families left behind. These activities are financed by fees collected from migrants: a P100 clearance fee from the National Bureau of Investigation and a P3,000 processing fee charged by the POEA, whose governing board includes representatives of the recruitment industry.

For the migrants, fees to private recruiters are the biggest cost of working overseas. The POEA limits recruiter fees to one month's wages abroad, but migrants who know that there are more applicants than jobs sometimes pay more, often the equivalent of two to four months wages, to get a two-year contract. There are active campaigns to stop illegal recruitment and to avoid recruitment overcharges, but there are almost daily press reports of migrants paying fees for non-existent overseas jobs or paying one month's wages for contracts and then having to wait four, six, or ten months before going abroad.

Between 1992 and 2002, the POEA filed 650 cases alleging illegal recruitment, but only 66 of the cases that were recommended for prosecution resulted in criminal convictions. The National Bureau of Investigation attributes few convictions to the inefficiency of the system of justice and reluctance on the part of victims to file formal charges.[12] Some victims refuse to testify because the illegal recruiter is a relative, friend, or resident of their town. Many violations occur overseas, as when a migrant is required to sign a supplemental contract once abroad that requires the payment of additional fees. Most migrants sign, fearing that if they do not, they will be dismissed and have to return to the debts they incurred to go abroad.

Filipino recruiters are jointly liable with foreign employers for the provisions of the contracts that the POEA reviews for each worker, under the theory that it will be difficult for the migrant to recoup funds from the foreign employer. This can put recruiters in a difficult position, since their revenues and profits depend on deploying migrants to employers abroad whom they may not know well.

The POEA provides pre-departure orientation for migrants financed by migrant-paid fees and issues a number of booklets that outline living and working conditions in various countries. Most migrants leave from Manila by air, and they must have a POEA-issued "balik manggagawa" certificate certifying that they are leaving with a contract to work for a foreign employer; some migrants leave with forged certificates.

The Overseas Workers Welfare Administration (OWWA), funded by a $25 fee collected from each migrant, provides emergency services and in some places medical care from offices at twenty-eight Philippine embassies.[13] The OWWA also operates shelters abroad for migrants who run away from abusive employers and is expanding its activities for returned migrants. Both migrants and their foreign employers contribute to a fund that helps returning migrants to reintegrate. (The problems of migrants seem most severe in their first three months abroad.) Some recruiters and migrants would like to eliminate the OWWA and its fees.[14]

A major issue is whether there is too much regulation of recruitment or not enough. Most recruiters as well as the Union of Filipino Overseas Contract Workers (OCW-Unifil) want less government regulation of recruitment and deployment, arguing that government regulation and fees increase their costs at a time when countries such as China, Indonesia, and Vietnam are attempting to expand labor exports; migrants from these countries are willing to work for lower wages. The number-of-migrants versus rights-of-migrants issue promises to become more important as Saudi Arabia and other oil exporters step up drives to replace foreign with local workers.

Domestic Helpers, Nurses, and Seamen

About 60 percent of Filipino migrants are women. There are four main flows of female migrants from the Philippines—to the Gulf states as maids, to Southeast Asia as maids, to Japan as entertainers, and to other industrial countries as nurses, teachers, and domestic helpers. In most cases, the decision to migrate is a family decision linked to household survival strategies, but emigration is also encouraged by a highly competitive recruitment industry.

Some 25 to 30 percent of Filipino OFWs are domestic helpers, also known as maids, amahs, nannies, or caregivers, with the largest concentrations in Hong Kong and Saudi Arabia. The domestic helper industry allows well-educated local women to work for wages in Hong Kong, and to make life easier for often-large families in the oil-exporting Gulf states.[15]

The working conditions that domestic helpers encounter abroad vary enormously, from being treated as one of the family to being exploited and subjected to sexual abuse. The labor laws of many countries do not cover domestic helpers, and few countries have effective mechanisms that allow maids to report abuses and punish employers who abuse them. Many employers of domestic helpers hold the documents of their employees to keep them from running away, and some insist that the helpers do work that their permits do not allow, as when Hong Kong households have their maids work in shops. Space is tight in Hong Kong, so that some maids must sleep under tables or in closets.

Nonetheless, Hong Kong may be the most favorable Asian destination for Filipino domestic helpers because of relatively extensive laws and regulations; the government has a model contract and a hot line to receive complaints from maids. The minimum wage was HK$3,670 ($470) per month in 2002, and Filipino maids were far more likely to receive it than maids from Indonesia and Sri Lanka. In April 2003, despite protests from the Philippine government, the minimum wage for maids was cut to HK$3,270 ($420) per month. In the oil-exporting Gulf states, wages vary with nationality, with Filipino domestic helpers near the top of the wage ladder because of their English and their better knowledge of protective regulations.

Domestic helpers sometimes run afoul of the law while abroad. In March 1995, Singapore hanged a Filipina maid for killing another maid and the child in her care, and the Flor Contemplacion case became a cause celebre in the Philippines. When a Filipina maid, Sarah Balabagan, was sentenced to death soon after for killing her employer in the United Arab Emirates (UAE), three Filipino ministers went to the UAE and successfully pleaded for the government to spare her life.[16] Filipinos in the Middle East have run afoul of laws that prevent evangelical activities; preaching a faith other than Islam is a crime under Saudi Arabia's Shariah law. In Greece, a dictionary in 1998 included the term "Filipineza," a derogatory term for Filipino domestic helper, prompting a Filipino government protest.

After the contemplacion case, President Fidel Ramos briefly broke diplomatic relations with Singapore, used military aircraft to allow maids to return home, and for a time prevented women from leaving legally to work as maids in Singapore and the Gulf states.[17] The Manila demonstrations, some argued, reflected indignation about the need of the country's women to emigrate to support their families and the helplessness of the Philippine government to protect them abroad. The result of the Contemplacion case was the Migrant Workers and Overseas Filipino Act of 1995 (Republic Act 8042), the OFW's Magna Carta, to protect migrants. The Philippine government became far more active in urging the UN to convene a global conference on international migration and the Association of Southeasts Asian Nations (ASEAN) to accept freedom of movement.[18]

In 2001, some 13,536 nurses left the Philippines for jobs in thirty-one countries under the auspices of POEA, including 304 to the United States (these data do not include nurses who leave for the United States or Canada with immigrant visas). In the Philippines, some 6,500 to 7,000 nurses graduate each year, and many plan to go abroad for better pay, more professional opportunities, and because of ties to relatives abroad. The Philippine Nurses Association Inc. (PNA) estimated in 2002 that 150,885 Filipino nurses were abroad, and noted that experienced nurses with specialty training were most in demand overseas.

In 2003, pay for Filipino nurses abroad was reported to be $3,000 to $4,000 a month, versus $170 per month in urban areas of the Philippines, and $75 to $95 per month in rural areas. Some Filipino doctors, who earn $300 to $800 per month, are reportedly retraining as nurses so they can emigrate. Within the Philippines, the government is the major employer of nurses, and pays better than private hospitals. Some Filipino hospitals recruit local nurses by arguing that a year's experience will help them to obtain an overseas job; in the early 1990s, there were reportedly 31,000 unemployed nurses in the Philippines.

Most U.S. hospitals require foreign nurses to speak English, have a degree in nursing, and to have worked at a hospital with at least 150 beds for at least two years. In 2001, 75 percent of the 17,000 foreign nurses who took the U.S. certification exam were from the Philippines. The dean of a nursing school in Manila said that about half the graduates of her school pass this U.S. exam the first time they take it, but noted that one part of the exam had to be taken in Saipan, the closest U.S. territory. For this reason, some nurses go first to Canada or the UK, and from there to the United States.

Labor Secretary Patricia Sto. Tomas says that nurses are "the new growth area for overseas employment," and that Filipinas have a comparative advantage because of their care-giving skills and competence in English. She minimized the danger of a shortage of nurses in the Philippines: "We won't lose nurses. The older ones, those in their mid-40s, are not likely to leave. Besides, the student population reacts to markets quickly. Enrollment is high. We won't lack nurses."[19] Marilyn E. Lorenzo of the University of the Philippines College of Public Health agrees in part: "There is no shortage. There are enough warm bodies here, but there is a shortage in terms of quality" since the most skilled and experienced nurses are the most likely to emigrate.[20]

The Philippines had about 200,000 sailors on the world's ships in 2000, accounting for 20 to 25 percent of the world's seafarers.[21] Almost half of the Filipino seafarers are employed on cruise ships, where they earn $450 to $600 a month for 70 to 90 hour workweeks; most stay at sea for four to ten months. Since July 1, 2000, the minimum salary of Filipino able-bodied seamen leaving for jobs aboard foreign sea vessels has been US$435 per month[22] for a 70-hour workweek.[23] The 200,000-plus seamen deployed each year go abroad with the help of recruiters or manning agencies with contracts with ship owners. There is, however, increasing competition from Eastern Europe and the ex-USSR as well as China and Vietnam, which puts downward pressure on wages.

The Associated Marine Officers' and Seamen's Union of the Philippines (AMOSUP) has been a leader in training, protecting, and re-integrating Filipinos employed as contract workers on ships. An ordinary seaman is a high-school graduate who has completed several basic courses on seafaring. AMO-SUP (www.amosup.org/), with 40,000 members, provides more advanced training in an academy with a four-year program, graduating 3rd mate junior officers who can earn $900 per month plus $500 in overtime. AMOSUP has a "seamen's village" with over 400 homes about an hour south of Manila that allows members to move in with no down payment and repayment over fifteen years. The union also operates hospitals and dormitories for members and their families.

Remittances and Returns

Remittances averaged $575 million per month in 2003, a total of $7.5 billion, with the major sources the United States, Saudi Arabia, Japan, United Kingdom, Hong Kong, Singapore, and the United Arab Emirates; by some estimates, half of the remittances are from Canada and the United States, countries in which Filipinos tend to be immigrants rather than temporary foreign workers. Remittances are almost 10 percent of the Philippines' $80 billion GDP; beginning in 1999 the government issued small-denominated Treasury Bonds for migrants overseas as a way to earn interest on their savings. "Bagong Bayani" (New Heroes) $100 bonds allow Filipinos working abroad to earn 4.5 percent interest for funds that are spent to improve the infrastructure in the Philippines.[24]

Migration has become deeply entrenched in Filipino society, and is often portrayed in books and movies. The 2000 movie *Anak*, or "Daughter," tells the story of a mother who returned from working as a maid in Hong Kong and found her family torn apart by her absence. Another movie, "Homecoming," portrays a Filipina caregiver returning after five years in Toronto to marry her childhood sweetheart. She brings hope to her village, but also a virus that could wipe it out. The virus exposes the many weaknesses of individuals, governments, and institutions but also highlights the strengths of Filipinos. Stories of domestic helpers in Hong Kong are the basis of "Homebound." With the help of a migrant assistance organization, they pool their savings to launch small businesses when they return, making them agents of change.

A weekly radio program, *Babaeng Migrante, May Kakampi Ka* (Women Migrant, You Have an Ally) discusses issues relevant to women thinking of emigrating.

The Philippine Human Development Report 2002 concluded that: "No solid evidence on loss of skilled manpower, due to labor migration, has surfaced. The consensus is, going abroad increases the return on investments in education and skills. Overseas work . . . should be encouraged." According to the report, there were 6.4 million Filipinos employed overseas, and 31 million employed in the Philippines. Those abroad included 2.1 million Filipino workers in the United States, 400,000 in Canada, and 260,000 in Australia and New Zealand.

Most Filipino migrants return after their overseas contracts expire, often with the goal of starting a small business, and there are a variety of migrant coops and private businesses to help them invest their savings from overseas work.[25] According to the Office of Reintegration of OFWs, most unskilled migrants must work abroad at least three years to repay the debts they incurred to become OFWs, so those with the most savings have been out of the Philippines the longest. Typically, a woman will go abroad under a series of two-year contracts when she is between twenty-five and forty-five, and then return to retire.

Among the most common investments made by returning migrants are small stores or "jeepneys," the 20-passenger vehicles with facing rows of seats that transport riders up to 4km for 4 pesos ($0.08). A used jeepney can be bought for 250,000 pesos or about $4,500, can generate fares of 500 pesos a day, and after paying a driver and maintenance, will have paid for itself in a year or two. Other popular investments made by returned migrants are raising pigs or poultry or developing handicraft businesses.

There are several government and nongovernmental organization (NGO) efforts to promote the re-integration of migrants. The OWWA has an Expanded Livelihood Development Program (ELDP) that provides advice to returning OFWs who want to launch small businesses—sewing garments, making furniture, going into pig or poultry farming, or opening small stores or service establishments such as tailoring or beauty parlors. The Social Security System (SSS) launched the OFW Flexi-Fund provident fund to provide a retirement protection scheme for OFWs.

There is a growing business in helping migrants to invest their savings. For example, a man named Carlito Balita travels to Hong Kong to give courses to Filipina domestic helpers on their days off to become "Entrepinoys," a play on entrepreneur and the Tagalog word for Filipino. He says that Filipinos must "get away from this employment mentality, working just so our children can get better work, and see the other side of the coin, see the beauty of creating your own life through business."[26] Balita says that too many Filipinos prefer "a safe salary" to taking the risks of opening a business, but others say that Balita is simply an inspirational speaker who extracts fees from maids who dream of running businesses. One reporter concluded: "There are precious few success stories of former maids who saved their money and made good."[27]

The Wall Street Journal on May 22, 2001,[28] described the impact of remittances on Pozorrubio, a city of 60,000 with 6,000 residents overseas. Western Union plays a central role in the city's life, bringing remittances from migrants overseas that have spruced up the city; Pozorrubians of Greater Los Angeles donated supplies to a local hospital. The Rural Bank of Pozorrubio says that remittances have given it more savings than can be lent locally.

The emigration wave began in the 1980s, and remittances brought concrete houses and appliances—even before there was electricity, some homes put dishwashers, refrigerators, and televisions on the porch. However, education for children seemed to be the priority of many families, second only to daily expenses in remittance spending. Proud of what they had achieved, residents posted their degrees on houses, such as "Certified Public Accountant," "Attorney at Law" or "Registered Nurse."

The reporter concluded that, despite the focus on education, the children of overseas workers usually become overseas workers themselves, largely because remittances have not been able to create good-paying local jobs. Instead, some residents complain that remittances have fueled a boom in gambling and karaoke clubs. Children educated with their parents' remittances often say, when asked about their hopes for the future: "I want to work abroad as a domestic helper." Press reports and research literature suggest a troubling trend of families becoming accustomed to living chiefly from OFW remittances. There are many reports of "too much" spending on imported consumer items and other "misplaced priorities," and a growing sense that upward mobility is best achieved by leaving to work.

Migration and Development?

There is general agreement that for the foreseeable future large numbers of Filipinos will emigrate for jobs. The government's position is that emigration is an "option" for migrants, but not the country's "official development strategy." Labor Secretary Patricia Sto. Tomas says, "Overseas employment is a choice made by individuals. But once they leave for overseas, the government is duty bound to assure that migrants' contracts have ample provisions for their protection."[29]

Some experts have concluded that even if per capita incomes rise, Filipinos will still emigrate because of strong demand for them in overseas labor markets. Economist Bernardo M. Villegas, in a book *The Philippine Advantage*, argues that foreign employers prefer Filipinos: "It is highly probable that, even as our per capita income improves and the poverty incidence is reduced, Filipinos will continue to migrate to other countries." Villegas noted that 80 percent of Filipino nurses are employed abroad, and said that migrants "will be the focus of the Philippine economy at least for the next 100 years."[30]

Sto. Tomas seems to agree, saying in 2001: "Look at it this way. Part of the reason we're [Filipino migrants] so in demand is because we have this unique characteristic where we send all our children to school. The net result is we have a lot of educated persons and this pool of educated persons is what makes us in demand all over the world. . . . It is a distinctly Filipino characteristic to make sacrifices for their families so that they can send their children to school, buy their necessities—even if this is at the expense of them being away." Sto. Tomas said those who choose to become domestic helpers abroad "make a choice for more money but less prestige."[31]

The Philippines may have the world's most diversified portfolio of foreign labor markets for its workers, and aims to send more professionals abroad. However, labor migration is, at best, a palliative for Filipino economic underdevelopment.

China

The CEME trip to the People's Republic of China in June 2004 included discussions at the Canadian Embassy, the Ministry of Public Affairs, the Fuzhou offices of the Border Defense Patrol, the detention center in Fuzhou and the resource restoration plant of an entrepreneur returnee in Beijing. A tour of the areas in and around Fuzhou showed clearly that remittance monies were invested in new ventures as well as in "conspicuous consumption" homes.[32]

China is experiencing all the major trends associated with internal migration and emigration: rapid growth, displacement, and increased inequality both across regions and between urban and rural areas. There is increased emigration, particularly of students and other temporary resident categories, more government efforts to manage migration, decreased irregular migration by sea, increasingly sophisticated fraud, and stronger bilateral cooperation on migration management and law enforcement with other countries, particularly Japan, Korea, Australia, Canada, UK, France, and United States.

China's migration management challenges are in one sense no different from those of other countries, but they seem greater given the rapid pace of economic and social change and the sheer scale of population movements. Earlier fears of Chinese hordes spilling over borders as a logical consequence of internal migration seem unfounded. The success of some returning entrepreneurs and the government's efforts to support apparently increasing "brain circulation" between China and industrial countries warrants special attention. For example, one entrepreneur we visited demonstrated how policies in origin and destination areas can combine in a "co-development" way to benefit the returnee, the home community and the sending country government.

Who Leaves and Why?
The Chinese Ministry of Public Security (MPS) reported that migration management has become complex, with rapid growth and rising living standards stimulating more emigration from China, particularly from the area

around Fuzhou in Fujian Province, and also of more educated, entrepreneurial Chinese looking for expansion, new technologies, new skills, and business opportunities. However, Chinese authorities believe that much of this migration is temporary, not permanent.

The MPS reports that the majority of Chinese go abroad with legal documents, either for tourism, to visit relatives, study, or to work/do business (although the Ministry could not corroborate this). Many return, but a large, indeterminate number overstay their visas. The Canadian Embassy observed two migration streams: the unskilled Chinese tend to move internally while the skilled migrate across international borders. The main push/pull factors for international migration are: well-established familial and other networks in the countries of destination; education opportunities for children abroad; relative ease of exit from China nowadays; global business opportunities and, for many, the services provided by smuggler agencies. Tourism has grown—some 20 million Chinese went abroad in 2003, as tourism agreements with destination countries foster and regulate tourist movements.

With some 120 million migrants estimated to be on the move internally, there was considerable debate about the potential spillover to international migration, but little evidence to suggest a significant link between the two. No systematic research has been done on the topic, but research on international migrants indicates that the majority are from the coastal regions of China, not from the hinterland areas from which internal migrants come. Research on internal migration indicates that rather than spill across international borders, the opposite may well be happening, at least in the short term, with rural-to-urban migration helping to take up the slack in some lesser skilled sectors caused by the departure of urban dwellers for other countries.

The economic boom has stimulated migration, but emigration flows are being tempered by such factors as improved tertiary education opportunities in China and stricter post September 11, 2001, entry procedures in many destination countries. For the United States, there is a five-year backlog in the family migration visa category; and many Chinese decide to enter as visitors or students or illegally. For Canada and Australia, there are also lower numbers for the family categories, as the major focus is on skilled migration.

In calendar year 2000, 36,718 People's Republic of China (PRC) nationals became permanent residents of Canada (5,741 were members of the family class). This rose to 40,315 in 2001 (6,472 were members of the family class) and fell back to 33,231 in 2002 (9,016 were members of the family class). In 2003, 36,115 PRC nationals became permanent residents and members of the family class accounted for 9,813 of this number. Given the growing proportion of family class immigrants globally, Canada decided to place a cap on the movement of parents and grandparents to ensure a 60:40 ratio between economic and family class movements. In 2004, the Canadian visa offices in Hong Kong (which deal overwhelmingly with PRC nationals) and Beijing have a combined target of 27,300 economic class visas and 8,270 family class visas. Australia issued just over 3,000 family visas in FY 2002/2003, compared with 5,000 five years ago. Some 9,800 skilled migrant visas were issued in 2002/2003, three times the family visa numbers, and 8.5 percent of the total skilled migration intake.

There is a high incidence of fraud in both the immigrant and non-immigrant categories reported by the destination countries; a key reason for stricter procedures and high rejections. Canada reported 43 percent fraud in some areas of the family class program—e.g., over-age dependents and adoptions of blood relatives. Canada waives the interview requirement in about 73 percent of the spousal cases and refuses 18 percent primarily because they are found to be "marriages of convenience." The refusal rate for student applications has fallen in recent years from 49 percent in 2002 to 35 percent in 2004. Canadian embassy staff believes that Canada may be receiving fewer but better applicants.

The refusal rate for business delegations in 2004 has been running at 17 percent. The Canadian Embassy's Migration Integrity Unit undertakes site visits to collect information and verify documentation, because of the lack of state control of authenticity of documents in China.

Many who leave are educated, have had a job in China, earned low pay, and have children whose education and job prospects would be enhanced abroad. Scientists and science researchers still have fewer opportunities in China, and are attracted by the greater opportunities to pursue research in line with their own interests in the United States and other foreign countries. To enter the United States, they often apply for B1/B2 (business/tourist) visas and then adjust status to a work visa.

Once in the destination country, many over-stay their visas and become illegal; many apply for asylum. According to Canadian Embassy statistics, China was the fourth largest source country of asylum seekers in 2002; the fifth largest in 2003, and the third largest in 2004. But, as MPS also pointed out in its claims that destination country policies may also need to be reviewed, there is a high asylum approval rate in Canada (76 percent), which may act as an incentive. Australia reported that, despite a drop in overstay rates, China was third on its list of overstayers.

Chinese Overseas Students and Tourists

Canada receives around 120,000 (in Beijing, Shanghai, and Hong Kong) visitor applications a year, mostly for business purposes, and going abroad for business is one way for Fujianese to transit to the United States and other destinations. Australia expects some 160,000 Chinese tourists in 2004 alone, and has experienced rapid growth. The Australian Tourism Forecasting Council predicts that by 2010 there may be up to a half million Chinese tourists visiting the country annually. The Approved Destination Status Agreement (ADS) with China, which facilitates tourist entry to Australia, has just been expanded to cover 9 provinces/regions in China.

According to an editorial in the *China Daily* (July 6, 2004), China has signed similar ADS agreements with some twenty-six countries around the world, and by September 1, 2004, this number is expected to grow by a further twenty-seven European countries. The article explains that travel abroad has increased because in 2004 Chinese GDP surpassed USD1,000 per capita and total foreign currency savings of Chinese residents topped USD90 billion. Since February 2002, people no longer need to produce letters from overseas groups in order to get permission from local public security authorities to travel abroad. "Passports are available on demand and citizens can join outbound tourism groups. Last year (2004) there were 20.2 million outbound Chinese tourists, despite the impact of the SARS crisis." The article explains "Chinese tourists were not allowed to travel to the European Union (EU) in the past except for Germany. People had to travel on different types of visas, such as for business or family visits."[33]

Study abroad is one of the four main reasons for Chinese emigrating and is increasingly used as a springboard for more permanent migration. It is also fraught with fraud, both of travel and other supporting documentation. While generally considered a growth sector for many destination countries, the number of Chinese students has been declining for some, such as United States, Canada, New Zealand, and Ireland, in part following stringent control measures introduced after September 11, 2001. They are growing elsewhere, such as for Australia, and generally shifting toward Europe.

For Australia, China is the biggest source of overseas students—14,215 visas in 2002/2003; and 18,000 in 2003/2004 of the total 100,000 visas issued per year. Most of them are undergraduates, but there is also a growing school sector. Add to this some 25,000 Chinese who study at Australian educational institutes within China. This makes Australia the highest per capita recipient of Chinese students, both in- and out-of-country. Australia also claimed to be the number one provider of overseas education within China.

The Australian Skilled Migration program has a provision for overseas students, and as a result, many Chinese students are able to change their status to permanent residence and work in Australia. In all, 40 percent of Australia's skilled migrants are now drawn from the overseas student caseload. This is also the trend in Canada, United States, and Europe, although still not on the same scale.

In the UK, the overwhelming numbers of Chinese migrants are students. In FY 2002/2003, there were 22,161 student applications, and a visa issuance rate of 73 percent. In 2003/2004, there were 22,828 applications and an issuance rate of 63 percent. UK colleagues in Beijing report that while the travel documents are usually genuine, the biggest problem are forged documents relating to educational qualifications and institutions, bank statements, stock market forms, employment records, etc. A number of students end up in the asylum pipeline, and some sell their multiple entry visas. The UK hopes to enter an ADS agreement with China this year and is seriously debating the possibility of issuing only single entry/fixed period visas, to avoid recycling of multiple entry visas.

The UK does not expect any notable increase in student numbers in the future, as Chinese students now have more opportunities to study at universities in China. This generally does not fit with other indications that Chinese interest in study is shifting from the traditional destination countries to Europe. According to the International Organization for Migration (IOM), some 20 percent of Chinese students were studying in Europe a few years ago—mainly in the UK, Germany, and France (only 30 percent of them ever returning home). In Germany, Chinese apparently accounted for the third largest foreign student group in 2000/2001.

In the United States, student numbers are down, and there are fewer self-funded students from China. A combination of factors have caused the downturn, including post–September 11 processing delays and the "dot.com" recession that reduced post-graduation employment opportunities for foreign students. The embassy in Beijing anticipated some 22,000 applicants in 2004, with a likely visa issuance rate of 70 percent. This is a reduction over previous years. The embassy reports that there are currently some 68,000 Chinese students in the United States, of which 75 percent are likely to stay.

There is a higher prevalence of graduate study by Chinese in the United States than in any other destination country. The numbers are down, but the quality is up. There is a high prevalence of document fraud—up to 30 percent of applications—or the use of valid documents (e.g., for MBA "refresher" courses) and overstay. U.S. authorities are moving to more monitoring and reporting by the universities and educational institutes on the behavior and regular status of students—a method already applied in Australia. Numbers have been dropping in the United States: 17,000 applications in 2001, and only 8,000 for the first six months in 2004.

In Canada, most Chinese students are undergraduates or English as a second language (ESL) candidates. The primary concern is overstaying. Many students travel to New York or apply for asylum in Canada (250 claimants in 2003). With high numbers, Canadian and Chinese interlocutors have set up a multi-departmental Canada-China Working Group (established after the arrival of four Chinese boats on the west coast of Canada in 1999). The Ministry of Public Security represents the Chinese side, while Citizenship and Immigration, the recently constituted Canadian Border Services Agency, and the Royal Canadian Mounted Police represent Canada. A wide range of issues is discussed.

As interest grows in study options in Europe, and the European states increasingly seize the student market opportunities, the latter are also strengthening their document checking and fraud control mechanisms. The team learned through the contact of one of its members with senior French Embassy officials in Beijing that the embassy has created a special agency to check Chinese student applications. Each application costs EUR300, and the money is used to hire Chinese and French employees to check the documents and assess the academic backgrounds and projects. By embassy accounts, fraud in this area seems to have decreased from 40 percent to 10 percent. The German Embassy apparently has the same kind of mechanism.

The Special Case of Fujian

Fuzhou, the capital of Fujian province, is a major source for migrants to countries like the United States, and beneficiary of migrant remittances (and allegedly also smuggler profits). Economic growth clearly stimulates out-migration, mostly of Fujianese who have relatives and contacts in the United States and elsewhere and leave with proper documents but overstay once abroad and/or enter the asylum systems. Many also travel with false documents. Travel agencies play a large part in this as do the transport agencies, which are subject to criminal sanctions if caught.

There are more than eighty counties in Fujian, but most irregular migrants are from two or three, each with more than twenty towns, and each town covers up to twenty administrative villages. It is difficult to gauge the exact number of exits/entries of the province. Policy and practice are divided between the Entry/Exit Bureau of the MPS and the Border Defense Force (BDF) of the same ministry. With three thousand kilometers of coastline and many thousands of boats, it is difficult to monitor and record all entries and exits.

The provincial director of the Border Defense Force judged that international emigration from this area could be explained partly by surging incomes, which enabled many to afford the high costs related to international migration (whether regular or irregular), but partly also by the in-migration from other provinces, as some counties in Fujian were still quite poor and backward. The team assessed that the extent and direction of causal links between internal and international migration still required considerably more research.

Interestingly, at the same time that Fujian produces migrants, its growth attracts increasing numbers of irregular immigrants. The economic strength of Fujian attracts investment from Hong Kong, Macao, Taiwan, and other countries, which in turn boosts Fujian's visitor statistics—and with these, illegal immigration. Since 2002, the Border Defense Force has apprehended around two thousand illegal entries and overstayers in the province, many from Iran, Bangladesh, and Pakistan.

The Government and Irregular Migration

Following the surge in boat arrivals in Australia, Canada, and the United States in the late 1980s to early 1990s, and the September 11 bombings, the government demonstrably increased efforts to reduce irregular Chinese migration in recent years. Laws covering the control of irregular migration have been strengthened,[34] and the passport law is also about to be amended. Document production has been enhanced with improved security features, especially in the new passport that came into use in 1999 and generally stronger information technology (IT) applications. Information campaigns have been launched, using media, lectures, village discussions, etc. to inform people about the risks of irregular migration. Detention facilities have been upgraded and a joint Committee for Anti-Illegal Migration set up, involving the Public Prosecutor, MPS, Ministry of Foreign Affairs (MFA) and Ministry of Civil Affairs.

But the government has focused most of its control efforts on the sea borders, as it is easier to control irregular migration by sea than by air. By the end of the 1990s, a marine police team was formed, and management control resources and mechanisms at the borders were strengthened.

MPS reports great success in controlling potential irregular migration through its emigration checks at the sea borders. There have been virtually no irregular migrants arriving in Australia, Canada, or Europe by boat in recent years, and fewer fake documents are coming to light, as a result of either modern technology or better fake documents.

MPS reported that during its concerted campaign against irregular migration in and out of China in the six-month period October 2003 to March 2004, there were approximately 5,500 Chinese attempting to leave in an irregular way (fake or no documents) and around 5,000 attempting to enter China illegally (e.g., from Vietnam, Pakistan, North Korea, Burma).

Regarding smuggling and trafficking, there have been repeated strikes in main source areas, targeting the organizers (loosely termed "snake heads" by the authorities). Countless seminars and information campaigns have been held, and legislation against smuggling and trafficking strengthened. Persons convicted of organizing smuggling or trafficking can be fined, or, if convicted, sentenced to two, five, ten years or life imprisonment. Where possible, finances owing to the victims are recovered from the organizers. There was little confirmation of larger efforts at confiscating assets, which, it was reported, would in any case go back into public revenue and not into any further supportive efforts in this area. MPS reported that the organizers are often a mixture of locals and migrants abroad, most of ethnic Chinese origin.

The Border Defense Force in Fuzhou also reported that rewards are now offered for information and assistance in capturing smugglers or traffickers. Last year some 50,000 to 80,000 Yuan were paid per informant for ten such cases.

Both the law and practice show a clear preference for punishing the perpetrators rather than the victims, including the smuggled, who are often sufficiently badly treated by the smugglers as to be victims. Nevertheless, both MPS in Beijing and its border defense force unit in Fuzhou confirmed that returnees who left with fraudulent or no documents or in some way violated Chinese law in immigrating illegally to other countries can be punished (up to six months in jail), educated, and monitored after return. Canadian Embassy staff informed that Canada deports hundreds of Chinese every year, mostly without escort and fanfare, as this is both quicker and easier and tends to go unnoticed and unpunished by the authorities.

Statistics on irregular Chinese migration are virtually impossible to obtain, because so much of the "illegality" or "irregularity" occurs at destination after the migrants have left China with proper documents (passport and visa) and under a regular temporary immigration program. Also, there are innumerable fake documents that are never brought to light. This information would need to be gathered at the destination end.

From statistics provided by MPS, in the period 1991–2003 some 38,691 persons were captured trying to migrate illegally, and 6,149 organizers were caught and punished. Some 8 organizers have apparently received life sentences. The Border Defense Force in Fujian advised that in 2003 some 750 smuggling organizers/transporters were arrested and imprisoned; among them a number of foreign snake heads from such places as the United States, South Korea, and Singapore. While China does not strictly distinguish between smuggling and trafficking of migrants, there is a difference in the severity of punishment. Smugglers are usually fined or imprisoned for two to seven years or for life, depending on the seriousness of the offense.[35] Trafficking in persons can involve the death penalty.

The Border Defense Force in Fuzhou is also increasingly confronted with irregular immigrants at the borders, hailing from countries in the larger Asian region such as Vietnam, North Korea, and Pakistan. Most do not have valid ID and travel documents. The Vietnamese and Pakistanis are seldom imprisoned, but simply quickly repatriated. The BDF claims to enjoy good law enforcement cooperation with neighboring countries, particularly on ID checking at borders.

Bilateral forms of cooperation in combating migrant smuggling have been established or strengthened with more than forty other countries, in particular countries of destination. China has especially good cooperation arrangements with Australia, Canada, UK, Netherlands, Japan, Germany, France, and Italy. An agreement exists between France and China for exchange of police, and similar cooperative arrangements exist between China and Japan. An MPS liaison officer has been seconded unofficially to the Chinese Embassy in Ottawa for several years, and two MPS officers will shortly be officially assigned to Canada. In 2003, three experts from MPS were sent to the UK to work with Home Office counterparts in identifying Chinese illegally in the country for eventual removal. Through direct interviews with the migrants, local dialects could be identified, and some sixty persons were deported. Joint operations with the Japanese authorities in 2001 resulted in the capture of one hundred smuggling organizers.

MPS reiterated the need for countries of destination to change their approach and policies to irregular migration, so that there is less encouragement to stay illegally. Some aspects of current policy in destination countries are problematic. In the case of the Dover deaths, for example, the UK authorities knew about the illegally present migrants, but preferred, for reasons of economies of scale, to address the problem at the back end, after the migrants had been through all available options, and their deportation was more assured. At earlier stages of the migration experience this is less possible. Also, multiple entry visas for temporary categories have tended to encourage multiple recycling of visas.

To better monitor irregular Chinese migration, the UK and Netherlands were testing the fingerprinting of applicants in China; and the Chinese government was also starting to test fingerprinting both for customs control and for business facilitation purposes in South China. When asked if the government was intending to use fingerprinting for migration management purposes, MPS was doubtful, claiming the government was more concerned to protect personal privacy at this stage.

The Government and Regular Migration

MPS claims to have issued 300,000 passports in 2003, but for a complete picture, one would need to add the "public affairs" passports issued by MFA in the same year. There is no clear evidence that all holders of such documents actually traveled, and judging by the visas issued by countries of destination in any given year, this in no way reflects either the level of interest or actual engagement in travel abroad. It can only be a reflection of new interest in such emigration. Actual departures from China could only be gauged by a systematic assembly of visa and entry statistics from countries of destination.

One progressive way for the government to address the issue of irregular migration has been to facilitate and promote legal, regular forms of migration, for example by simplifying application procedures for passports and by signing cooperation agreements with countries of destination, such as the Approved Destination Status Agreements (ADS) on tourism with Australia and some twenty-seven others around the world. These can be accompanied by cooperation on identifying illegal migrants, such as between UK and China.

While principally an agreement on tourism flows between China and Australia, the ADS agreement helps to foster legitimate forms of migration to a country that in the past experienced high levels of non-return of Chinese visitors and students and now enjoyed among the lowest non-return levels of all destination countries. The agreement combines in a balanced way few controls up front and high visa issuance rates with travel agency accountability and strict monitoring of departures via travel agency accountability.

Detention Center in Fuzhou

The main Fujian detention center just outside Fuzhou can accommodate up to three hundred persons—both foreigners caught entering the country illegally and Chinese returning from illegal migration activities abroad. Managed by the Border Defense Force, the center is intended to detain persons returned and those awaiting the outcome of administrative investigation for up to fifteen days. It offers information; awareness raising through newspapers, TV, and discussions; recreation; medical attention; and individualized "ideological education." The team was told that detainees are allowed one to three hours "free activity" every day, and that their dietary needs are taken into account.

The center has on a number of occasions been presented as a model to immigration officials (including ministers) from Australia, Canada, and the United States. It appeared clean, well kept, and managed but was unoccupied at the time of the CEME visit (indeed seemed only to have housed some two hundred occupants in the year). It offers excellently presented displays of its history, including distinguished visits from other countries, and a rousing documentary video of its purpose, history, and operation.

The team found the center to be a conspicuous demonstration by the government to the world of how heavily it is investing in combating irregular forms of migration. However, given that the center was unoccupied, the team speculated about how much it was actually used for the purposes and to the extent claimed.

Circular Migration—Turning Night Soil into Pay Dust

The team met with Mr. J. C. Yu, an entrepreneur who had returned to China after studying and working in Canada for ten years and acquiring Canadian citizenship, as an example of the effects of return migration on economic development. Mr. Yu, an environmental engineer with a Masters Degree from the University of Alberta, clearly hailed from an educated, well-to-do family. His sister also apparently attained her qualifications in organic chemistry in Canada. His brother, a geophysicist, chose to remain in China. Mr. Yu appeared to straddle the interests of both siblings—personal development abroad and national development at home.

It appears that the governments of both countries of residence helped him achieve a convergence of these aspirations—wittingly or unwittingly.

Mr. Yu had the good fortune of being in the right place at the right time and seizing the opportunity as it arose. In Canada, he profited from the "amnesty" policies after the Tiananmen Square events of 1989 and could acquire Canadian citizenship, which gave him the confidence and empowerment to return to China ten years later and try his luck with new qualifications and skills from abroad. When, after studying and working in the environmental protection area in Canada for years, he was unable to realize his entrepreneurial dreams there, he seized the new opportunities presenting themselves in China in 2000.

Mr. Yu returned to China in 2000 and opened up a business in solid waste management, setting up a "resource recovery center" in Beijing, in response both to a general urgent need to upgrade this facility in that vast metropolis and to specific needs of the upcoming Olympic Games in Beijing. The center helps service the 8,000 public toilets in Beijing and successfully combines immediate utility with future planning. The night soil processing plant rids the city of its waste, restores the basic resources water and soil, and produces methane gas to power the center. It thus serves multiple purposes for the community, the government, other businesses, and the entrepreneur himself: solid waste management, water restoration (sold to a nearby cement factory), clean-earth production (for local landfill), and power generation. It thus also serves a range of general sanitation and ecological purposes.

The association between Mr. Yu and the Chinese government is indicative of current trends in China. The technology used in the plant (which is only one of ten processing waste from Beijing) was developed by Mr. Yu, and, in his words, is the most efficient applied to date in China. The plant was designed and built under the responsibility of Mr. Yu and his private company, which now has an operating contract with the government of Beijing. The plant, however, is government-owned. But in addition to the operation fee, he has rights to additional profits made from the sale of fertilizer and other by-products. The team wanted to find out whether the Chinese government was providing financial incentives for returning Chinese professionals to help them get established in China, and Mr. Yu said he had asked for such incentives and talked to the government about the creation of financial programs for returning migrants, but so far none had been created. With this arrangement, however, there is little need for risk capital from the entrepreneur, and still he is able to make an entrepreneurial profit.

Mr. Yu built his business within two years, with some basic funding support from the private sector, to a multi-million RMB enterprise employing some forty workers, and it is growing. Mr. Yu is a celebrity in Beijing and China. He is currently honorable chairman of the Canada-China Society of Science and Technology. In true reflection of the circular nature of migration in a globalized world, Mr. Yu plans to return to Canada and expand his business interests there.

Important in this whole saga is the role that his Canadian citizenship played in giving Mr. Yu the confidence to return and "speculate" in his home country at a time of great opportunity, knowing that he could always return to Canada. With this policy, the Canadian government is indirectly fostering a "co-development" scenario to the advantage of the country of origin (see chapter 9). The Chinese government has also played a part in this regard by exercising discretion in regard to Mr. Yu's dual citizenship status, which strictly speaking is not permissible in China.

While the gains for the migrant and his home community and country seemed clear, the team speculated about the immediate or longer term benefits for the destination country, which had educated the migrant, bestowed citizenship, and then seen him leave to do business in the country of origin. Are destinations like Canada factoring this kind of circular migration into their migration/development policy thinking and planning?

It is also unclear how representative this case is of the experience of the majority of return migrants. The Beijing municipal government is undertaking an assessment of the impact of the considerable incentives—subsidized loans, tax breaks, etc.—offered to returning entrepreneurs in recent years. But given the number of sectors involved and the lack of a control group of people who did not leave, it is hard to assess the value added by such programs.

Internal and International Migration

There appears to be less of a flow-on from internal to external emigration than may be feared by countries of destination. Discussions with a Chinese researcher, Dr. Xiang,[36] confirmed that the major places of origin for internal migration (Sichuan, Hunan, Jiangxi, Henan, Gansu, etc.) have hardly produced any international migration. But the most important places of origin for international migration (Zhejiang, Fujian, and to some extent Guangdong provinces) are among the key places of destination for internal migration. This is also borne out by other ongoing research in this area.[37]

Large-scale internal migration began in the late 1980s, and international emigration from China resumed at the end of the 1970s and increased significantly after 1986 with a new law that relaxed exit control. Thus both internal and international migration have been growing for more than two decades now; however, to date the two streams have developed along separate lines.

The researcher reported that there are some new trends in both internal and international migration. Internally, more hinterland places are now involved in migration, though from early 2004 with the implementation of favorable rural policies, some migrants have started returning to their home places to resume farming activities. Internationally, some new emigration communities have appeared in places without international migration (most notably northeast China), but the new migrants are mainly urban-based citizens with medium- to high-level education. Again, this shows that in terms of future trends, the two migration streams are likely to remain separate: different types of people involved in internal or international migration.

Dr. Xiang's long-term fieldwork in one of the largest places of origin of Chinese immigrants to Europe, Wenzhou Prefecture, Zhejiang Province, southeast China, suggests that even within one county, one township may specialize in internal migration and the other in international mobility.

The two streams do converge in some cases: A) Merchants in the migrant community in Beijing (mainly garment producers and traders from Zhejiang province in southeast China), some traveling to Russia, Mongolia, and other East European countries to sell their products. This trend continues now, but the size is relatively small. B) Highly skilled, who often move to big cities first and then find opportunities to go overseas. C) International migration leads to internal migration to fill the vacancies; this is almost universal across the world. D) Organized labor export, in cases such as seafarers and laborers to the Middle East (particularly Israel), Far East Russia, Korea, and reportedly Mongolia. Some persons who could have become internal migrants may instead have embarked on international migration through this means.

The team felt there were many issues where the information and knowledge were deficient. The team saw great potential for exploring the internal/international migration nexus further, and particularly how China could fare better with organized labor exports—a rather under-researched topic.

Future Chinese Migration?

Why do migrants continue to choose the "illegal" route over the legal options available to them, particularly in view of the apparent ease with which most people who apply for a passport actually acquire it? Illegal routes involve extraordinary high risks: payments to smugglers/organizers, potential exploitation and further loss of family money, degradation of health, and possible loss of life. It is difficult for Chinese to leave their country without a passport, and it is often more difficult than to receive it in another country. If caught without a passport, Chinese law can punish emigrants. Even the threat of six months in detention in Fuzhou sets those "perpetrators" apart from persons who began their migration odyssey with legal documents.

Perhaps the majority of irregular Chinese abroad begin their saga in a regular, documented way, but the rejection rates in regular temporary visa categories still act as an incentive to opt for the illegal route, which if successful can be quicker. They are spurred on by others' success stories, and taken in by the sales pitches of smugglers. High asylum approval rates, such as 76 percent in Canada, can also be an incentive to irregular immigration and to the use of asylum to prolong stay and gain residence, e.g., some Chinese asylum seekers in Canada reportedly are able to acquire a PRC passport and regularly return to China during the asylum process (although such return may hinder their eventual access to asylum if it can be demonstrated that they do not have a well-founded fear of persecution). These kinds of "flexible" circumstances must serve to encourage those wanting to go abroad quickly and illicitly.

Without policy/practice reviews by destination countries, this kind of irregular immigration is unlikely to change much, despite the belief of MPS that Chinese irregular migration will probably reduce in the coming years.

It would also seem that the government's efforts at deterring undocumented emigration, together with eased passport requirements, may have led to an increase in legal migration to third countries of easy entry, which then become departure points for irregular migration to more attractive destinations. MPS officials interviewed in Beijing noted that irregular migration away from third countries was beyond their jurisdiction, and involved foreign smugglers. The team believes this can be best followed up with research in countries of destination.

Emigration is certain to continue, even grow, with the increasing economic strength of China, but so are returns and emigré investments in the country. As the "education export" industries of Australia, Canada, United States, Europe, et al. become more competitive and flexible in their interface with more permanent skilled migration, they will continue to provide an entrée to other countries. Economic growth and greater education opportunities in the PRC may slow this down, but the circular migration opportunities opening up through the complementarities of origin-destination policies, as seen with the Yu case, will encourage further out-movement.

The benefits to be gained from policies at both origin and destination that facilitate such circular migration need more study to determine how much this is actually impacts out-migration from China and the development-needy regions of China and what the benefits are for the country of destination investing in this "brain gain" for China. An article in the June 25, 2004, edition of the *China Daily* about the gloomy job prospects for returning overseas students, whose salary expectations have become too high in relation to locally educated graduates, confirm the sense that the re-integration of returnees is not always smooth and that some are having difficulty finding work.

There are also social impacts of the internal migration in China ("rural orphans struggle as parents leave in search of jobs"). The Chinese state, despite its size and power, places emphasis on its "legitimacy," which may be one reason for the government's determination to demonstrate to a wider world that it is tackling the issue of irregular migration.

As a new player in co-managing international migration, the Chinese government has been demonstrative in efforts to curb irregular migration—mostly since 2000, at the height of the boat movements and attendant anxiety of countries of destination. There have been some measurable results—reduced boat movements and fewer non-return cases from Australia—but little evidence that fraud and overstaying of visas were diminishing. On the contrary, MPS admits that document fraud has become more sophisticated and that increased captures and convictions of smugglers and traffickers are more attributable to enhanced resources and capacities than to weakening of the fraud industry. But the signals from the government are clear: it, too, has become sophisticated in its methods, and is an increasingly strong dialogue partner with other countries on migration. It has come of age in international migration diplomacy.

In response, the attitude of destination countries to Chinese migration has also changed, becoming more receptive to the mutual benefits to be gained and relaxing old fears that all Chinese migration is illegal and likely to flood other countries. Bilateral cooperation frameworks like the ADS agreement between China and Australia are worth watching and emulating, as they base their success in returning irregular migrants and lowering overstays on the principle that more regular immigration (even of visitors/tourists) can help curb irregular immigration. This approach (albeit largely unproven) can also benefit China in its emerging role as a destination country for other immigrants.

Finally, there is a need for more systematic research across sectors and portfolios to gain a more complete picture of the scale and impact of net migration in China. Emigration was the traditional focus of concerned countries of destination, but immigration and all its attendant illicit facets seemed to be rising in proportion to the economic growth of China. And the enormous returns to China—of people, skills, investments—need to be measured and weighed against the equally massive needs of this evolving economy.

This leaves us with five major questions: What are the connections between China's internal and external migration flows? What are the institutional architecture and longer-term planning objectives of the burgeoning labor migration from China, currently driven disparately by labor agreements, private company initiatives, and individual visa categories offered by destination countries? What does the Chinese experience tell us about the relationship between migration and development (ranging from the "villa envy" phenomenon to returnee enterprises like Mr. Yu's)? And has the recent focus on migration-development linkages downplayed the role of cultural and social factors in determining migration movements? What social and political controls are exerted over the smugglers/traffickers? Presumably in a society such as China, these are known to the authorities and to other members of society. How much is transnational migration offering a basis for real cooperation to mutual benefit of both China and countries of destination?

Conclusion

The Philippines and China demonstrate the global nature of international migration. With migrants traveling from these countries to all parts of the world for work and study, the Philippines and China have established ties with principal destination countries in the Americas, Europe, Australia, and the Gulf States. The development context in which this migration takes place is, however, quite distinct for the two source countries. China has been experiencing very high economic growth rates, providing opportunities for investment by return migrants and members of the Diaspora. The Philippines, on the other hand, has promoted overseas work in the context of slow economic growth and few prospects for economic advancement at home. In this sense, it is representative of a number of the sites discussed in previous chapters. In the next chapter we explore the benefits and mechanisms of cooperation in migration management, particularly as it relates to "co-development" in both of these contexts.

Notes

1. The Citizenship Retention and Re-Acquisition Act of 2003 allows Filipinos to retain or regain their citizenship after naturalizing in another country.

2. Anti-poverty programs, such as "rolling stores" selling subsidized rice, sugar, meat, and canned food from small trucks, spend much of their funds in Manila, not in the rural areas with the most extreme poverty.

3. Globally, a 10 percent increase in income growth means a 10 percent gain in the incomes of the poor. In the Philippines, 10 percent overall growth means a 4 percent gain for the poor.

4. Unions are fragmented—there were about 8,800 unions and 170 federations of unions in 2002, and the lawyers who lead many unions prefer to litigate disputes rather than settle them informally.

5. For example, Eduardo M. Cojuangco Jr. obtained a monopoly on coconut exports from Marcos and used the profits to buy farmland as well as the beer and food conglomerate San Miguel. Instead of selling his land to peasants, Cojuangco persuaded peasants working his land to let him retain land titles and to become shareholders in what he calls a "corporative."

6. Sabah was leased by the Sultan of Sulu to the British East India Company during Spanish colonial rule but was not claimed by the Philippines until the time of Marcos.

7. Some 70,000 Filipinas per year leave, and 95 percent go to Japan as entertainers with 3-month contracts. Since 1995, women leaving the Philippines as entertainers have to be at least 23 years old, have one year's performing experience in the Philippines, and obtain artists' record books that certify to their training. In September 1996, Japan made it harder for entertainers to receive an extension of their three-month visas after finding that 93 percent of entertainers who were supposed to be singing or dancing were instead attending to customers as hostesses or guest relations officers (GROs).

8. About nine hundred recruitment agencies specialize in placing Filipinos in land-based jobs abroad, and three hundred in sea-based jobs.

9. POEA recognized fifty-five recruitment agencies as top performers in 2003.

10. Most police stations in the Philippines have an OFW desk to receive complaints.

11. Filipino migrants have protested the charges levied by Philippine consulates for passports and employment contract authentication.

12. In November 1998, a Malaysian, a Briton, and an Australian were arrested after they recruited Filipinos for jobs in a fictitious country, the Dominion of Melchizedek, said to be in the South Pacific (in the Old Testament, Melchizedek was a model priest to whom Abraham and others paid tithes).

13. OWWA reported 1,400 emergency returns and the return of 600 bodies in 2003.

14. The Saudi government ordered the fifty OWWA-run shelters in Saudi Arabia closed in 2002, saying that only the Saudi Arabia Social Welfare Administration could operate shelters for runaway migrant workers.

15. In the Gulf States, maids report being required to work up to fifteen hours per day. Most local women who work are in government services and have short careers. For example, married women in Kuwait can retire after age forty and fifteen years of employment with full benefits; about 90 percent of Kuwaitis work for the government.

16. Instead of being hanged, Balabagan was given one hundred lashes and made to pay $40,000 blood money. Balabagan said she was seventeen, although her documents say she is thirty. Balabagan received more than a million pesos from a French non-government group called "Save Sarah Balabagan Movement."

17. Many Filipina women went "illegally" as tourists to Malaysia and then further to work, or paid bribes to board flights directly to their destinations in Manila. Many recruitment agents use escorts to get migrants onto flights to their destinations.

18. For example, under the Act, a migrant illegally dismissed overseas can recover up to three months' wages for every year of service from the foreign employer. A Filipino was hired by the Asian Center for Career and Employment System and Services, Inc. (ACCESS) to work as a mason in Jeddah, Saudi Arabia, in February 1995 for 1,200 Saudi rials a month. In mid-1996, he took a 30-day home vacation. His employer fired him with eight months to go on his contract, and he sued for the eight months' remaining wages. The Philippine court ruled that he could collect a maximum of three months' wages from the local recruiter.

19. Quoted in Patricia L. Adversario, "Philippines Suffers from Hemorrhage of Nurses," *Manila Times*, April 21–23, 2003 (three-part series).

20. Quoted in Patricia L. Adversario, "Philippines Suffers from Hemorrhage of Nurses," *Manila Times*, April 21–23, 2003 (three-part series).

21. The Philippines maritime industry does not want seafarers on foreign vessels defined as migrant workers, and International Labor Organization Convention No. 97 of 1949 specifically excludes seamen or seafarers from its definition of migrant worker.

22. Many seafarers work under collective bargaining agreements that have higher minimum wages.

23. The ILO recommends a minimum wage of $435 per month for 70-hour work weeks, extending a tradition of regulating wages and working conditions dating from thirteenth century Europe, when the Rules of Oleron required ship owners to provide free medical care for sick or injured seamen.

24. Between 1974 and 1986, migrants had to remit 80 percent of their earnings, and there is still a remittance requirement for seafarers.

25. There are reported to be over two hundred cooperatives, associations, and self-help groups that have managed to pool their remittances for small and medium enterprises.

26. Quoted in John Krich and Eric Bellman, "Empowerment Guru Helps Thousands of Filipinas, but Not as Much as Hoped," *Wall Street Journal*, April 20, 2001.

27. Quoted in John Krich and Eric Bellman, "Empowerment Guru Helps Thousands of Filipinas, but Not as Much as Hoped," *Wall Street Journal*, April 20, 2001.

28. Robert Frank, "Pozorrubians Find the Road to Riches Is Paved by Workers Far From Home," *Wall Street Journal*, May 22, 2001.

29. Quoted in Jeremaiah M. Opiniano, "Maximizing Benefits of OFW Remittances," *Philippine Daily Inquirer*, May 14, 2003.

30. Bernardo M. Villegas, *The Philippine Advantage* (University of Asia and the Pacific, 2001), pp. 7–8.

31. Quoted in Jeremaiah M. Opiniano, "Maximizing Benefits of OFW Remittances," *Philippine Daily Inquirer*, May 14, 2003.

32. The famous multi-level "villas" on the outskirts of Fuzhou, and along the main route between the airport and the city, can cost a migrant's family around RMB300,000 (CAN50,000; USD35,000), the equivalent of more than forty-one years of local wages (average monthly wages are RMB600).

33. The *China Daily* newspaper can be read at: www.chinadaily.com.cn/english/home/index.html.

34. The detention center provides information about how in March, 1994, the Standing Committee of the National People's Congress introduced supplementary provisions to ensure that the criminal law covers the organization of smuggling and illegal transporting of smugglees abroad, with sanctions ranging up to life imprisonment.

35. Life imprisonment would apply where large numbers have been smuggled, and/or in very dangerous circumstances.

36. Dr. Biao Xiang is currently working in the COMPAS program in Oxford, and has for years been undertaking field work in one of the largest places of origin of Chinese migrants to Europe, Wenzhou Prefecture, Zhejiang Province, Southeast China, as well as major receiving places of internal migration, Beijing and the Pearl River Delta in south China. He will be engaged over the coming year in research on northeast China.

37. Frank N. Pieke, Paul Nyiri, Mette Thumo, and Antonella Caccagno. *Transnational Chinese: Fujianese Migration in Europe* (Stanford: Stanford University Press, 2004).

PART THREE

CHAPTER NINE

❦

Toward a Cooperative Framework for Managing Migration

The case studies and analyses presented in this book demonstrate the need for greater cooperation between receiving and source states in the management of migrant flows—also known as co-development—in order to effect positive outcomes for host nations, countries of origin, and for immigrants themselves. During the past decade, there has been growing recognition among states about the need for greater cooperation. As discussed earlier, the European Union's (EU) October 1999 summit in Tampere emphasized the need for their countries to work more effectively with source countries of immigration to reduce emigration pressures while attending to the integration of legal immigrants into European society:

> The European Union needs a comprehensive approach to migration addressing political, human rights and development issues in countries and regions of origin and transit. This requires combating poverty, improving living conditions and job opportunities, preventing conflicts and consolidating democratic states and ensuring respect for human rights, in particular rights of minorities, women and children. To that end, the Union as well as Member States are invited to contribute, within their respective competence under the Treaties, to a greater coherence of internal and external policies of the Union.
>
> The European Council stresses the need for more efficient management of migration flows at all their stages. It calls for the development, in close cooperation with countries of origin and transit, of information campaigns on the actual possibilities for legal immigration, and for the prevention of all forms of trafficking in human beings.[1]

The EU Commission re-emphasized these conclusions in November 2000, asserting:

> The Member States at the Tampere Council acknowledged the principle that an EU asylum and immigration policy must necessarily involve co-operation with the countries of origin and transit of migrants. . . . With today's increasingly mixed flows of migrants caused by economic and other reasons and with populations straddling two cultures as part of survival strategies it is possible to develop policies which use migration to the mutual benefit of the country of origin and the receiving country.[2]

The need for significant changes in migration policy becomes strikingly clear when we consider the failures and dissatisfactions of the current approach.

The Problems: Crossing Complaints and Failures

Concerns of Receiving Countries

Over the past twenty years, policymakers in a number of developed countries have attempted to implement policies of "zero immigration." Others have sought to manage migration through quotas and ceilings on admissions that have led to long waiting lists and backlogs in legal admission categories and an explosion of unauthorized movements. These respective policies have largely failed to manage movements into the destination countries.

The European recruitment stops of 1973–1974 affected only the arrival of new non-skilled and non-EU migrants seeking jobs, but exempted EU nationals and their spouses, families of resident legal aliens, recognized political refugees, and often-skilled non-EU workers. Some states have attempted further to restrict immigration by limiting access to family reunification and refugee migration, but these efforts have often resulted in debacles for the host state and immigrants alike by erecting barriers to individuals who have legitimate reasons for entering the receiving country.

France in the mid-1990s provides a concrete recent example of the problems associated with restrictive policies. In an effort to combat "fraud," additional screens were established for French-foreigner marriages as well as family reunification. France often violated the fundamental rights of those involved, and the restrictive strategy did not work because the police were overloaded with work. Forced to choose, police often denied visas to those least likely to complain: students, businesspersons, families, or future spouses, often the individuals with the most legitimate claim to immigrate and who could bring some of the greatest benefits to France.

The U.S. experience with its large-scale legalization program in the 1980s is a further example. Legal status was granted to about three million unauthorized migrants but the legalization program did not include their spouses and minor children who had to apply through the regular immigration program. Legislative restrictions on the number of visas available per year for these family members soon led to a backlog of more than one million applications and waits as long as five years for legal admission.

When countries implement restrictive laws that curtail access to legal entrance, some migrants simply arrive without authorization and remain in the receiving state. Since the migration of many of these migrants (for instance those who are attempting to re-unify with their families) is perceived as legitimate by a large part of the population, those without papers benefit from widespread sympathy and, after some delay, governments often legalize their status. Highly restrictive immigration policies thus call into question the host country's commitment to basic human rights and are ineffective, as it is simply not possible for receiving states to limit legitimate immigration flows.

Rather than attempting to exclude immigration as much as possible, it is clearly in the best interest of immigrants and of host countries to develop policies that allow a reasonable number of individuals to immigrate through the three main traditional avenues of family reunification, refugee status, and meeting labor force demands.

Demographic and labor market needs also dictate the need for legal avenues of admission. Although unemployment is still high in much of Europe, many firms are facing labor shortages and a number of businesses and economic experts have called for more immigration. Advocates of a more liberal immigration policy have seen their cause bolstered by a UN report on "Replacement Migration"[3] which demonstrates that Europe must increase immigration in order to maintain its active or total population. It is important to note that demographic situations vary between countries, especially in Europe, but virtually all developed states will need some immigration to maintain active populations large enough to pay pensions at current levels to larger retired populations. Immigration is not a panacea but will likely need to be a significant element of any policies adopted to address population aging and decline.

Such balanced approaches to migration will still not obviate the problem of unauthorized entrants, where cooperation with the source countries can play a key role. Unless host states implement a policy of totally open borders for anyone who wishes to immigrate, some persons will not qualify for legal admission. Some will migrate illegally, and a combination of legal norms and lack of administrative resources means that forced repatriation of these irregular migrants is extremely difficult. For instance, Parisian police in 1997 questioned an average of one hundred undocumented migrants per day, but released eighty within an hour because there were no places to detain them or they could not in any event be returned to their countries of origin. The United States typically apprehends about one million migrants per year who are attempting to enter the country without authorization, with most returned immediately to Mexico where they seek to re-enter the United States as quickly as possible.

In short, as long as there are large inequalities between developed and undeveloped nations, significant levels of irregular immigration will persist, and lack of cooperation between source and host states intensifies the phenomenon of undocumented immigration since the country of origin can be a major obstacle to host states' efforts to deport illegal entrants. In particular, source nations sometimes refuse to give migrants necessary documentation for their repatriation. This causes major difficulties for host states that must follow various procedures designed to respect human rights in their deportation of unauthorized migrants. The bottom line here is that experience has shown that it is simply not possible for receiving states to limit immigration flows effectively by themselves.

Concerns of Source Countries

Source countries object to the additional immigration restrictions imposed by virtually all European and North American states in recent decades because emigration has been an important safety valve. The money that emigrants send back to their relatives can also have major benefits in terms of the economic development of specific communities or of the source state as a whole.

Source countries do not entirely benefit from their citizens' emigration, however. In fact, a commonly discussed phenomenon is brain drain, including the emigration of the most talented individuals who leave their home countries for higher education abroad and then never return. From the point of view of sending countries, this type of emigration obviously deprives them of a major resource. Often, African countries accuse European states of draining their professionals for their own selfish needs. However, developing countries cannot reduce this problem by simply asking developed ones to deny work permits to these individuals after they finish their studies. If foreign students with degrees from European universities do not want to return to their countries of origin, they will not do so, since graduates can seek jobs in a global labor market. And if European countries refuse work permits to these individuals, they will simply receive job offers in the United States, Japan, Canada, or Australia.

Concerns of Immigrants

One of the most unfortunate aspects of today's situation is that policymakers and the public tend to view all foreigners from developing nations as potential illegal migrants. More specifically, host countries often limit access to travel visas for foreigners, which limits the ability of settled migrants to circulate. Besides the hardship this creates for tourists, such a restrictive policy toward visa distribution has more serious consequences in terms of limiting travel access for individuals with business, intellectual, or family contacts in the host country.

Migrants often have an interest in maintaining relations with their home country, either permanently moving back or making frequent trips between their host and home nation. A permanent worker might want to retire in his country of origin, and still receive his pension, and have the option to return for visits and medical care, just as a seasonal worker could be ready to return home at the end of the season if there is a guarantee of a new contract the following year. However, many countries continue to behave as *l'Etat inerte* of the nineteenth and early twentieth centuries,[4] meaning they want stable populations without frequent movements over borders. However, such attitudes mean that many migrants are forced to choose permanent settlement or returning and losing the stake they may have in industrial countries.

A major obstacle for immigrants who wish to use the resources and skills they have gained abroad is the lack of reliable financial and banking systems in many source nations. The problems range from the extraordinarily high commissions to send remittances to their relatives to being unable to find loans and other sources of investments for business projects in their countries of origin.

Creating Cooperative Policies

A strategy of cooperation between host countries and countries of origin can address the problems of the three major immigration actors through a series of tradeoffs that facilitate the improved management of legal migration flows and better deal with illegal flows. This cooperation should be based on the recognition that the best migration policy is one that seeks not to block but to regulate smoothly international flows of people.

Cooperation as a strategy to manage international migration is in an early stage of evolution. A conference on what is sometimes referred to as co-development, organized by the French government in July 2000, discussed three components of a cooperative strategy:

Managing Flows. There are a number of ways to manage flows. For example, France and Mali have established a binational committee that meets regularly to discuss visa policy, return of unauthorized migrants, and smuggling and trafficking. The United States and Mexico have a similar binational working group that discusses border issues, visa policy, documentation, cooperation in combating smuggling and trafficking, protection of the rights of Mexican migrant workers in the United States, removal of criminal aliens, and other similar issues. These mechanisms are not meant to undermine the sovereign responsibility of each government to manage the movements of people into or out of their countries, but they provide an opportunity to discuss and to negotiate changes to policies and procedures. They also enable countries to cooperate against smuggling and trafficking, so that the net effect is the expansion of legal channels for emigration/immigration and better controls over unauthorized movements.

Diaspora-led Development. Migrants can contribute to economic development through their financial resources as well as their skills, entrepreneurial activities, and support for democratization and human rights. Co-development seeks to ensure that policies do not preclude such contributions and, to the extent possible, support the initiatives of migrants. For example, associations of migrants often band together to raise and transmit funds for infrastructure development and income generation activities in their home communities. Individual remittance transfers are an important source of subsistence for many families in developing countries. Governments can cooperate to facilitate such transfers, provide technical assistance to ensure their effective use, match the funds to stimulate additional contributions, regulate transfer fees and exchange rates to reduce transaction costs, and take other steps to promote effective use of remittances for economic development.

Co-development also seeks to increase the potential for migrants to bring needed skills to their home countries. For example, migrants with long-term residence permits may be more willing to return home if they do not fear the loss of their residence permits. Programs that identify migrants with specific skills needed by their home countries and facilitate return and reintegration also contribute to co-development, as does support for return migrants who plan to open small businesses upon reintegration. The skills may be needed for economic development, but they may also be required to help move the source country toward greater democratization and respect for human rights. For example, migrants who have legal training may be helpful in developing new judicial systems and establishing the rule of law.

Targeting Assistance. Providing the means by which people can stay home and enjoy greater economic opportunities is another aspect of co-development. Targeted aid includes micro-credit for would-be migrants to invest in their home communities, income generation opportunities for women left behind by migrating spouses, infrastructure development to create new markets and economic opportunities, and education and health care services. It is important to ensure, however, that targeting aid, trade, and investment at high emigration areas does not divert it from equally needy places with low levels of emigration.

Benefits of Cooperation for the Country of Origin

Cooperation can have a positive impact on countries of origin and their citizens in three major domains: 1) increased circulation of non-immigrants through better access to visas; 2) greater impact of remittances; 3) return and re-circulation of skilled persons, retirees, and seasonal workers.

Nationals of many developing countries face problems obtaining visas, which can limit the capacity of their citizens to increase trade and intellectual exchange. A prime goal of a sustained, dedicated policy of cooperation is to encourage rather than discourage travel by nationals of developing countries, which means that denials of visas should be submitted to some formal, independent review body.[5] When a citizen, resident legal immigrant, or domestic business is seriously affected by a decision to refuse a visa, governments should be required to justify the denial.

Cooperation aims not simply to increase remittances, but also to augment the impact that these remittances have on individuals and the economy of the source nations. A dedicated policy of cooperation would include guarantees by the countries of origin to tackle the corruption that often skims off large portions of the remittances and would also involve mechanisms to allow immigrants to send remittances to their families more efficiently and cheaply. Finally cooperation means encouraging persons who receive remittances to put the money toward projects that would foster economic development, such as building factories in addition to or rather than repairing churches. To cite one example, France and Mali have signed a convention designed to address many of these issues that would increase the impact of remittances from Malians working in France. Mexico has pioneered the three for one program that matches the contributions of hometown associations to the development of their communities.

Cooperation would bring benefits to the source country through measures that will permit immigrants—depending on their status—to re-circulate far more easily than they can as of now. Some retirees are relatively young but fear returning to their countries of origin because they worry that they will not receive their pensions and they will not be able to return to the host country to visit friends or get medical care. If such individuals had permanent visas to circulate and re-circulate, and guarantees of continued payments of pensions and access to medical assistance in the host country, they would probably return home. Retirees could rejoin their families and contribute to their home nation's economic development, and share with their local communities any relevant education and skills they gained while abroad.

In 1998, France promulgated a law that granted foreigners a *carte de retraité* after fifteen years of professional activity in France. This encouraged circulation, since these persons are guaranteed their pensions and access to the French medical care. Mr. Yu, who returned to China after receiving Canadian citizenship to become a successful entrepreneur in Beijing is a further example of the benefits of circulation, with potential benefits for both countries, particularly if he follows through on his intent to establish a similar business in Canada (see chapter 8, pp. 215–17).

Cooperation can also encourage seasonal workers to return. The fear in host countries is that seasonal workers will stay permanently, and there is the added complication of high unemployment rates among domestic unskilled workers. Seasonal worker programs should be implemented only if there is an adequate level of control over unauthorized entry and incentives are in place for employers to hire domestic workers or take other actions, such as mechanization, to reduce dependence on foreign workers.

Even with these measures, there are likely to be labor shortages—in part because there are various jobs that domestic workers refuse to fill. For instance, despite very high unemployment rates in certain regions, Italy signed agreements with Morocco, Tunisia, and Albania allowing the entry of seasonal workers. Spain signed similar agreements with Morocco, Ecuador, and other countries. Cooperation could involve giving seasonal migrants renewable visas that would allow them to work for several consecutive years in the host country on the condition that they return home after each season. Guaranteed return the following season can reduce incentives to migrate illegally, and the wages a seasonal laborer can earn working a few months in a developed country can often support him and his family for an entire year in the country of origin.

Re-circulation can also affect the behavior of skilled workers. Foreign students who receive university degrees in American and European countries could be encouraged to circulate between their host countries and their home states by modifying foreign aid disbursements so that more is available to these skilled individuals who wish to initiate development projects in their home country, perhaps in the form of low interest loans and granting permanent visas (or an equivalent) so that skilled persons know they can go home without worrying about returning. Such policies could encourage skilled individuals to make contributions to both their host and home countries and, by fostering intellectual exchanges and economic growth in both states, could become crucial private agents of cooperation.

Benefits of Cooperation for the Receiving Country

Receiving countries can gain in several ways from cooperation, including from migrant contributions to the labor force and cooperation to control illegal migration. Countries differ today in their willingness to admit foreign workers. Some policy makers fear that liberalizing skilled migration would lead to a brain drain. More prevalent, though, is a concern about competition that foreign workers might pose for native-born workers. Some European states today prefer to regularize the position of undocumented and unskilled migrants rather than allow the legal entrance of foreigners who could compete with skilled native workers. Thus, it can be difficult for a foreigner with a degree from a European university to obtain permission to work in a European country even if he or she has a job offer from a local company. On the other hand, the United States has numerous admissions categories for highly skilled foreign workers, but few for lesser-skilled workers, instead tolerating large-scale unauthorized migration.

An appropriate policy of cooperation would allow host countries to reap the benefits of highly skilled migration. Such a policy would welcome highly skilled foreigners to contribute to the labor force while putting in place mechanisms that would encourage these migrants to contribute as well to their home countries' economies. Migrants should retain the capacity to return to the host country and have access to sources of investment for development projects they seek to undertake at home.

Formal admission policies for lesser-skilled workers are also beneficial to the receiving country, particularly in the face of large-scale demand for this type of labor. Rather than rely on unauthorized migration, destination countries should seek to manage and regulate these flows. Seasonal workers can benefit the host country by filling jobs in agriculture, construction, and services. They can be admitted on the basis of single or multi-annual permits, the latter providing a guarantee of recurrent seasonal jobs if they go back home at the end of each year's work. By allowing documented seasonal immigrants to fill these posts, employers will be able to hire the labor they need legally, and host states can regulate migration in these sectors instead of attempting control.

As part of a general policy of cooperation, source countries would cooperate with host countries to accept the return of seasonal workers who are apprehended when they do not depart as required. If such individuals attempt to stay illegally because they worry they will never be able to return, a policy of renewable visas for seasonal workers would obviate this motivation for illegal migration. Italy used this reasoning in developing its policies towards economic migrants. In 2000, the Italian government authorized the entrance of 20,000 migrants for seasonal work, especially in agriculture and the hotel industry, and negotiated agreements with Albania, Morocco, Tunisia, and India that establish quotas for legal migrants.

These policies work only if there is little irregular migration. Experience has demonstrated that host countries frequently have a very difficult time deporting undocumented migrants who enjoy various legal rights to stay in the host state. However, when countries of origin are committed to working with host countries to prevent irregular migration flows, they can often make significant progress in preventing undocumented individuals from emigrating in the first place. When Italy put its quotas into place, it also established cooperative arrangements with key transit points for irregular migration, such as Albania, to conduct joint enforcement missions to deter smuggling into Italy. Ensuring a meaningful right to re-circulate for various types of migrants could improve migration management and foster cooperation between sending and receiving countries that is key cooperative migration management in the twenty-first century.

Policies must also recognize, however, that many migrants fill jobs in the permanent labor force and are likely to remain permanently in the host country. While a right to re-circulate helps immigrants to retain ties to their home countries, destination countries must also take steps to facilitate longer-term integration of these migrants. In an increasingly globalized world, circulation and integration are not mutually exclusive concepts. Immigrants who have fully adapted to their new societies nevertheless may send remittances home on a regular basis, travel back and forth to their countries of origin, and invest when given the opportunity in home country economies and infrastructure development. At the same time, they and their children learn the languages of their new countries, develop new skills to make them economically productive, buy homes and otherwise invest in their new communities, and eventually become citizens who participate fully in the political life of the new country. Policies that enable immigrants to take on these roles with minimal disruption will benefit both destination and source countries.

Institutionalizing Cooperation

This book advocates a "bottom-up" approach to promoting cooperation among states in the management of migration, building on successful examples to define modes of cooperation that can be institutionalized. Our analysis focuses on three levels of cooperation: bilateral, regional, and global.

Bilateral Cooperation

Many of these strategies involve bilateral agreements between receiving and source countries of migration. The case studies have described agreements reached between the United States and Mexico, the United States and the Dominican Republic, Italy and Albania, Spain and Morocco, France and Mali—to name only a few.

In some cases, cooperation has been institutionalized through continuing processes of consultation and coordination. For example, Presidents Reagan and Lopez Portillo established the U.S.-Mexican Binational Commission in 1981 as a forum for cabinet-level officials from both countries. The U.S. Secretary of State and the Mexican Secretary of Foreign Relations chair the one-day conference. Each delegation includes numerous cabinet-level officials and other agency directors. Meeting in plenary and working groups, they discuss a complex and diverse range of bilateral issues that have international and domestic impact, including migration and border relations. Members of the working groups often gather between meetings of the Commission to develop joint policy proposals.

The working group on migration proved extremely useful in the mid-1990s when immigration became an explosive political issue in both countries. In addition to serving as a forum to exchange information and help the other country's officials understand the nature of the concerns about migration, the working group reached a number of agreements on cooperation in improving border safety, increasing the Mexican consular presence in the United States, conducting joint operations against smugglers and traffickers, returning third country nationals transiting Mexico to their home countries, piloting commuter lanes to speed travel across the border, and other similar initiatives.[6] At the meeting of the Binational Commission in November

2004, U.S. Secretary of State Colin Powell and Secretary of Homeland Security Tom Ridge told their counterparts of the Administration's intent to press for new legislation for a temporary work program, and with their counterparts, Foreign Secretary Luis Ernesto Derbez and Government Secretary Santiago Creel, announced a new Cyber-Security Working Group and infrastructure protection strategy for the border. The Binational Commission also reviewed the progress of the Partnership for Prosperity (P4P), one of the aims of which is to reduce the fees on remittance transfers.

In a similar fashion, France has established binational commissions to consult with Mali and other Francophone countries in Africa about migration issues. As discussed in chapter 6, Mali and France established the Mali-France Consultation on Migration, an annual binational consultation on migration between the two countries in 2000. The two countries agreed to meet at least once a year at the ministerial level to deal with the integration of Malians who want to remain in France, co-management of migration flows, and cooperative development. Co-management has focused on a number of issues regarding both unauthorized and legal movements.

Regional Processes

In 1997, United Nations Secretary General Kofi Annan addressed the possibility of convening a conference on international migration and development. Upon consulting with UN member governments, he found insufficient consensus about what such a conference could accomplish and reported: "The disparate experiences of countries or subregions with regard to international migration suggest that, if practical solutions are to be found, they are likely to arise from the consideration of the particular situation of groups of countries sharing similar positions or concerns with the global international migration system. In the light of this, it may be expedient to pursue regional or subregional approaches whenever possible."

Since 1997, regional processes have matured. Perhaps most developed is the Regional Migration Conference, the so-called Puebla Group, which brings together all the countries of Central and North America for regular dialogue on migration issues, including an annual session at the vice-ministerial level. The Puebla Group's Plan of Action calls for cooperation in exchanging information on migration policy, exploring links between development and migration, combating migrant trafficking, returning extra-regional migrants, and ensuring full respect for the human rights of migrants, as well as reintegrating repatriated migrants, equipping and modernizing immigration control systems, and training officials in migration policy and procedures. Discussions have led law enforcement officials of the United States, Mexico, and several Central American countries to cooperate in arresting and prosecuting members of large-scale smuggling and trafficking operations that move migrants illegally across borders and then force them to work in prostitution, sweatshops, and other exploitive activities.

Similar regional groups are working in East and Southeast Asia. The "Manila Process" focuses on unauthorized migration and trafficking in East and Southeast Asia. Since 1996, it has brought together each year seventeen countries for regular exchange of information. The Asia-Pacific Consultations include governments in Asia and Oceania and focus on a broad range of population movements in the region. A 1999 International Symposium on Migration hosted by the Royal Thai government strengthened both ongoing dialogues. In the resulting Bangkok Declaration on Irregular Migration, nineteen Asian countries agreed to cooperate to combat smuggling and trafficking.

Other such groups are operating in the Southern Cone of South America, in western and southern Africa, and in the Mediterranean. The intent is to bring together the governments of all countries involved in migration, whether origin, transit, or receiving. At present, the groups are forums for exchanging information and perspectives, although the more developed ones, such as the Puebla Group, are leading to joint action as well. Given the lack of shared information or consensus about migration policies and practices, the discussion stage is a necessary first step in developing the capacity for joint efforts.

Steps toward Global Cooperation
While a great deal of migration occurs within defined regions, other migration is truly global in nature. As this book has demonstrated, Filipino and Chinese migrants can be found throughout the world. We have also found, however, that nationals of countries with very defined patterns of movement often move outside of these frameworks—Malians migrate not only to France but also to the Cote d'Ivoire and the United States, Ecuadorians migrate mostly to the United States but in increasing numbers to Spain. Regional consultative mechanisms will have only limited effectiveness in managing these movements. During the past few years, there have been a number of attempts to identify existing best practices, consistent with international law, and to recommend policies that would promote cooperation at the global level. This section discusses three such efforts: the Berne Initiative, the Hague Declaration, and the Global Commission on

International Migration. These are attempts to build consensus among governments and within civil society.

The Berne Initiative, launched by the Swiss government in 2001, is "a States-owned consultative process with the goal of obtaining better management of migration at the regional and global level through co-operation between States. As a process, the Berne Initiative enables governments from all world regions to share their different policy priorities and identify their longer-term interests in migration, and offers the opportunity of developing a common orientation to migration management, based on notions of cooperation, partnership, comprehensiveness, balance and predictability."[7] Through regional and international consultations, the Berne Initiative has developed an International Agenda for Migration Management, which includes "common understandings for the management of international migration" and "Effective Practices for a Planned, Balanced, and Comprehensive Approach to Management of Migration." Twenty common understandings are listed:[8]

1. The movement of people across borders is a feature of modern life.
2. Orderly and humane management of migration benefits both states and migrants.
3. All states share a common interest in strengthening co-operation on international migration in order to maximise mutual benefits.
4. The prime responsibility for the management of migration lies with states: each State has the right to develop its own legal framework on migration and to protect the security of its population, consistent with existing international principles and norms.
5. The implementation of comprehensive and coherent national migration policies is a prerequisite to effective international migration policy and cooperation in this field. Support for capacity-building in those states lacking adequate resources, infrastructure or expertise can make a useful contribution in this regard.
6. According to customary international law, states are bound to protect and respect the fundamental human rights of all migrants, irrespective of their status; the special needs of women and children, the elderly and the disabled require particular attention. Such protection and respect are central to the development of effective migration management systems.
7. Relevant international and regional instruments provide a solid starting point for the development of co-operative approaches to migration management.
8. Compliance with applicable principles of international human rights, refugee, humanitarian, migrant workers and crime control law is an integral component of any migration management system, at the national, regional and international levels.

9. Co-operation and dialogue among all interested stakeholders including states, international organizations, non-governmental organizations, the private sector, civil society, including migrant associations, employer and worker organizations, are important elements for effective migration management partnerships and the development of comprehensive and balanced migration management policies.
10. Bilateral, regional and inter-regional consultative processes are key to the development of co-operative migration management and contribute to co-operation at the global level.
11. Effective migration management is achieved through balanced consideration of economic, social, political, humanitarian, developmental and environmental factors, taking into account the root causes of migratory flows.
12. There is a close relationship between migration and development; properly managed, that relationship can reap benefits for the development of states.
13. Providing adequate channels for legal migration is an essential element of a comprehensive approach to migration management.
14. Reduction of irregular migration is a shared responsibility among all states.
15. Enhanced efforts are needed at all levels to combat human trafficking, organized migrant smuggling and other forms of international criminality affecting migrants and to provide support to victims of trafficking.
16. The family is the basic unit of society and as such deserves special attention. In the context of migration, family separation has to be avoided. Facilitation of family reunion can contribute to maximizing the positive effects of social and cultural integration of migrants in the host community.
17. Integration of migrants is essential to foster social and political stability, to maximize the contributions migrants can make, and to reduce instances of racism and xenophobia.
18. The dissemination of accurate, objective and detailed information on migration policies and procedures enables migrants to make informed decisions. It is necessary for informed public opinion and support for migration and migrants.
19. The systematic collection, analysis and exchange of timely, accurate and comparable data on all aspects of migration, while respecting the right to privacy, are important for migration management at national, regional and international levels.
20. Research on all aspects of migration is needed to better understand the causes and consequences of international migration.

The effective practices focus on mechanisms to promote international cooperation; specific policies to regulate entry and stay for work purposes, family union, study, humanitarian resettlement; prevent irregular migration; protect human rights of migrants; protect refugees from refoulement; integrate immigrants; regulate naturalization and citizenship; and manage return. The effective practices also address the nexus between migration and such issues as development, trade, security, health, and the environment.

The strength of the Berne Initiative is the consultative process that has brought source, transit, and destination countries together to build consensus on the common understandings and effective practices. The Common Understandings briefly restate or give adherence to international law, but they go well beyond conventions to achieve consensus on a framework for international cooperation. This framework recognizes the benefits of legal avenues of migration and the integration of immigrants, but also emphasizes the need to reduce irregular migration and curb such abuses as smuggling and trafficking as well as racism and xenophobia.

The weakness of the Berne Initiative is its emphasis on state participation in the consultations. Although nongovernmental organizations and academic experts participated in the international and regional meetings, the process has been dominated—purposefully—by states. Since the state participants usually have a vested interest in the issues (coming from ministries with specific responsibilities for migration), convincing the broader political spectrum as well as public opinion as to the wisdom of the common understandings and effective practices may be difficult.

By contrast, the Hague process has been a nongovernmental effort launched by the Society for International Development's Netherlands chapter in 2000. It brought together about five hundred persons from government, intergovernmental organizations, nongovernmental organizations, and academia, and the Hague Declaration lists twenty-one principles for managing migration. It begins by recognizing that the primary responsibility for migration and refugee policy rests with states, but it asserts that states cannot act alone and succeed in managing migration. The Declaration emphasizes, "Coherent orderly migration programs are key instruments in a new approach to migration" because they clarify rights and obligations of migrants, strengthen public confidence, and reduce the constraints and costs of unauthorized migration. Placing great focus on refugees and displaced persons, the Declaration calls for conflict prevention measures, respect for human rights and international humanitarian law, adherence to the UN Convention Relating to the Status of Refugees and the Guiding Principles on Internal Displacement, and "new, inclusive, bottom-up approaches to post-conflict situations."[9]

The Declaration also promotes integration and social inclusion of migrants, emphasizing "refugees and migrants have skills, knowledge, experience and strong aspirations for a better life." Accordingly, the Declaration includes a specific reference to the corporate sector, calling on business leaders to "actively ensure the inclusion into the labor force of refugees and migrants in host countries and thereby reinforce the integration process." The Declaration's 20th Principle recognizes that "powerful instruments of human rights, international humanitarian law, and refugee law already exist to protect refugees, and to a lesser extent migrants. The priority for the future is to ensure their effective implementation." The Declaration ends with a call for re-examination of the institutional arrangements for population movements at the global and regional levels.

The third initiative is the Global Commission on International Migration (GCIM), organized at the request of the UN secretary general to do precisely what the Hague Process recommended. The Commission's mandate is:[10]

1. *Placing International Migration on the Global Agenda* by promoting a comprehensive debate among governments, international organizations, academia, civil society, private sector, media and other actors on all aspects of migration and issues related to migration.
2. *Analyzing Gaps in Current Policy Approaches to Migration and Examining Inter-linkages with Other Issue-Areas* by focusing on various approaches and perspectives of governments and other stakeholders in different regions, and by addressing the relationship of migration with other global issues that impact on and cause migration.
3. *Presenting Recommendations to the United Nations Secretary-General and other Stakeholders* on how to strengthen national, regional and global governance of international migration.

It is composed of nineteen commissioners from both source and receiving countries of immigration. The members are all distinguished persons with long histories of public service in their own countries and at the international level. They have held regional hearings and commissioned substantive research to guide their deliberations. The work of the commission is also supported by a core group of states that have provided financial support and policy perspectives.

As of this writing, the commission had not issued its final report. It is expected to provide guidance on a wide range of issues, ranging from the interconnections between migration and such issues as development, security, and human rights, to concrete recommendations regarding management of labor migration, control of unauthorized migration, and the integration of migrants in destination countries. Perhaps the most controversial recommendations will be those that focus on the legal and normative framework for managing migration and the institutional arrangements for promoting greater cooperation and gaining greater coherence on migration issues within the United Nations system.

Institutional Implications

Weak institutional arrangements make international cooperation in managing international migration difficult to achieve. Institutional responsibilities are spread across many organizations, none having a clear mandate to work with states to manage flows of people across borders, enhance compliance with existing international law, or to fill gaps where they exist.

To date, much of the consensus building has taken place through ad hoc, informal mechanisms such as the Berne Initiative, at the international level, and the various consultative mechanisms established at the regional level. These mechanisms provide useful forums for discussion but they do not seek to enforce norms of behavior on their members. They may identify gaps in international law and even set out normative frameworks (or common understandings, as in the Berne Initiative), but members may choose to ignore the norms.

Moving from the current arrangements to a more robust international regime may be premature, however. While there has been progress in setting out common understandings, there continue to be fundamental disagreements among states as to causes and consequences of international migration and the extent to which it is in the interests of states to liberalize or restrict flows of migrants. This situation contrasts sharply with the general consensus that governs movements of goods, capital, and services—that it is in the ultimate interest of all states to lessen barriers to the movements of these factors.

Yet, there does appear to be growing consensus that managing migration—whether in a more liberal or restrictive direction—is in the best interests of states. Uncontrolled movements—particularly when dominated by organized criminal smuggling and trafficking networks—harm states as well as those migrating via these unauthorized channels. In this context, there also appears to be growing consensus—as witnessed by the broad ratification of the UN Convention Relating to the Status of Refugees, the Smuggling and Trafficking Protocols, and even the less impressive ratification of the Migrant Rights Convention—that persons crossing borders have special needs and that the protection of their rights is of international concern. However, with the exception of the UN High Commissioner for Refugees in relationship to refugees, there is no international organization with a clear mandate to help states manage the movements or to protect the rights of the migrants.

Should one international organization seek to cover all of the issues raised by international migration? The international legal framework would argue for keeping the institutional arrangements for refugees distinct from those for voluntary migrants. The Refugee Convention covers individuals who cannot or will not accept the protection of their own countries because of a well-founded fear of persecution on the basis of one of five protected grounds. By contrast, labor or family migrants can presumably call upon their own country's protection, either via consular protection or by return to their home territory. The role of the international community is far more limited in the case of voluntary migrants than it is in the case of refugees because of these distinctions. Yet, it is also true that the line between migration and asylum is often blurred and states have difficulties determining who qualifies for international protection.

One possible option arising from the differences in international law would be to continue to assign responsibility for protection and assistance to refugees to the UN High Commissioner for Refugees while identifying and assigning to a separate organization or set of organizations (for example, the International Organization for Migration [IOM], International Labor Organization [ILO] and UN High Commissioner for Human Rights [UNHCHR]) responsibility for helping states manage migration and protect the rights of migrants.[11] IOM already provides technical assistance to states in the management of immigration and development of policies and programs, while ILO and UNHCHR already have mechanisms in place to address violations of the rights of migrants. A coordination mechanism could then be established to address issues that arise at the nexus between refugee and migration issues.

Conclusion

Migration is generally a force for individual and global betterment. Individuals crossing national borders to take advantage of higher wages and more opportunities generally benefit themselves, their host countries, and sometimes the countries they left behind, as when remittances and returns hasten an economic takeoff. There is no basis for calculating an optimal rate of international migration, which means that there is no agreement on whether the current 3 percent of the world's residents who are migrants is too high, too low, or just right. What is clear, however, is that no country is an island in the global migration system, and dialogue and cooperation are the keys to effective migration management.

Notes

1. Conclusions of the European Council at Tampere, Finland, 15 and 16 October 1999 (available at www.europarl.eu.int/summits/tam_en.htm#a).

2. Communication from the Commission to the Council and the European Parliament on a Community Immigration Policy, Brussels, 22.11.2000, COM(2000) 757 final.

3. United Nations Population Division, Replacement Migration, 2000.

4. Weil Patrick, "Populations en mouvement, Etat inerte," in Roger Fauroux, Bernard Spitz (dir.), Notre Etat, le livre vérité de la Fonction publique, Paris, 2000, Robert Laffont, pp. 413–433.

5. See Transatlantic Learning Community, Migration in the New Millennium (Gütersloh: Bertelsmann Stiftung and the German Marshall Fund of the United States), 2000, p. 52.

6. Susan F. Martin, "Migration and Foreign Policy: Emerging Bilateral and Regional Approaches in the Americas" in Myron Weiner and Sharon Stanton Russell, eds., Demography and Security. Oxford: Berghahn Books, 2001.

7. The Goal of the Berne Initiative, April 2003 (www.iom.int//DOCUMENTS/OFFICIALTXT/EN/Goal_E.pdf).

8. International Agenda for Migration Management, distributed at final meeting of the Berne Initiative, Berne, Switzerland, December 13–15, 2004.

9. Declaration of The Hague on the Future of Refugee and Migration Policy, Society for International Development, Netherlands, adopted in 2002.

10. See GCIM website: www.gcim.org/en/a_mandate.html.

11. In other writings, one of the authors, Susan Martin, has recommended that a single international organization—dubbed the UN High Commissioner for Forced Migrants—take responsibility for both refugees and internally displaced persons who share similar characteristics with refugees—that is, a need for international protection because their own countries are unwilling or unable to protect them.

APPENDIX I

CEME Participants and Activities

The CEME group includes people who influence policymaking and public opinion regarding international migration. The participants in CEME site visits and discussions include:

Philip Martin, University of California, Davis, Co-Chair
Susan Martin, Georgetown University, Co-Chair
Thomas Straubhaar, HWWA-Hamburgisches Welt-Wirtschafts-Archiv, Co-Chair
Patrick Weil, University of Paris1-Sorbonne, Co-Chair

Manolo Abella, International Labor Organization
Joaquin Arango, Fundacion Ortega y Gasset, Madrid
Philippe Barret, French Codevelopment Office
Jean Louis de Brouwer, European Union
Agustin Escobar, Director, Ciesas Occidente
Peter Fischer, Neue Zuercher Zeitung
Kay Hailbronner, University of Konstanz
Elmar Honekopp, German Labor Ministry
Diane Lindquist, San Diego Union Tribune
Irena Omelaniuk, International Organization of Migration
Ferrucio Pastore, CeSPI, Rome
Mark Schlakman, University of Florida
Sharon Stanton Russell, Massachusetts Institute of Technology

Peter Schatzer, IOM

Michael Teitelbaum, Sloan Foundation

Robert Trempe, Immigration Canada (Quebec)

Gerry van Kessel, Intergovernmental Consultations on Immigration, Refugees and Asylum

Jonas Widgren, International Centre on Migration Policy and Development

APPENDIX II

※

Site Visits and Meetings

CEME *Site Visits*	*Dates*	*Co-Sponsors/Assistance*
Istanbul	March 29–31, 2001	German government
Belgrade-Timisoara	June 4–10, 2001	IOM
Mali-Senegal	January 7–13, 2002	French government
Dominican Republic	March 7–9, 2002	US government, IOM
Italy-Albania	June 5–9, 2002	Cespi
San Diego-Tijuana	January 9–11, 2003	US government
Spain-Morocco	April 9–13, 2003	Fundacion Ortega y Gasset
Manila	February 1–4, 2004	ILO
Vienna-Bratislava	April 29–May 1, 2004	ICMPD
China	June 20–24, 2004	Canadian government

CEME *Policy Briefings*	*Dates*	*Co-Sponsors*
Geneva-International Organizations	December 17, 2002	ILO
Mexico City	March 23–24, 2003	IOM, Mexican government

Reports of these events are at: migration.ucdavis.edu/ceme/index.html

Bibliography

Abel, David. "Haiti's Poorest Cross Border, Face Backlash." *Boston Herald*, November 28, 1999.

Adams, R. H., Jr., and J. Page. "International Migration, Remittances and Poverty in Developing Countries," World Bank Policy Research Working Paper, no. 3179 (Washington, D.C.: World Bank, 2003).

Adversario, Patricia L. "Philippines Suffers from Hemorrhage of Nurses," *Manila Times*, April 21–23, 2003.

Albania, Status/Progress Report, Working Table III. Stability Pact for South Eastern Project, 2001.

Arango, Joaquín. "Becoming a Country of Immigration at the End of the Twentieth Century: The Case of Spain," pp. 253–76 in Russell King, Gabriella Lazaridis, and Charalambos Tsardanidis, eds., *Eldorado or Fortress?—Migration in Southern Europe*. London: Macmillan, 2000.

———. La fisonomia de la inmigracion en España. Pp. 237–62 in *El Nuevo Orden Demográfico*, edited by Pedro Reques. Madrid: El Campo de las Ciencias y de las Artes, 2002.

Atkins, G. Pope. *The Dominican Republic and the United States: From Imperialism to Transnationalism*. Athens: University of Georgia Press, 1998.

Ayala, César J. *American Sugar Kingdom: The Plantation Economy of the Spanish Caribbean, 1898–1934*. Chapel Hill: University of North Carolina Press, 1999.

Bean, Frank R., R. G. Chanove, R. G. Cushing, et al. *Illegal Mexican Migration and the United States Border: The Effects of Operation-Hold-the-Line on El Paso/Juarez*. Austin, TX: Population Research Center, University of Texas–Austin, 1994.

Beattie, Alan. "Seeking Consensus on the Benefits of Immigration," *Financial Times*, July 22, 2002, p. 9.

Bensinger, Ken. "Mexico's Other Migrant Wave," *Christian Science Monitor*, October 8, 2004.

Bhagwati, Jagdish. "Borders beyond Control." *Foreign Affairs*, Jan./Feb. 2003.

Bhagwati, Jagdish, and T. N. Srinivasan. "On Reanalyzing the Harris-Todaro Model: Policy Rankings in the Case of Sector-Specific Sticky Wages," in *American Economic Review* 64, no. 3 (1974): 502–8.

Böhning, W. Roger. *The Migration of Workers in the United Kingdom and the European Community.* Oxford: Oxford University Press for the Institute of Race Relations, 1972.

Borjas, George J. "The Economics of Immigration." *Journal of Economic Literature* 32, no. 4 (December 1994): 1167–1717.

Castles, Stephen, and Mark Miller. The Age of Migration. International Population Movements in the Modern World. New York: Guilford Press, 1998.

Castro, Max, and Thomas Boswell. "The Dominican Diaspora Revisited: Dominicans and Dominican-Americans in a New Century." Miami: University of Miami North-South Center, 2002.

Commission of the European Communities. "Communication from the Commission to the Council and the European Parliament: Integrating Migration Issues in the European Union's Relations with Third Countries." COM(2002)703 final, 3 December 2002.

———. "Governance and Development." Brussels: Communication COM(2003)615, October 20, 2003.

Conclusions of the European Council at Tampere, Finland, 15 and 16 October 1999 (available at www.europarl.eu.int/summits/tam_en.htm#a).

Congressional Research Service. "Temporary Worker Programs: Background and Issues." Prepared for the Senate Committee on the Judiciary, February 1980.

Cornelius, Wayne A. "Spain: The Uneasy Transition from Labor Exporter to Labor Importer" in *Controlling Immigration: A Global Perspective*, edited by Wayne A. Cornelius, Philip L. Martin, and James F. Hollifield. Stanford, CA: Stanford University Press, 2004.

Cornelius, Wayne, Takeyuki Tsuda, Philip L. Martin, and James F. Hollifield. *Controlling Immigration: A Global Perspective*, 2nd edition. Stanford: Stanford University Press, 2004.

Council of the European Union, High Level Working Group on Asylum and Migration. *Action Plan for Albania and the Neighboring Region.* Brussels: European Union, June 2000.

Declaration of The Hague on the Future of Refugee and Migration Policy, Society for International Development, Netherlands, adopted in 2002.

della Rocca, R. Morozzo. Albania: le radici della crisi. Milan: Guerini e Associati, 1997.

Dugger, Celia W. "In Africa, an Exodus of Nurses," *New York Times*, July 12, 2004.

Economist Intelligence Unit Ltd. *Albania: Country Profile.* London: The Economist, 2001.

———. *Albania. Country Report*, London: The Economist, April 2001.

Ellerman, David. "Policy Research on Migration and Development." Mimeo. 2003.

Findley, Sally E., Dieudonne Ouedraogo, Nassour Ouaidou. "From Seasonal Migration to International Migration: An Analysis of the Factors Affecting the Choices Made by Families of the Senegal River Valley" in African Population Conference/ Congres Africain de Population, Dakar, Senegal, November 7–12, 1988, vol. 2 (Liege, Belgium: International Union for the Scientific Study of Population [IUSSP], 1988, pp. 4.3.39–53.

"Fox Visits Bush." *Migration News* 8, no. 10 (October 2001).

Frank, Robert. "Pozorrubians Find the Road to Riches Is Paved by Workers Far From Home," *Wall Street Journal*, May 22, 2001.

Gelbard, Alene, Carl Haub, and Mary M. Kent. *World Population. Beyond Six Billion.* Washington, DC: Population Reference Bureau 54, no. 1, March 1999.

Ghosh, Bimal, editor. *Managing Migration: Time for a New International Regime?* New York: Oxford University Press, 2000.

Government Accounting Office (GAO), INS' Southwest Border Strategy: Resource and Impact Issues Remain After Seven Years. GAO-01-842. Washington: GAO, August 2, 2001.

"Government Sets Up Task Force on Health Tourism." *Financial Express*, January 11, 2004.

Greenlee, David, Special Coordinator for Haiti, State Department, Statement at Hearing of the House International Relations Committee, December 9, 1997.

Hamilton, Bob, and John Whalley. "Efficiency and Distributional Implications of Global Restrictions on Labour Mobility." *Journal of Developmental Economics* 14 (1984): 61–75.

Hartlyn, Jonathan. *The Struggle for Democratic Politics in The Dominican Republic.* Chapel Hill: University of North Carolina Press, 1998.

Hatton, Timothy, and Jefffrey Williamson. "What Drove Mass Migrations from Europe in the Late Nineteenth Century?" *Population and Development Review* 20, no. 3 (September 1994): 533–59.

———. *The Age of Mass Migration: Causes and Economic Impact.* Oxford: Oxford University Press, 1998.

Howard, David. *Dominican Republic: A Guide to the People, Politics and Culture.* Brooklyn, NY: Interlink Publications Group, 1999.

Ingco, Merlinda, and John D. Nash, editors. *Agriculture and the WTO: Creating a Trading System for Development.* Washington, DC: World Bank, March 2004.

Inter American Development Bank. "Remittances and Development: The Case of Mexico," Washington: IADB, June 28, 2005, available at: idbdocs.iadb.org/wsdocs/ getdocument.aspx?docnum=561166.

International Centre for Migration Policy Development. *Report From The Evaluation Mission to Albania 2–5 July 2000, Undertaken in the Framework of the Budapest Process, to Examine the Albanian-Italian Co-operation to Stem Illegal Migration.* Vienna: ICMPD, 2000.

International Helsinki Federation for Human Rights (IHF-HR), Women 2000: An Investigation into the Status of Women's Rights in the former Soviet Union and Central and South-Eastern Europe. Vienna: IHF-HR, 2000.

International Labor Organization. *International Labor Migration Database.* Geneva, 1999.

International Organization for Migration, "L'inserimento lavorativo e l'integrazione sociale degli albanesi in Italia, Research Report" unpublished, 2000.

IOM Sarajevo, IOM *Trafficking in Migrants-Quarterly Bulletin*, no. 22. Autumn, 2000.

Johnson, H. G. "Some Economic Aspects of the Brain Drain" in *Pakistani Development Review* 7 (1967): 379–411.

Jovanovic, Dragana. "Gateway to Opportunity." Available at moreabcnews.go.com/ sections/world/DailyNews/yugo_chinese000710.html, July 13, 2000, accessed on 4/18/2001.

Juntunen, Marko. "Between Morocco and Spain: Men, Migrant Smuggling and a Dispersed Moroccan Community." Thesis, University of Helsinki, 2002.

Kaufman, Jonathan. "China Reforms Bring Back Executives Schooled in U.S." *Wall Street Journal*, March 6, 2003.

Khadria, Binod. *The Migration of Knowledge Workers: Second-Generation Effects of India's Brain Drain.* Thousand Oaks, CA: Sage Publications, 2000.

Kindleberger, Charles P. *Europe's Postwar Growth: The Role of Labor Supply.* Cambridge, MA: Harvard University Press, 1967.

Krauss, M. B. "The Economics of the 'Guest Worker' Problem: A Neo-Heckscher-Ohlin Approach." *Scandinavian Journal of Economics* 78 (1976): 470–76.

Krich, John, and Eric Bellman, "Empowerment Guru Helps Thousands of Filipinas, but Not as Much as Hoped." *Wall Street Journal*, April 20, 2001.

Kyle, David, and Rey Koslowski, editors. *Global Human Smuggling: Comparative Perspectives.* Baltimore: Johns Hopkins University Press, 2001.

"Latin America: DR-Haiti, Argentina," *Migration News* 8, no. 8 (August 2001).

Levitt, Peggy. *The Transnational Villagers.* Berkeley, CA: University of California Press, 2001.

Lewis, W. Arthur. "Economic Development with Unlimited Supplies of Labour." *Manchester School of Economic and Social Studies* 22 (1954): 139–91.

Luo, Yu-Ling, and Wei-Jen Wang. "High-skill Migration and Chinese Taipei's Industrial Development" in OECD, *International Mobility of the Highly Skilled.* Paris: OECD, 2002.

Maingot, Anthony P. "Emigration Dynamics in the Caribbean. The Cases of Haiti and the Dominican Republic." Pp. 178–231 in volume 3 of *Emigration Dynamics in Developing Countries. Mexico, Central America and the Caribbean.* Edited by Reginald Appleyard. Brookfield, VT: Ashgate, 1999.

Martin, Philip L. *Bordering on Control: A Comparison of Measures to Combat Irregular Migration in North America and Europe.* Geneva: International Organization for Migration, 2003.

———. *Trade and Migration: NAFTA and Agriculture*. Washington, D.C.: Institute for International Economics, 1993.

———. *The Unfinished Story: Turkish Labor Migration to Western Europe, With Special Reference to the Federal Republic of Germany*. Geneva: International Labor Office, 1991.

Martin, Philip, and Jonas Widgren. *International Migration: Facing the Challenge*. Washington, DC: Population Reference Bureau, 2002.

Martin, Susan. "Migration and Foreign Policy: Emerging Bilateral and Regional Approaches in the Americas," in *Demography and National Security*, edited by Myron Weiner and Sharon Stanton Russell. New York and Oxford: Berghahn Books, 2001.

———. "Protecting Refugees and Internally Displaced Persons: The Need for Comprehensive Reform," in *Towards a Comprehensive Regime for Refugees and Internally Displaced Person*, edited by Migration Policy Institute and Brookings Institution. Washington, DC: Migration Policy Institute, 2005.

Martin, Susan, Patricia Weiss Fagen, Kari Jorgensen, Lydia Mann-Bondat, and Andrew Schoenholtz. *The Uprooted: Improving Humanitarian Responses to Forced Migration*. Lanham, MD: Lexington Books, 2005.

Martin, Susan, Andrew Schoenholtz, and Deborah Waller Meyers. "Temporary Protection: Towards a New Regional and Domestic Framework." *Georgetown Immigration Law Journal* 12, no. 4. Summer 1998.

Martínez, Samuel. *Peripheral Migrants: Haitians and Dominican Republic Sugar Plantations*. Knoxville: University of Tennessee Press, 1995.

Massey, Douglas S., Joaquin Arango, Graeme Hugo, Ali Kouaouci, Adela Pellegrino, and J. Edward Taylor. *Worlds in Motion: Understanding International Migration at the End of the Millennium*. New York: Oxford University Press, 1998.

Meyers, Deborah Waller. "Does 'Smarter' Lead To Safer? An Assessment of the Border Accords with Canada and Mexico" in MPI Insight no. 2, June 2003.

Ministero degli Affari Esteri, *Il ministero degli esteri in cifre. Annuario statistico*, 2001.

Morozzo della Rocca, R. *Albania: le radici della crisi*. Milano: Guerini e Associati, 1997.

Mundell, Robert A. "International Trade and Factor Mobility." *American Economic Review* 47 (June 1957): 321–35.

Opiniano, Jeremaiah M. "Maximizing Benefits Of OFW Remittances," *Philippine Daily Inquirer*, May 14, 2003.

Organization for Economic Co-operation and Development. *International Mobility of the Highly Skilled: From Statistical Analysis to the Formulation of Policies*. Paris: OECD, 2002.

———. *Migration, Growth and Development*. OECD, Paris. 1978.

———. *Trends in International Migration*. Paris. OECD, annual.

Orozco, Manuel, B. Lindsay Lowell, and Micah Bump. *Transnational Engagement, Remittances and their Relationship to Development in Latin America and the Caribbean*. Washington, DC: Institute for the Study of International Migration, 2005.

Pastore, Ferruccio. *Conflicts and Migration. A Case Study on Albania*, CeSPI Occasional Papers. Rome: CeSPI, 1998.

Pastore, Ferruccio, P. Romani, and G. Sciortino. *L'Italia nel sistema internazionale del traffico di persone*, Commissione per l'integrazione, working paper n.5, 2000.

Pastore, Ferruccio, and G. Sciortino. *Tutori lontani, Il ruolo degli stati d'origine nel processo di integrazione degli immigrati. Ricerca svolta dalla commissione per le politiche di integrazione degli immigrati*, CeSPI, Rome 2001.

Pieke, Frank N., Paul Nyiri, Mette Thumo, and Antonella Caccagno. *Transnational Chinese: Fujianese Migration in Europe*. Stanford: Stanford University Press, 2004.

Piperno, F. *From Albania to Italy: Formation and Basic Features of a Binational Migration System*, background paper for the CEME visit to Italy and Albania, available on www.cespi.it, 2002.

Pons, Frank Moya. *The Dominican Republic: A National History*. Princeton, NJ: Markus Wiener Publishers, 1998.

Population Reference Bureau. *The 2004 World Population Data Sheet: 2004*. Available at www.prb.org/Template.cfm?Section=PRB&template=/Content/ContentGroups/Datasheets/2004_World_Population_Data_Sheet.htm%20%20.

"Prop. 187 Approved in California," *Migration News* 1, no. 12, December 1994.

Ranis, G., and J. C. H. Fei. "A Theory of Economic Development," *The American Economic Review* 51 (1961): 533–65.

Ratha, Dilip. "Workers' Remittances: An Important and Stable Source of External Development Finance" in World Bank, *Global Development Finance 2003*. Washington, DC: World Bank, 2003.

Remarks by Mrs. Sadako Ogata, United Nations High Commissioner for Refugees, Conference of the Carnegie Commission on the Prevention of Deadly Conflict and UNHCR, on a Humanitarian Response and the Prevention of Deadly Conflict, Geneva, February 17, 1997.

Report: A Comprehensive Examination of the International and Domestic Law on Asylum and Migration Issues vs. the Albanian Procedural Rules and Actual Practices Carried Out at the Border Crossings. Tirana, Albania. October 7, 2000 (consulted during site visit).

"Robust Growth in Revenue for Health Tourism Sector," *Business Times* (Malaysia), February 4, 2004.

Shacochis, Bob. *The Immaculate Invasion*. New York: Viking, 1999.

Silj, A. "Albanian Immigration to Italy: A Criminal Invasion?" *Ethno Barometer*, CCS-ERCOMER, working paper n.1, 1997.

Sokoli, N., and S. Axhemi, "Emigration in the Period of Transition in Albania," *Studi di Emigrazione*, XXXVII, n.139, 2000.

Stalker, Peter. *Workers Without Frontiers: The Impact of Globalization on International Migration*. Boulder, CO: Lynne Rienner Publishers, 1999.

Stolper, Wolfgang F., and Paul A. Samuelson. "Protection and Real Wages." *Review of Economic Studies* vol. 9 (November): pp. 58–73, reprinted in *Readings in the Theory of International Trade*, edited by H. S. Ellis and L. A. Metzler. Philadelphia: Blakiston, 1941.

Straubhaar, Thomas. *On the Economics of International Labor Migration*. Bern/ Stuttgart: Paul Haupt, 1988.

Taran, Patrick, and Eduardo Geronimi. "Globalization, Labour and Migration: Protection is Paramount." *Perspectives on Labour Migration Paper No. 3*. Geneva: International Labour Organization, 2003.

Taylor, J. Edward. "The New Economics of Labour Migration and the Role of Remittances in the Development Process," *International Migration* 37 no. 1 (1999): 63–88.

Teitelbaum, Michael. "Do We Need More Scientists?" *The Public Interest*, no. 153 (Fall 2003): 40–53.

Tempest, Rone. "China Tries to Woo Its Tech Talent Back Home," *Los Angeles Times*, November 25, 2002.

Todaro, Michael P. "A Model of Migration and Urban Unemployment in Less-developed Countries," *American Economic Review* 59 (1967):138–48.

Transatlantic Learning Community, Migration in the New Millennium. Gütersloh: Bertelsmann Stiftung and the German Marshall Fund of the United States, 2000.

UN Division on the Advancement of Women. *2004 World Survey on the Role of Women in Development: Women and International Migration*. New York: United Nations, 2004.

UN Population Division. *International Migration Report 2002*. ST/ESA/SER.A/220, New York: United Nations, 2002.

———. *Replacement Migration: Is It A Solution to Declining and Ageing Populations?* New York: United Nations, 2000.

———. *Trends in Total Migrant Stock: The 2003 Revision*. New York: United Nations, 2003.

U.S. Commission for the Study of International Migration and Cooperative Economic Development, *Unauthorized Migration: An Economic Development Response*, Washington, D.C.: U.S. Government Printing Office, 1990.

U.S. Committee for Refugees, *World Refugee Survey: 2001*. Washington DC: U.S. Committee for Refugees, 2001.

U.S. Office of Immigration Statistics, *U.S. Legal Permanent Residents: 2004*, at uscis .gov/graphics/shared/statistics/publications/FlowReportLegalPermResidents 2004.pdf.

Villegas, Bernardo M. *The Philippine Advantage*. University of Asia and the Pacific, 2001.

Weil Patrick. "Populations en mouvement, Etat inerte," in Roger Fauroux, Bernard Spitz (dir.), *Notre Etat, le livre vérité de la Fonction publique*, Paris, 2000.

Wiarda, Howard J., and Michael J. Kryzanek. *The Dominican Republic, a Caribbean Crucible*. Boulder, CO: Westview Press, 1992.

Winters, Alan, Terrie Walmsley, Zhen Kun Wang, and Roman Grynberg. "Negotiating the Liberalization of the Temporary Movement of Natural Persons." *Discussion Paper 87*. Brighton: University of Sussex, October 2002.

World Bank. *Albania. Interim Poverty Reduction Strategy Paper*. Tirana: World Bank, 2000.

———. *Dominican Republic: A Poverty Assessment.* Santo Domingo: World Bank, June 5, 2001.

———. *Global Development Finance Report.* Washington, DC: World Bank, 2003.

———. *Globalization, Growth and Poverty.* Washington, DC: World Bank, 2002.

———. *World Development Report 2003: Sustainable Development in a Dynamic World.* New York: Oxford University Press, 2003.

Wucker, Michele. *Why the Cocks Fight: Dominicans, Haitians, and the Struggle for Hispaniola.* New York: Hill & Wang, 2000.

Index

Korea, 35
Kosovo, 66, 97, 100, 108
Kostunica, Vojislav, 97
Kurds, 79
Kuwait, 222n15

labor abundance, 54n34
labor force: agriculture and, 36–37; in
    Austria, 113; in Dominican
    Republic, 153–54; in Europe, 73;
    foreign direct investment and, 91;
    in Haiti, 162; in Mali, 135, 138;
    men in, 36–37; in Mexico, 169,
    176, 179–83; in Morocco, 124–25;
    in Philippines, 194–95, 202;
    remittances and, 36–37; in Romania,
    89–90, 91, 92; in Senegal, 146n32; in
    Slovak Republic, 114, 116; in Spain,
    126–28; in Turkey, 75, 76, 78, 86–87;
    women in, 19, 160; worldwide, 15,
    17. See also labor migration; specific
    industries; unskilled labor
labor migration: agriculture and, 15–17,
    163, 164, 165, 166–67, 170, 178;
    Albania and, 110–11, 112; Austria
    and, 113, 114–16; children and,
    141–42, 157–58; China and, 218,
    220; cooperation and, 123, 131–32,
    229, 234–37; Dominican Republic
    and, 150, 152, 154–55, 156–58, 163,
    164, 165, 166–67; economic
    development and, 2–3, 236–37;
    European Union and, 2, 229, 235;
    families and, 157–58; France and,
    126; freedom of movement and, 2–3;
    Germany and, 86; Haiti and, 152,
    163, 164, 165, 166–67; Hungary and,
    94; illegal migration and, 31–32,
    236; income and, 15–17; Italy and,
    108–9, 110–11, 112, 234–35, 236;
    Ivory Coast and, 141–42, 145n31;
    Mali and, 141–42; maquiladoras and,
    182–83; Mexico and, 2–3, 170–73,
    178–79, 182–83; Morocco and, 126,

127, 128, 129–33; North American
    Free Trade Agreement (NAFTA)
    and, 2–3; Philippines and, 19, 20,
    25n20, 30, 195–201, 204–5, 221;
    remittances and, 236–37; returns
    and, 236–37; Romania and, 87, 94,
    95–96; Slovak Republic and, 113,
    116; Spain and, 127–28, 129–33,
    234–35; trade and, 40–41;
    transnationalism and, 156–58;
    Turkey and, 79–80, 81–82, 83, 86;
    United States and, 2–3, 150,
    154–55, 156–58, 170–73, 178–79,
    182–83. See also labor force;
    recruitment; specific industries
language, 88, 93
Latortue, Gerald, 162
legal migration: Australia and, 214;
    China and, 205–11, 214, 218–21;
    cooperation and, 233, 245;
    Dominican Republic and, 150,
    154–55, 160–61, 163–64; France
    and, 137, 228; fraud in process of,
    161, 207, 208, 209, 210, 212, 220;
    Haiti and, 154–55, 163–64; Italy
    and, 108–10, 110–11; Mali and, 137;
    Mexico and, 168–69, 170–73, 178;
    Morocco and, 131–33; Philippines
    and, 191–92, 195–99; restriction of,
    228–30, 231; rights and, 23–24, 132,
    196–98; Slovak Republic and, 117;
    Spain and, 128–30, 131–33; Turkey
    and, 84; United States and, 154–55,
    160–61, 168–69, 170–73, 178, 229;
    women and, 18–19
Leontief Paradox, 54n34
Levitt, Peggy, 156–59
Lewis, W. Arthur, 36, 153
Lorenzo, Marilyn E., 201

Maastricht Treaty, 74
Macedonia, 121n45
Maingot, Anthony, 154, 163
Malaysia, 30, 196

About the Contributors

Philip Martin earned a PhD in economics from the University of Wisconsin-Madison and is Professor of Agricultural and Resource Economics at the University of California-Davis. Dr. Martin has worked on labor and immigration issues for 25 years in the U.S. and abroad. He has worked for UN agencies around the world, with assignments that included assessing the prospects for Turkish migration to the European Union and evaluating the effects of foreign workers on the economies of Thailand and Malaysia. He has studied the effects of NAFTA on Mexico-U.S. migration and the effects of migration on U.S. agriculture.

Susan Martin is Visiting Professor and the Director of the Institute for the Study of International Migration in the School of Foreign Service at Georgetown University. Previously Dr. Martin served as the Executive Director of the U.S. Commission on Immigration Reform, established by legislation to advise Congress and the President on U.S. immigration and refugee policy, and Director of Research and Programs at the Refugee Policy Group. She is the author of numerous books, articles and monographs on labor and forced migration issues. She earned her MA and PhD in American Studies from the University of Pennsylvania and her BA in History from Douglass College, Rutgers University. She is the President of the International Association for the Study of Forced Migration.

Patrick Weil is a senior research fellow at the French National Research Center (CNRS) in Paris. He also serves as director of the Center for the Study of Immigration, Integration, and Citizenship Policies (CEPIC) at the University of Paris1, Panthéon–Sorbonne and, since 2005, as a transatlantic fellow at the German Marshall Fund of the United States. In 2003, Dr. Weil served on the French presidential commission on secularism established by Jacques Chirac. Dr. Weil was also appointed by the French government in 1997 to prepare a report on immigration and nationality policy reform, which served as the basis of immigration and nationality legislation passed by the French parliament the following year. Since 2005, Dr. Weil holds a PhD in political science from the Institut d'Etudes Politiques de Paris and an MBA from the ESSEC Business School. He received a BA in public law from the University of Paris1, Panthéon–Sorbonne.